PREPARING AND USING FINANCIAL REPORTS

JOEL G. SIEGEL, *Ph.D., CPA*

JAE K. SHIM, *Ph.D.*

ANIQUE AHMED QURESHI, *Ph.D., CPA, CIA*

ANTHONY GAMBIN, *CPA*

THOMSON
™

Australia · Canada · Mexico · Singapore · Spain · United Kingdom · United States

THOMSON
™

The Manager's Handbook to Preparing and Using Financial Reports
Joel G. Siegel, Jae K. Shim, Anique Ahmed Qureshi, Anthony Gambin

Editor-in-Chief:
Jack Calhoun

Vice President/ Executive Publisher:
Dave Shaut

Acquisitions Editor:
Steve Momper

Channel Manager, Retail:
Bari Shokler

Channel Manager, Professional:
Mark Linton

Production Editor:
Alan Biondi

Production Manager:
Tricia Matthews Boies

Manufacturing Coordinator:
Charlene Taylor

Compositor:
Edgewater Editorial Services

Editorial Associate:
Michael Jeffers

Production Associate:
Barbara Evans

Printer:
Edwards Brothers, Inc.
Ann Arbor, MI

Cover Designer:
Chris Miller

ISBN: 0-538-72679-2

DEDICATION

Barbara M. Evans
An Excellent Editor

Roberta M. Siegel
Loving Wife, Colleague, and Partner

Chung Shim
Dedicated Wife

Shaheen Qureshi
Wonderful Wife

Anna Gambin
Loving Wife

ACKNOWLEDGMENTS

We are very grateful and appreciative to Barbara Evans for her outstanding editorial assistance on this book. She worked very hard and made a major contribution to the project.

Thanks also to Roberta M. Siegel for her important input and editorial suggestions.

TABLE OF CONTENTS

About the Authors . . . . *vi*
What This Book Will Do For You . . . . *viii*

Chapter 1—Cash Management and Analysis Reports 1
Chapter 2—Accounts Receivable 12
Chapter 3—Inventory Reporting and Analysis 19
Chapter 4—Reports for Investments 33
Chapter 5—Sales Efficiency Reporting 43
Chapter 6—Reporting on Sales and Service Revenue 50
Chapter 7—Reporting on Salespersons 59
Chapter 8—Customer Service Reporting 66
Chapter 9—Geographic Area Reporting 72
Chapter 10—Analysis and Reporting of Purchasing 81
Chapter 11—Analysis and Reporting of Distribution 88
Chapter 12—Employee Performance Reporting 93
Chapter 13—Manager Performance Reports 99
Chapter 14—Segmental Reporting 114
Chapter 15—Managerial Accounting and Reporting 122
Chapter 16—Planning and Control Reports 132
Chapter 17—Budget Reporting and Control 139
Chapter 18—Capital Budgeting Analysis and Reporting 152
Chapter 19—Analysis of Capital Expenditures 160
Chapter 20—Manufacturing Cost Reports: Material 171
Chapter 21—Manufacturing Cost Reports: Labor 180
Chapter 22—Manufacturing Cost Reports: Ovehead 191

Chapter 23—Manufacturing and Production Reports. 199
Chapter 24—Cost Analysis and Allocation Reporting 217
Chapter 25—Plant Reporting 233
Chapter 26—Research and Development 242
Chapter 27—Marketing. 249
Chapter 28—Financial Statements. 254
Chapter 29—Financial Statement Analysis 264
Chapter 30—Reporting on Operating Expenses. 275
Chapter 31—Financial Analysis 282
Chapter 32—Valuation of a Business 284
Chapter 33—Financing the Business. 286
Chapter 34—Reporting on Liabilities 292
Chapter 35—Audit Reporting and Controls. 294
Chapter 36—Insurance Analysis 303
Chapter 37—Operations Management Reports 308
Chapter 38—Quantitative Analysis, Business Statistics and
    Mathematics 332
Chapter 39—Forecasting. 342

ABOUT THE AUTHORS

JOEL G. SIEGEL, Ph.D., CPA, is a self-employed certified public accountant and professor of accounting and finance at Queens College of the City University of New York. He was previously employed by Coopers and Lybrand, CPAs, and Arthur Andersen, CPAs. Dr. Siegel has been a consultant in accounting and finance to many organizations, including Citicorp, International Telephone and Telegraph, United Technologies, and the American Institute of CPAs. Dr. Siegel has written 65 books and more than 200 articles on accounting and financial topics. His books have been published by Glenlake Publishing Company, Ltd., Prentice-Hall, Richard Irwin, Probus, Macmillan, McGraw-Hill, HarperCollins, John Wiley, International Publishing, Barrons, American Management Association, and the American Institute of CPAs. His articles have been published in many accounting and financial journals including *Financial Executive, The Financial Analysts Journal, The CPA Journal, Practical Accountant,* and *The National Public Accountant.* In 1972, he was the recipient of the Outstanding Educator of America Award. Dr. Siegel is listed in *Who's Where among Writers* and *Who's Who in the World.* He served as Chairperson of the National Oversight Board.

JAE K. SHIM, Ph.D., is an accounting consultant to several companies and professor of accounting at California State University, Long Beach. He received his Ph.D. degree from the University of California at Berkeley. Dr. Shim has 40 books to his credit and has published over 50 articles in accounting and financial journals including *The CPA Journal,*

Advances in Accounting, International Accountant, and *Financial Management.*

ANIQUE AHMED QURESHI, Ph.D., CPA, CIA, is a consultant in accounting and associate professor of accounting at Queens College. Dr. Qureshi has authored books for Prentice-Hall, and has contributed chapters to books for McGraw-Hill. His articles have appeared in *The CPA Journal, National Public Accountant, Management Accounting,* and *Internal Auditing.* He has made presentations at the American Accounting Association, American Association of Accounting and Finance, and INFORMS.

ANTHONY GAMBIN, MBA, CPA, is research director at the National Association of Accountants. He formerly served as both a technical manager and editor at the American Institute of CPAs, editor at Warren, Gorham and Lamont, director of accounting standards at the American Insurance Association, a financial analyst at Berkey Photo, Inc., a budget supervisor at Lever Brothers, and a public accountant and auditor at both Laventhol, Krekstein, Horwath and Horwath, CPAs and Warshaw and Clarke, CPAs. His publications include research reports, articles, and chapters published by the National Association of Accountants, Society of Management Accountants of Canada, Prentice-Hall, and the National Society of Accountants.

WHAT THIS BOOK
WILL DO FOR YOU

The Manual of Accounting Reports, Formats, and Designs may be used by financial executives including financial managers, managerial accountants, financial accountants, auditors, and financial analysts. The financial executive must present and communicate numbers and reports to management. Ninety percent of the book covers accounting reports. The other 10 percent includes such items as: forms, figures, tables, charts, diagrams, checklists, ideas for different formats, sample documents, and ways and ideas to enhance the appearance of reports. The users will have a better picture of what is going on in the entire company, divisions, departments, responsibility centers, and other business segments and units. The book is a how-to, real-life, user-friendly business application text.

The business reports presented may be used to guide improvements in profitability, financial status, performance, productivity, efficiency, effectiveness, cooperation, coordination, and the management information system.

Benefits to be gained by the reader from this book follow:

- The *Handbook* gives you over 300 model accounting reports that can be used "as is" or adapted.

- The reports have been successfully used in businesses for many years.

- The reports will help you tackle difficult reporting questions.

- The *Handbook* covers every operation of a company (all types and size companies).

- Readers will get such reports as: reports for investments, geographic area reporting, distribution reports, employee performance reports, valuation reports, financing reports, reports on potential mergers and acquisitions, reports for manufacturing and service activities, reports on liabilities, break-even analysis reporting, analyzing and reporting on revenue and expenses, profitability reporting, reports on managing assets, analysis of rate of return, variance analysis reporting, salesperson reporting, reports on advertising and promotion, capital expenditure reporting, insurance appraisal and reporting, risk evaluation and reporting, financial analysis reports, and budgets and planning reports.

- The *Handbook* includes all the accounting reports needed to evaluate and improve operational performance for any type and size of business.

- The *Handbook* aids in understanding the financial status and operating results and enables better communication on what is essential in the firm for accomplishing both short-term and long-term goals.

- The *Handbook* will enable better decision making on the part of management and users of financial statements including investors and creditors.

- The *Handbook* includes reports to analyze business situations and problems such as reports to evaluate business proposal projects, operations, activities, and functions.

- The *Handbook* includes how the reports are to be used, by whom and for what purpose, how often, what other reports may be related, and who to route the report. Applicable rules of thumb, ratios, and formulas are also provided.

- The recommended formats are logical, useful and easily comprehensible.

- All types of accounting and financial reports in proper format to facilitate an organized flow of sequential information along with evaluative implications are at your fingertips.

- The *Handbook* covers all areas of accounting and financial management. It enhances understanding and minimizes the risk of incomplete or misleading information.

- The *Handbook* considers the ever-changing business world and the latest up-to-date advances in quantitative, technological, and computer areas. New and emerging trends in report formats are included.

- Financial reports emphasizing trend and ratio analysis to appraise, for example, a company's liquidity, solvency, asset utilization, profitability, earnings quality and market value are included.

- Illustrative reports are provided to facilitate the analysis of the company's product lines, services, customer service base, suppliers, and geographic regions (domestic and international). The model reports will also aid communication so sub-units know what is expected of them.

Keep this valuable reference guide handy for daily use. It is comprehensive, informative, authoritative, and practical. The content of this *Handbook* is clear, concise, and to the point. The uses of this book are as varied as the topic areas presented.

CHAPTER 1

Cash Management and Analysis Reports

Cash management reporting is the basis for cash planning and control, because cash flow is the lifeblood of a business.

Cash flow indicates whether you will be able to pay your bills on time. Not only does failure to make timely payments have a detrimental impact on the credit standing of the business, especially in the case of a bank loan or bond it may cause a default that leads to involuntary bankruptcy. Bankruptcies are caused by lack of cash, not lack of profit.

Look carefully at the trend in your cash balance each month. A declining trend may foretell a looming cash crisis.

- Exhibit 1-1 shows popular methods for (1) accelerating cash receipts and (2) delaying cash payments.

- Exhibit 1-2 lists key cash ratios that indicate the adequacy of a company's liquid funds to meet obligations.

- Adequate cash flow is needed not only for a company to stay afloat but to achieve capital growth. Exhibits 1-3 through 1-9 analyze cash flow movement, cash balance, cash budgeting, and cash variances.

- Exhibit 1-10 schedules projected payments by month and quarter for all budgeted material purchases.

EXHIBIT 1-1
CASH MANAGEMENT SYSTEM

Acceleration of Cash Receipts	**Delay of Cash Payments**
Lock box system	Pay by draft
Concentration banking	Requisition more often
Preauthorized checks	Disbursing float
Preaddressed stamped envelopes	Make partial payments
Obtain deposits on large orders	Use charge accounts
Charge interest on overdue receivables	Pay employees less often

Purpose: To show popular methods for (1) accelerating cash receipts and (2) delaying cash payments

Distribution: Cash manager, treasurer, controller, CFO, CEO

Use: To help cash managers like treasurers manage cash efficiently

Action to be taken: Pick the right approach. The idea is "accelerate cash inflow and stretch your payments as long as you can."

EXHIBIT 1-2
CASH RATIOS

1. $\dfrac{\text{Cash flow}}{\text{Total debt}}$

2. $\dfrac{\text{Cash flow}}{\text{Long-term debt}}$

3. $\dfrac{\text{Cash + marketable securities}}{\text{Total current assets}}$

4. $\dfrac{\text{Cash + marketable securities}}{\text{Total current liabilities}}$

5. $\dfrac{\text{Cash + marketable securities + receivables}}{\text{Year's cash expenses}}$

6. *Cash flow-to-capital expenditures ratio:*

$$\frac{\text{Cash flow from operations - dividends}}{\text{Expenditures for plant and equipment}}$$

7. *Cash flow adequacy ratio:*

$$\frac{\text{Five-year sum of cash flow from operations}}{\text{Five-year sum of capital expenditures, inventory additions,}}{\text{and cash dividends}}$$

EXHIBIT 1-2
CASH RATIOS, *Cont'd*

Purpose: To list key cash ratios for assessing the adequacy of a company's liquid funds to meet obligations (Adequate cash flow is needed not only for a company to stay afloat but to achieve capital growth)

Distribution: Cash manager, treasurer, controller, CFO, CEO

Use: To help cash managers like treasurers manage cash efficiently

Action to be taken: Calculate cash ratios to find out whether the company can pay its debts. They are useful in predicting financial distress (even bankruptcy):

- Cash flow to long-term debt appraises the adequacy of available funds to meet noncurrent obligations.

- The ratio of cash plus marketable securities to current liabilities indicates the amount of cash available to satisfy short-term debt and tells whether a company's immediate liquid resources are sufficient to meet current expenses.

- The cash flow-to-capital expenditures ratio indicates a company's ability to maintain plant and equipment from cash provided from operations, rather than from borrowing or issuing new stock.

- The purpose of the cash flow adequacy ratio is to determine whether an enterprise has generated sufficient cash flow from operations to cover capital expenditures, net investment in inventories, and cash dividends. A five-year total is used to remove cyclical and other erratic influences. If the ratio is 1, the company has covered its needs based on attained levels of growth without the need for external financing. If the ratio drops below 1, internally generated cash may be inadequate to maintain dividends and current operating growth levels. This ratio may also reflect the impact of inflation on the company's requirements.

EXHIBIT 1-3
DAILY CASH MOVEMENT REPORT

| | Downey National—General | | | Donna Park—Payroll | | | | |
	Book Balance	Collected Balance per Bank	Float	Book Balance	Collected Balance per Bank	Float	Lockbox #1 Chicago	Lockbox #2 New York
1-Oct	$84,500	$106,789	$22,289	$6,000	$47,635	$41,635	$16,666	$6,134
2	69,800	79,860	10.060	6,000	46,579	40,579	22,546	8,965
3	134,500	149,327	14,827	6,000	23,333	17,333	38,297	9,067
4	170,840	119,820	(51,020)	6,000	12,685	6,685	14,620	28,796
5	97,233	118,438	21,205	6,000	7,975	1,975	18,211	7,890
6	136,788	81,540	(55,248)	6,000	2,344	(3,656)	19,821	21,657
7	145,670	178,235	32,565	6,000	970	(5,030)	47,800	6,785
8	98,750	162,720	63,970	6,000	899	(5,101)	31,222	1,679
9	136,789	168,940	32,151	6,000	423	(5,577)	5,789	2,888

(cont'd)

Purpose: To display the amount of cash in each bank account for cash management purposes

Distribution: Treasurer, cash manager, accountant, controller, CFO

Use: To monitor book cash balances, collected cash balances, and cash float by account on a daily basis

Action to be taken: Make sure the company can minimize cash float periods.

EXHIBIT 1-4
DAILY CASH BALANCE REPORT

Date	Beginning Cash	Cash Receipts	Cash Disbursements	Bank Loans	Investments	Ending Balance
1	$1,37,000	$24,320	$33,465			$127,855
2	127,855	56,433	45,300			138,988
3	138,988	87,900	4,570		(100,000)	122,318
4	122,318	33,400	56,400			99,318
5	99,318	46,700	95,460			50,558
6	50,588	43,200	56,000		(100,000)	(62,242)
7	(62,242)	25,400	87,500	150,000		25,658
8	25,658	112,300	67,500			70,458

Purpose: To summarize cash activity by daily receipts, disbursements, loans, investments, and cash balances

Distribution: Treasurer, cash manager, accountant, controller, CFO

Use: To monitor daily cash balances

Action to be taken: Make sure the firm is always liquid enough to pay expenses.

EXHIBIT 1-5
CASH FLOW VARIANCE ANALYSIS

	Previous Week Budget	Actual	Year-to-Date Budget	Actual
Cash receipts				
Collection from customers	$,111,000	$109,000	$990,000	$979,000
Investment income	2,400	2,500	33,000	32,500
Royalty	3,000	3,000	60,000	60,000
Total cash receipts	$116,400	$114,500	$1,083,000	$1,071,500
Cash disbursements				
Material purchases	$26,300	$18,410	!76,000	$226,000
Payroll	27,500	29,000	400,000	412,800
Property taxes	5,500	5,540	5,500	5,500
Group insurance premium	13,000	13,200	39,000	39,600
Bank note—interest	4,320	4,320	15,000	12,960
Lease payment—building	5,475	5,475	16,425	16,425
Dividend payment	1,232	1,232	3,696	3,696
Rent	6,897	6,897	20,691	20,691
Total disbursements	63,924	65,664	500,312	511,672
Net increase (decrease) in cash	$47,076	$43,336	$489,688	$467,328

EXHIBIT 1-5
CASH FLOW VARIANCE ANALYSIS, *Cont'd*

Purpose: To show cash receipts and disbursements for the week and year-to-date compared to budget

Distribution: Treasurer, cash manager, accountant, controller, CFO

Use: To monitor cash inflow and outflow for planning purposes

Action to be taken: Make sure the firm is always liquid enough to pay expenses and to see if borrowing is necessary.

EXHIBIT 1-6
QUARTERLY CASH FLOW ANALYSIS

	1st Quarter		Last Year's 1st Quarter
	Actual	Budget	Actual
Net income	$254,000	$280,000	$134,500
Depreciation	67,900	67,000	56,000
Short-term debt	134,000	85,000	250,00
New long-term debt	50,000	40,000	--
Total cash available	$505,900	$472,000	$440,500
Property, plant and equipment purchase	78,000	49,000	38,000
Retirement of short-term debt	30,000	30,000	25,000
Retirement of long-term debt	38,500	40,000	43,650
Receivable requirements—increase (decrease)	100,000	114,500	165,000
Inventory requirements—increase (decrease)	178,000	190,000	125,000
Accounts payable—increase (decrease)	(77,000)	(60,000)	14,000
Accrued expenses—increase (decrease)	21,000	9,000	20,000
Total cash requirements	368,500	372,500	430,650
Net cash flow	$137,400	$ 99,500	$ 9,850
Total outstanding short-term debt	140,000	90,000	34,000
Total available short-term debt	500,000	500,000	400,000
Net short-term debt still available	$360,000	$410,000	$366,000

Purpose: To analyze cash flow for planning purposes

Distribution: Treasurer, cash manager, accountant, controller, CFO

Use: To monitor cash inflow and outflow quarterly for planning purposes

Action to be taken: Make sure the firm is always liquid enough to pay expenses.

EXHIBIT 1-7
MONTHLY BANK BALANCE ANALYSIS REPORT

Bank	Balance per Books	Budgeted Balance	Above (Below) Plan	Balance per Bank
Norwood				
Regular	$98,750	$100,000	$(1,250)	$111,250
Payroll	32,250	32,250		21,320
Savings	125,000	125,000	--	125,000
U.S. National	17,650	20,000	(2,350)	9,950
Merchant Bank	15,478	20,000	(4,522)	13,970
Norman Hanover	15,677	15,000	677	8,550
	$304,805	$312,250	$(7,445)	$290,040

Purpose: To compare cash balances per book with balances per budget and bank account

Distribution: Treasurer, cash manager, controller, CFO, CEO

Use: To monitor (1) any discrepancies between cash balance per book and per budget and (2) differences between book cash and bank balances

Action to be taken: (1) Determine reasons for any overspending and take remedial actions; (2) reconcile differences between book and bank balances.

EXHIBIT 1-8
MONTHLY CASH BUDGETS

		December (actual)	November (actual)	October (actual)	January
Expected sales		$510,000	$457,500	$375,000	$410,000
Cash receipts:					
Cash sales	10%				41,000
Collection from sales:					
One month ago	75%				382,500
Two months ago	15%				68,625
Three months ago	8%				30,000
Bad debts	2%				
	100%				522,125
Other cash receipts					11,000
Beginning of month cash					80,000
Total available cash					613,125
Cash disbursements:					
Material					138,000
Labor and wages					182,000
Selling costs					175,000
General/administrative costs					46,000
Income taxes					
Capital equipment					28,000
Interest expense					15,000
Total cash disbursements					584,000
Ending cash balance (deficiency) before additional borrowings/ (repayments) or (investments) redemptions					29,125
Bank borrowing/(repayments) (investments)/redemptions					
Ending cash balance					$ 29,125

Purpose: To project cash receipts and disbursements by month

Distribution: Budget analyst, treasurer, cash manager, controller, CFO, CEO

EXHIBIT 1-8
MONTHLY CASH BUDGETS, *Cont'd*

February	March	April	May	June
$385,000	$580,000	$600,000	$600,000	$625,000
38,500	58,000	60,000	60,000	62,500
343,125	281,250	307,500	288,750	435,000
56,500	61,500	57,750	87,000	90,000
32,800	30,800	46,400	48,000	48,000
470,675	431,550	471,650	483,750	635,500
7,600	18,500	12,000	16,500	8,100
29,125	4,000	17,350	38,600	17,350
507,400	454,050	501,000	538,850	660,950
145,000	150,000	125,000	140,000	150,000
110,000	169,000	105,000	150,000	172,000
169,000	181,000	168,500	177,000	165,000
49,500	48,000	47,000	47,000	43,000
28,500			28,500	
5,200	21,200		13,000	4,800
16,200	17,500	16,900	16,000	14,300
523,400	586,700	462,400	571,500	549,100
(16,000)	(132,650)	38,600	(32,650)	111,850
20,000	150,000	--	50,000	(100,000)
$ 4,000	$ 17,350	$ 38,600	$ 17,350	$ 11,850

Use: To manage cash inflow and outflow on a timely basis

Action to be taken: If deficit, arrange borrowings ahead of time and in case of surpluses, plan temporary investments in short-term securities.

EXHIBIT 1-9
MONTHLY BANK RECONCILIATION

Balance per book		$22,190
Add: Deposits in transit	3,680	
Bank error	175	3,855
		26,045
Less: Outstanding checks		
#410	3,450	
#423	1,551	5,001
Adjusted bank balance		$21,044
Balance per book		20,502
Add: Proceeds on note	600	
Error in recording check #2343	180	780
		$21,282
Less:		
NSF check	220	
Collection fee	8	
Service charge	10	238
Adjusted book balance		21,044

Purpose: To reconcile bank statement balance and book cash balance

Distribution: Treasurer, cash manager, controller, CFO, CEO

Use: To assure that the company's records agree with the bank's records after accounting for all reconciling items

Action to be taken: If the reconciliation shows a discrepancy, an investigation should be made to uncover any errors or irregularities (such as a fraud perpetrated by a bookkeeper or an accountant).

EXHIBIT 1-10
MONTHLY PROJECTED PAYMENTS FOR MATERIAL PURCHASES REPORT

		Payments							Payables Balance
	Total	January	February	March	1st Quarter	2nd Quarter	3rd Quarter	4th Quarter	Next Jan. 1
Beginning of fiscal year payable balance	$132,000	$87,000	$52,500		$132,000				
Budgeted purchases:									
January	236,000	11,000	175,000	42,000	236,000				
February	175,000		10,000	140,000	140,000	35,000			
March	312,000			20,000	12,000	300,000			
1st Quarter	723,000	11,000	185,000	202,000	388,000	335,000			
2nd Quarter	825,000					389,000	436,000		
3rd Quarter	890,000						426,000	464,000	
4th Quarter	612,000							397,000	215,000
Total	$3,182,000	$98,000	$237,500	$202,000	$520,000	$724,000	$862,000	$861,000	$215,000

Purpose: To schedule projected payments by month and quarter for all budgeted material purchases

Distribution: Stock manager, treasurer, cash manager, accountant, controller, CFO

Use: To plan for when budgeted purchases will be paid

Action to be taken: Make sure projected payments are in line with the company's overall cash receipts and disbursements budget.

CHAPTER 2

Accounts Receivable

Prompt recording of sales and collections is one of the most important activities of any business. A firm that does not perform these functions on a timely basis may be forced out of business. Part of successful accounts receivable management is careful granting of credit. All the reports in this chapter are designed tools to help insure prompt collection and the maintenance of an appropriate credit policy.

EXHIBIT 2-1
AGED RECEIVABLES REPORT

Customer	Invoice #	Current	Under 30	Over 30	Over 90	Total	Last Collection Date
			Days Overdue				
Abbot Corp.	1492			1,520		1,520	
	1553			755		755	
	1559		520			520	
	1621	2,550				2,550	
		$2,550	$520	$2,275	$0	$5,345	
Delewis Inc.	1294				250	250	8/25
	1525			275		275	
	1561		1,295			1,295	
		$0	$1,295	$275	$250	$1,820	
Rawis Bros.	1550		1,250			1,250	
	1610	1,560				1,560	
		$1,560	$1,250	$0	$0	$2,810	

Purpose: To monitor collections and the granting of credit

Distribution: Collection manager, credit manager

Use: To decide on policies to deal with overdue invoices

Action to be taken: Aggressively pursue collection of accounts more than 90 days overdue; decide whether to grant more credit to slow paying accounts.

EXHIBIT 2-2
ALLOWANCE FOR BAD DEBT REPORT

Bad debt allowance, opening $725,000

Subtractions:
  Write-offs:

Premier Corp.	$2,200	
Harmony Co.	3,200	
United Enterprises	890	
Estes, Inc.	1,300	
Total write-offs		(7,590)

Additions:
  Recovery of amounts previously written off:

Danlop Corp.	1,225	
Keyes, Inc.	2,555	
Cyprus Corp.	950	
Total recoveries		4,730

Adjustment to allowance   120,000

Bad debt allowance, closing $842,140

Purpose: To monitor adequacy of bad debt allowance

Distribution: Controller. treasurer

Use: To reconcile bad debt allowance for period

Action to be taken: If recoveries of "amounts previously written off" seem excessive (which may be the case here), the firm may want to reevaluate a policy that is resulting in too many write-offs.

EXHIBIT 2-3
BUILD-UP OF ACCOUNTS RECEIVABLE BUDGET
For the quarter ending March 31, 20--

Month	Sales	Beginning Balance	Add: Billings	Less: Collections	Ending Balance	LY Balance
January	$1,060,000	$695,000	$954,000	$730,000	$919,000	$ 895,255
February	955,000	919,000	860,000	650,000	1,129,000	1,063,533
March	1,200,000	1,129,000	1,016,000	900,000	1,245,000	1,158,656
Total for quarter	$3,215,000	$695,000	$2,830,000	$2,280,000	$1,245,000	$1,158,656

Purpose: To set goals for billings, collections, and anticipated sales

Distribution: Sales managers, collections managers

Use: To help assess how well sales billings and collections are on target

Action to be taken: If ending balance builds in relation to sales, make sure credit policy is not too lax, and collection policy is sufficiently aggressive.

EXHIBIT 2-4
ANTICIPATED ACCOUNTS RECEIVABLE COLLECTIONS

	A/R balance, 1/1	January	February	March	First Qtr.	Second Qtr.	Third Qtr.	Fourth Qtr.	A/R balance, Year-end
A/R balance	$584,000	$475,000	$90,000	$19,000	$584,000				
Anticipated Collections:									
January	505,000		380,000	96,000	476,000	29,000			
February	325,000		12,000	241,000	253,000	66,000	6,000		
March	470,000			26,000	26,000	444,000			
First Qtr.	1,300,000				755,000	539,000	6,000		
Second Qtr.	1,835,000					948,000	835,000	52,000	
Third Qtr.	1,901,000						963,000	856,000	82,000
Fourth Qtr.	1,715,000							1,082,000	633,000
Total collections	$6,751,000		392,000	363,000	755,000	1,487,000	1,804,000	1,990,000	715,000

Purpose: To budget receivable collections for the year

Distribution: Collection manager, credit manager

Use: To record budgeted cash receipts by month and quarter

Action to be taken: Manage collections and prepare cash forecast.

EXHIBIT 2-5
ACCOUNTS RECEIVABLE SUMMARY REPORT

Month		Opening Balance	Add: Invoices	Less: Collections	Adjustments	Closing Balance
January	Dept A	$255,000	$141,000	($155,290)	($2,350)	$238,360
	Dept B	528,250	278,000	(365,000)		441,250
	Dept C	325,000	229,850	(256,000)	1,550	300,400
	Total	1,108,250	648,850	(776,290)	(800)	980,010
February	Dept A	473,500	525,290	(345,000)		653,790
	Dept B	482,560	328,520	(268,500)	2,690	545,270
	Dept C	419,820	248,000	(305,260)		362,560
	Total	1,375,880	1,101,810	(918,760)	2,690	1,561,620
March	Dept A	549,620	402,250	(398,125)		553,745
	Dept B	365,720	341,370	(255,340)		451,750
	Dept C	753,650	501,480	(562,820)		692,310
	Total	1,668,990	1,245,100	(1,216,285)	0	1,697,805

Purpose: To help manage credit and collection

Distribution: Credit manager

Use: To monitor AR balances, invoices, collections, and adjustments by month and department

Action to be taken: Take corrective action for any changes in collection trends.

EXHIBIT 2-6
RECEIVABLES WRITE-OFF REPORT

Customer	Amount Received			Total Write-off	% of Write-off of Total Rec.
	Current	Late	Total		
Abrams Enterprises	$2,846	$556	$3,402		
B.J. Auto Parts	10,840	226	11,066	107	0.97%
Case Stores		8,461	8,461		
Finest Decorators	340		340	4	1.18%
Greater Metro Supply	4,475	2,430	6,905	209	3.03%
Leonard's Favorite	2,569		2,569		
Shopper's Express	2,599		2,599		
Towne Mart	4,256	1,109	5,365		

Purpose: To monitor write-offs of accounts receivable

Distribution: Credit manager

Use: To manage business relationships with slow-paying customers

Action to be taken: When a portion of an account is written off, conduct additional business with that customer on a "cash only" basis.

EXHIBIT 2-7
CUSTOMER PAYMENT ANALYSIS (Year-to-Date)

Customer	Credit Category	Total Payments	Total On-Time	Aging Period				Ave. Days per Invoice	Write-off Amount
				1 to 30	31 to 60	60 to 90	Over 90		
Abrams Enterprises	A	$3,402	$2,846	$556				20	
B.J. Auto Parts	A	11,066	10,840	226				21	$107
Case Stores	B	8,461	8,461					26	
Finest Decorators	B	340	340					30	4
Greater Metro Supply	A	6,905	4,475	2,430				37	
Leonard's Favorite	B	2,569	2,569					37	
Shopper's Express	B	2,599	2,599					39	
Towne Mart	B	5,365	4,256	1,109				42	209

Purpose: To monitor customer payment pattern

Distribution: Credit manager, collection manager

Use: To manage receivables cash flow

Action to be taken: Change credit policy towards accounts that are slow-paying or in default.

CHAPTER 3

Inventory Reporting and Analysis

One of the most common problems for managers is inventory planning. Inventory usually represents a sizable portion of a firm's total assets-in fact, on average more than 30 percent of total current assets in U.S. industry.

Good inventory management leads to maximum return at minimum risk. Inventory buildup may indicate management uncertainty about future sales. Whether at a plant, a wholesaler, or a retailer site, buildup occurs whenever inventory increases faster than the sales.

A high ratio of sales to inventory means that inventory is being used efficiently to generate revenue. It is important to ascertain the turnover rate for each major inventory category and for each department. A low turnover rate may point to (1) overstocking, (2) obsolescence, or (3) deficiencies in the product line or marketing effort. Note, however, that a low rate of turnover may sometimes be appropriate, as when inventories are built up in anticipation of rapidly rising prices.

On the other hand, high turnover rate may indicate that the company does not maintain adequate inventory—a situation that could lead to a loss of sales if inventory is unavailable. Also, the turnover rate may be unrepresentatively high if a company uses its "natural year-end" as a basis for calculating turnover, since the inventory balance at that time of year would be exceptionally low. A decline in raw materials coupled with an increase in work-in-process and finished goods indicate a future production slowdown. Note, too, that creditors view a company with poor inventory turnover as a liquidity risk.

Too much money tied up in inventory is a drag on profitability; corporate funds that are tied up in inventory could be invested elsewhere.

Excess inventory is also associated with both high carrying costs for storing goods and with risk of obsolescence.

1. Exhibit 3-1 lists key ratios that reveal turnover and age of inventory.

2. Exhibits 3-2 through 3-10 are reports used to analyze inventory investment and control inventory.

3. Exhibits 3-11 and 3-12 show two popular inventory valuation methods used by retailers.

4. Exhibits 3-13 and 3-14 explain how to determine economical order quantities with and without quantity discounts.

EXHIBIT 3-1
INVENTORY RATIOS

1. Inventory turnover = $\dfrac{\text{Cost of goods sold}}{\text{Average inventory}}$

where

Average inventory = $\dfrac{\text{Beginning inventory + ending inventory}}{2}$

2. Number of days inventory held (age of inventory) = $\dfrac{365}{\text{Inventory turnover}}$

3. Sales to inventory: $\dfrac{\text{Sales}}{\text{Inventory}}$

Purpose: To provide key ratios that reveal turnover and age of inventories in, for example, raw materials, work-in-process (partially completed goods), and completed goods (Excess inventory (1) ties up corporate funds that could be invested elsewhere, (2) increases costs for storing unnecessary goods, and (3) increases the risk of write-offs due to obsolescence.)

Distribution: Inventory manager, treasurer, controller, CFO, CEO

Use: To help financial officers manage cash efficiently

Action to be taken: Ascertain the turnover rate for each major inventory category and for each department.

If the turnover rate is low, determine whether the cause is due to overstocking, obsolescence, deficiencies in the production line or marketing effort, or an anticipated rise in prices. Begin remedial process as appropriate for all but the last of these causes.

If the turnover rate is high, determine the reason and begin remedial process as appropriate.

EXHIBIT 3-2
MONTHLY STOCK STATUS REPORT

Part #	Description	Unit of Measure	Remaining On-Hand Qty.	Average Monthly	Usage Current Mo. For.	Current Mo. Act.	Current Mo. Issue Freq.	ABC Code	Unit Price
M	Water motor assembly	Ea	200	250	185	225	9	B	$189.00
F	Frame assembly	Ea	300	100	330	250	7	B	$58.00
H	Hose recpt. assembly	Ea	1,500	1,200	1,350	1,400	11	A	$65.00
M-A	Aluminum tube	Ea	30,000		122	130	10	C	$59.00
M-B	Metal screws	Ea	5,000	4,500	5,200	5,600	21	A	$23.00
M-C	Water motor	Ea	1,000		985	1,250	18	C	$65.00
F-D	Plastic cap	Ea	3,000		2,980	3,100	18	C	$32.50

Purpose: To analyze inventory by part on a weekly basis showing quantity on hand, quantity on order, usage, and unit prices

Distribution: Stock manager, treasurer, cash manager, accountant, controller, CFO

Use: To analyze inventory usage so adequate inventory levels can be maintained to meet demand

Action to be taken: Use material requirement planning (MRP) systems to avoid part shortage.

EXHIBIT 3-3
WEEKLY OPEN-TO-BUY REPORT

Description	Total	Class A	Class B	Class C
Desired ending inventory	$537,800	$146,000	$312,000	$79,800
Plus: Planned sales	690,000	198,000	325,000	167,000
Total stock required	1,227,800	344,000	637,000	246,800
Less: Beginning inventory on hand	522,000	165,000	245,000	112,000
Budgeted purchases	705,800	179,000	392,000	134,800
Outstanding orders	567,000	135,672	245,789	123,675
Open to buy	$138,800	$43,328	$146,211	$ 11,125

Purpose: To show desired ending inventory, budgeted sales, stock requirements, budgeted purchases, outstanding orders, and open to buy

Distribution: Purchasing agents, stock manager, inventory supervisor

Use: To help regulate purchases

Action to be taken: Make sure purchases are within budget.

EXHIBIT 3-4
MONTHLY INVENTORY TURNOVER REPORT

Department	Inventory Turnover	Percentage of Sales	Sales in Dollars	Average Stock at Retail
A	9.9	15%	$67,890	$6,842
B	8.9	10%	45,670	5,123
C	6.5	15%	65,456	10,001
D	11.5	20%	87,905	7,656
E	3.2	17%	78,123	24,532
F	8.7	23%	102,000	11,689
	6.8	100%	$447,044	$65,843

Purpose: To show inventory turnover rate and percentage of sales total

Distribution: Purchasing agent, cash manager, VP-production/operations, controller, CFO

Use: To help manage inventory by showing how much money is tied up in inventory

Action to be taken: Improve turnover by reducing investment in inventory.

EXHIBIT 3-5
QUARTERLY SEASONAL BUILDUP ANALYSIS REPORT

Month	Unit Sales Demand	Sales *Minus* Max. Plant Capacity	Inventory Buildup	Plant capacity = 20,000 units
March	16,700	(3,300)		
April	13,560	(6,440)		
May	22,500	2,500	2,500	
June	28,500	8,500	11,000	
July	25,000	5,000	16,000	
August	19,000	(1,000)	15,000	
September	18,000	(2,000)	13,000	
October	17,000	(3,000)	10,000	
November	19,500	(500)	9,500	
December	12,000	(8,000)	1,500	
January	12,000	(8,000)		
February	12,000	(8,000)		

Purpose: To schedule inventory buildup to meet seasonal demand

Distribution: Purchasing agent, cash manager, stock manager, inventory supervisor, VP-production/operations

Use: To analyze seasonal inventory needs for marketing and cash management purposes

Action to be taken: Monitor inventory buildup to avoid shortages.

EXHIBIT 3-6
MONTHLY APPRAISAL OF INVENTORY INVESTMENT REPORT

Month	Description	Inventory Dollars			Age of Inventory in Days*		
		Actual	Budget	Variance +(-)	Actual	Budget	Variance +(-)
April	Raw material	$546,789	$478,000	$(68,789)	43	41	-2
	Work in process	176,590	210,000	33,410	10	9	-1
	Finished	246,789	345,000	98,211	28	29	1
	Total	970,168	1,033,000	62,832	81	79	-2
May	Raw material	500,676	495,000	(5,678)	42	42	0
	Work in process	234,567	210,000	(24,567)	11	12	1
	Finished	412,678	420,000	7,322	27	30	3
	Total	1,147,923	1,125,000	(22,923)	80	84	4
June	Raw material	499,988	510,000	10,102	44	42	-2
	Work in process	231,456	230,000	(1,456)	9	11	2
	Finished	426,890	435,000	8,110	30	31	1
	Total	1,158,334	1,175,000	16,666	83	84	1

(365 days x cost of inventory)/use of inventory item (raw materials issued, work in process finished, or finished goods sold)

EXHIBIT 3-6
MONTHLY APPRAISAL OF INVENTORY INVESTMENT REPORT, *Cont'd*

Purpose: To show investment in inventory and average age of inventory in days compared to budget

Distribution: Treasurer, inventory supervisor, controller, CFO

Use: To analyze controls over inventory

Action to be taken: Keep inventories in line with budget and make sure inventory control procedures are working.

EXHIBIT 3-7
MONTHLY OBSOLESCENCE REPORT

Part No.	Description	Last Usage Date	Unit of Measure	On-Hand Quantity	Unit Price	Total Dollars
7963	Metal tube	2/14/87	ea	456	$145	$66,120
1556	Comtel hose heater	2/4/89	ea	211	78	16,458
3321	Plastic screws	12/23/90	ea	34	11	374
1678	Marble vanity	2/24/93	ea	34	211	7,174
4536	Hot water heater	3/7/93	ea	15	342	5,130
5436	Solar closet	1/294	ea	34	321	10,914
4563	Auto maid	4/8/94	ea	435	23	10,005
4352	Fitprice pump	2/5/95	ea	67	45	3,015
4432	Tub enclosine	4/6/95	ea	34	98	3,332
2768	Standard steamiest	5/6/95	ea	234	34	7,956
Total obsolete material						$130,478

Purpose: To show obsolete inventory, on-hand quantity, unit price, and total dollars, ranked by last usage dates

Distribution: Stock manager, inventory supervisor, sales manager

Use: To itemize obsolete inventory for planning and control purposes

Action to be taken: Minimize obsolete inventory.

EXHIBIT 3-8
MONTHLY INVENTORY CONTROL REPORT

Part No.	Description	ABC Code	Unit Price	Unit of Measure	Beginning of Month Balance	Receipts	Usage	On-Hand Quantity	On-Order Quantity	Current Mo. Issue Freq.	Ave. Mo. Usage	On-Hand Qty. in $
M	Water motor assem.	B	$38.50	ea	200	400	490	110	600	20	250	$4,235
F	Frame assem.	B	176.40	ea	300		200	100	500	10	185	17,640
H	Hose recpt. assem.	B	48.75	ea	1,500	200	375	1,325	400	10	330	64,594
M-A	Aluminum tube	A	58.00	ea	30,000		170	29,830	150	16	240	1,730,140
M-B	Metal screws	C	95.50	ea	5,000	275	200	5,075		16	122	484,663
M-C	Water motor	A	113.40	ea	1,000	350	925	425	500	24	820	48,195
F-D	Plastic cap	C	39.60	ea	3,000		1,890	1,110	1,500	21	985	43,956

Purpose: To show unit receipts and usage, quantity on hand in units, units on order, and quantity on hand in dollars

Distribution: Stock manager, treasurer, cash manager, accountant, controller, CFO

Use: To analyze inventory usage to maintain inventory levels needed to meet demand

Action to be taken: Use material requirements planning (MRP) systems to control inventory.

EXHIBIT 3-9
INVENTORY ITEMS IN ANNUAL-DOLLAR-VOLUME ORDER (20x2)

Stock #	Annual demand	Unit Cost	Annual Dollar-Volume	Percent	20x1 Percent
510	35,000	$30.50	$1,067,500	53.2	54.3
310	1,000	650.00	650,000	32.4	32.3
001	2,000	55.00	110,000	5.5	4.8
378	20,000	5.00	100,000	5.0	4.4
423	4,200	10.00	42,000	2.1	2.6
188	500	36.00	18,000	0.9	0.7
320	35	275.00	9,625	0.5	0.4
115	100	44.00	4,400	0.2	0.3
275	400	5.00	2,000	0.1	0.1
323	800	1.75	1,400	0.1	0.1
			$2,004,925	100.0	100.0

Purpose: To determine annual dollar volumes of inventory

Distribution: Inventory manager, plant manager, operations manager, controller, treasurer, CFO

Use: To perform ABC analysis for inventory control

Action to be taken: Assign priorities: A items should receive major, B items moderate, and C items little attention.

Keep records:

• class A items: permanent inventory records, which require frequent, often daily attention.

• class B items: less expensive than A items but still important, which require intermediate control.

• class C items include most inventory items, usually less expensive and less used. There is usually a high safety stock level for C items.

There should be blanket purchase orders for A items and only "spot orders" for Bs and Cs. Examples of inventory controls that may be based on ABC classification are:

1. Purchasing authorizations for class A items might be signed by the president, for class B items by the head of the purchasing department, and for class C items by any purchasing agent.

2. Physical inventory check: Count A items monthly, B items twice a year, and C items annually.

EXHIBIT 3-9
INVENTORY ITEMS IN ANNUAL-DOLLAR-VOLUME ORDER (20x2)
Cont'd

3. Forecasting: Forecast A needs by several methods with resolution by a prediction committee, B items by simple trend projection, and C items by best guess of the responsible purchasing agent.

4. Safety stock: No safety stock for A, one month's for supply B, and three months' for C items.

EXHIBIT 3-10
MONTHLY ANALYSIS OF INVENTORY REPORT

	Beginning of Year	End of Previous Month	End of Current Month	Current Month Over (Under) Beginning of Year $	%	Current Month Over (Under) End of Previous Month $	%	Budget— End of Current Month	Current Month Actual Over (Under) Budget $	%
Appliances										
Raw materials	458,900	396,000	406,000	(52,900)	-12	10,000	3	428,000	(22,000)	-5
Work in process	375,000	328,000	347,690	(27,310)	-7	19,690	6	350,000	(2,310)	-1
Finished goods	618,960	571,250	533,000	(85,960)	-14	(38,250)	-7	525,000	8,000	2
Total	1,452,860	1,295,250	1,286,690	(166,170)	-11	(8,560)	-1	1,303,000	(16,310)	-1
Electronics										
Raw materials	634,750	561,000	502,000	(132,750)	-21	(59,000)	-11	452,000	50,000	11
Work in process	211,680	241,500	256,750	45,070	21	15,250	6	130,000	126,750	98
Finished goods	165,890	98,740	125,600	(40,290)	-24	26,860	27	140,000	(14,400)	-10
Total	1,1012,320	901,240	884,350	(127,970)	-13	(16,890)	-2	722,000	162,350	22

Purpose: To show inventory on hand by departments, compared to budget

Distribution: Stock manager, inventory supervisor, controller, CFO

Use: To analyze inventory levels to measure the effectiveness of inventory planning and control, compared to budget

Action to be taken: Analyze variances so that proper corrective action can be taken.

EXHIBIT 3-11
RETAIL INVENTORY METHOD REPORT

	1 Cost	2 Retail	3 Markup
Beginning inventory	$88,000	$161,000	$73,000
Net purchases	670,000	1,108,690	438,690
Freight in	31,000		(31,000)
Additional markups		22,100	22,100
Total	789,000	1,291,790	502,790
Net sales		1,030,000	
Net markdowns		73,000	
Employee discounts		6,800	
Total retail deduction		1,109,800	
Ending inventory at retail		181,990	
Cost-to-retail percentage ($789,000/$1,291,790)			61.1%
Ending inventory at estimated cost ($181,990 x 61.1%)	111,156		
Cost of goods sold	677,844		

Purpose: To provide an efficient way to value a retailer's ending inventory and determine the cost of goods sold

Distribution: Cost accountant, controller, VP-merchandising, CFO

Use: To estimate the retailer's ending inventory

Action to be taken: A retailer's ending inventory is valued by applying a cost-to-retail price percentage to the retail value of the inventory. Accuracy depends on the assumption that the ending inventory contains the same proportion of goods at the various markup percentages as did the original group of merchandise available for sale. If the mix of markup percentages does not remain constant, the accuracy of the estimate is suspect, and the method should not be used.

EXHIBIT 3-12
GROSS PROFIT METHOD REPORT

	1	2	3
Beginning inventory		20,000	
Net cost of purchases		50,000	
Cost of goods available for sale		70,000	
Net sales	80,000		
Estimated gross profit	24,000		
Estimated gross profit percentage			30%
Estimated cost of goods sold		56,000	
Estimated ending inventory		14,000	

Purpose: To provide an efficient way to estimate ending inventory

Distribution: Cost accountant, controller, VP-merchandising, CFO

Use: To estimate ending inventory by deducting estimated cost of sales from the cost of goods available for sale

Action to be taken: For this method to be valid, the gross profit percentage used must be representative of the merchandising activity leading up to the date of this estimate. Use a statistical method such as *correlation analysis* to see if the percentage is reliable.

EXHIBIT 3-13
ECONOMIC ORDER QUANTITY REPORT

Annual demand: **6,400**

Cost per unit:	$40		Economic order quantity = 400
Ordering cost:	$100		
Carrying cost:	20%		

Order quantity:	**300**	**400**	**500**	**1,000**
Ordering cost:	$2,133	$1,600	$1,280	$640
Carrying cost:	1,200	1,600	2,000	4,000
Total cost:	$3,333	$3,200	$3,280	$4,640

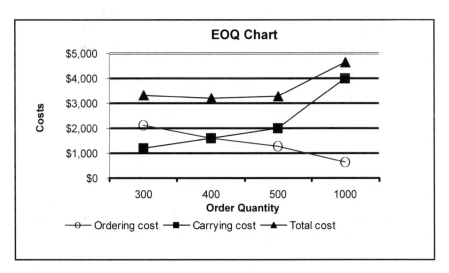

Purpose: To determine economic order quantity (EOQ)

Distribution: Inventory manager, production/operations manager, treasurer, cash manager, controller, CFO

Use: To ensure investment inventory is kept to a minimum

Action to be taken: Order the quantity of materials or finished goods that result in lowest total costs of carrying and ordering.

EXHIBIT 3-14
ECONOMIC ORDER QUANTITY WITH QUANTITY
DISCOUNT REPORT

		Price Discount Schedule	
Annual demand:	**6,400**	**Order Quantity**	**Unit Price**
		1 - 499 sets	40.00
Ordering cost:	$100	500 - 999	39.90
Carrying cost:	8	1,000 or more	39.80
Economic order quantity =		400	

Order quantity	400	500	1,000
Ordering cost	$1,600	$1,280	$640
Carrying cost	1,600	2,000	4,000
Product cost	256,000	255,360	254,720
Total cost	259,200	258,640	259,360

Purpose: To determine the most economic quantities to order given quantity discount options

Distribution: Inventory manager, production/operations manager, treasurer, cash manager, controller, CFO

Use: To ensure minimum investment in inventory

Action to be taken: Order the quantity of materials or finished goods that result in the lowest total carrying, ordering, and product costs.

CHAPTER 4

Reports for Investments

Many companies are concerned about how to manage surplus funds, temporary idle cash. The funds must be made available to cover any shortfall in cash flow or working capital and as a reservoir for capital spending and acquisition.

Corporate financial officers must be conservative in investing idle cash in financial securities, because the money should be on hand without loss in value.

- Exhibit 4-1 illustrates that integral to many business decisions is a risk-return trade-off.

- Exhibit 4-2 analyzes the return on short-term investments.

- Exhibits 4-3 through 4-5 relate to mutual fund investing.

- Investing in financial derivatives should only be done with a great deal of care, though they can be used for hedging. Exhibit 4-6 lists the types of financial derivatives available to corporate investors.

- Exhibit 4-7 is a checklist for risk management when using these futures contracts, in order to minimize currency risk, interest rate risk, market risk, etc.

EXHIBIT 4-1

RISK VERSUS RETURN TRADE-OFF REPORTING

		Case A ($)	Case B ($)
Cash	(a)	2,000	2,000
Marketable securities	(b)		20,000
Other current assets	(c)	50,000	50,000
Fixed assets		100,000	100,000
Total	(d)	152,000	172,000
Current liabilities	(e)	30,000	30,000
Long-term debt		50,000	50,000
Owners' equity		72,000	92,000
Total		152,000	172,000
Net income	(f)	20,000	20,800 (g)

Note: (g) During the year Case B held $20,000 in T-bills, which earned an 8% return ($1,600 for the year, or $800 after taxes).

Current ratio = [(a) + (b) + (c)]/(e)   1.73   2.4
Return on total assets (ROA) = (f)/(d) 13.16%   12.09%

Purpose: To illustrate that a risk-return trade-off is integral to many business decisions

Distribution: Treasurer, cash manager, controller, CFO, CEO

Use: To help evaluate a project's profitability-liquidity trade-off

Action to be taken: Assess and balance various risk-return trade-offs in order to create a sound financial and investment plan. In this example, to increase liquidity, you may opt for additional cash, short-term securities such as T-bills and commercial paper, or some combination of both, after analyzing trade-offs of liquidity and return.

EXHIBIT 4-2
QUARTERLY INVESTMENT REPORT

Description	Purchase Date	Maturity Date	Interest Rate	Face Value	Purchase Price	Premium=P (Discount=D)	Accrued Interest Earned
Treasury Bill	8/11/99	8/9/00	10.6757%	$325,000	$293,059	$(31,941.00)	$12,340.65
Treasury Note	8/19/99	2/29/2001	15.125%	100,000	100,000	4,312.50	5,125.71
Treasury Bill	8/11/99	2/9/00	10.23539%	110,000	104,672.46	(5,327.54)	4,225.92
				$535,000	$497,731	$(32,956.04)	$21,692.28

Purpose: To compare various aspects of alternative short-term investments

Distribution: Chief investment officer (CIO), treasurer, cash manager, controller, CFO, CEO

Use: To help manage temporary surplus funds

Action to be taken: First and most important, make sure that maturity dates match the timing of fund needs. Yield is a secondary consideration in short-term investments.

EXHIBIT 4-3
PORTFOLIO SELECTION REPORT

Year	Annual Return (%) ABC	XYZ	DEF
1	11.2	8.0	10.9
2	10.8	9.2	22.0
3	11.6	6.6	37.9
4	-1.6	18.5	-11.8
5	-4.1	7.4	12.9
6	8.6	13.0	-7.5
7	6.8	22.0	9.3
8	11.9	14.0	48.7
9	12.0	20.5	-1.9
10	8.3	14.0	19.1
11	6.0	19.0	-3.4
12	10.2	9.0	43.0
Average:	**7.64**	**13.43**	**14.93**

Covariance Matrix

	ABC	XYZ	DEF
ABC	0.00258	-0.00025	0.00440
XYZ	-0.00025	0.00276	-0.00542
DEF	0.00440	-0.00542	0.03677

	ABC	XYZ	DEF	Total
Portfolio	27.2%	63.4%	9.4%	100%

Expected return: 12.00%
Required return: 12.00%

Portfolio variance: 0.00112

Purpose: To design an optimal investment portfolio

Distribution: Chief investment officer, treasurer, cash manager, controller, CFO, CEO

Use: To choose a portfolio that minimizes risk as measured by variance

Action to be taken: In this example, the optimal portfolio has 27.2% of the fund in ABC stock, 63.4% in XYZ, and 9.4% in DEF stock.

EXHIBIT 4-4
FIGURING RETURN ON A MUTUAL FUND

1. The number of months for which the fund's performance is measured — 5

2. Investment value at the beginning of the period—total number of shared times the net asset value (NAV) — $2,500.00

3. The ending value of investment —number of shares currently owned times current NAV — $5,890.38

4. Total dividends and capital gains received in cash (not reinvested) — $0.00

5. Additional investments (minus redemptions) — $3,500.00

6. Computation of gain or loss:
   (a) Add line 2 to 1/2 of the total on line 5 — $4,250.00
   (b) Add lines 3 and 4, then subtract 1/2 of the total on line 5 — $5,140.38
   (c) Divide the (b) sum by the (a) sum — 1.2095
   (d) Subtract the numeral 1 from the result of (c), then multiply by 100 — 20.95%

7. Annualized return: 12 divided by the number of months in line 1; multiply the result by (d) % — 50.28%

Purpose: To calculate return on a mutual fund investment

Distribution: Chief investment officer, pension manager, treasurer, cash manager, controller, CFO

Use: To set the company's overall investment policy

Action to be taken: Based on past performance, the company must readjust its investment portfolio.

EXHIBIT 4-5
DOLLAR-COST-AVERAGING VERSUS LUMP-SUM INVESTING

	Dollar-Cost Purchase Plan			Lump-Sum Up-Front Investing		
	Amount	Share	Shares	Amount	Share	Shares
Period	Invested ($)	Price ($)	Purchased	Invested ($)	Price ($)	Purchased
1	100	12.50	8.00	1,000	12.50	80.00
2	100	8.00	12.50	–	8.00	–
3	100	10.00	10.00	–	10.00	–
4	100	8.00	12.50	–	8.00	–
5	100	10.00	10.00	–	10.00	–
6	100	12.50	8.0	–	12.50	–
7	100	14.28	7.00	–	14.28	–
8	100	12.50	8.00	–	12.50	–
9	100	16.67	6.00	–	16.67	–
10	100	20.00	5.00	–	20.00	–
	$1,000	$124.45	87.00	$1,000	$124.45	80.00

Average share price = $124.45/10 = $12.45	= $12.45
Total shares owned = 87	= 80
Average share cost = $1,000/87 shares = $11.49	= $1,000/80 shares = $12.50
Total market value = 87 shares x $20 = $1,740	= 80 shares x $20 = $1,600

Purpose: To compare a dollar-cost-averaging investment plan with a lump-sum up-front plan

Distribution: Chief investment officer, treasurer, cash manager, controller, CFO, CEO

Use: To stabilize a firm's surplus funds. Dollar-cost-averaging will work as long as prices of the stocks targeted rise over time

Action to be taken: Do not use this strategy if high transactions costs would lower returns over time. (That is why mutual funds, which often charge either no sales fee or a flat fee are a popular way to implement this strategy.)

EXHIBIT 4-6
GENERAL CHARACTERISTICS OF MAJOR TYPES OF
FINANCIAL DERIVATIVES

Type	Market	Contract	Definition
Option	OTC or organized exchange	Custom* or Standard	Gives the buyer the right but no obligation to buy or sell a specific amount at a specified price within a specified period.
Futures	Organized exchange	Standard	Obligates the holder to buy or sell at a specified price on a specified date.
Forward	OTC	Custom	Same obligation as futures. Not standardized. Delivery required.
Swap	OTC	Custom	Agreement between the parties to make periodic payments to each other during the swap period. Examples are interest swaps and currency swaps.
Hybrid	OTC	Custom	Incorporates various provisions of other types of derivatives.

Custom contracts are negotiated between the parties with respect to their value, period, and other terms.

Purpose: To show financial derivative alternatives available to corporate investors

Distribution: Chief investment officer (CIO), treasurer, CFO, CEO

Use: To choose which to use for hedging purposes

Action to be taken: Use these contracts only to minimize certain risks, such as currency, interest rate, or market risk.

EXHIBIT 4-7
CHECKLIST FOR MANAGING DERIVATIVES RISK

1. General

- Does the company use derivatives? If so, which types?
- Has the company objectives for the use of derivatives?
- Are the objectives linked at different company levels?
- Are the objectives consistent with each other?

2. The Board of Directors

- Was the risk management plan approved by the Board of Directors?
- Does the board receive periodic reports on derivatives activity?
- Does the board make timely, corrective actions on audit recommendations?

3. Audit Committee

- Does the Risk Management Committee oversee audit programs?
- Does the committee oversee both internal and external auditors?
- Does the committee periodically report to the board on audit results?

4. Senior Management

- Is there a risk management plan?
- When was the risk management plan last reviewed?
- Has there been a change in business or market circumstances since the last review? If so, when will it be incorporated into the risk management plan?
- Does the risk management plan clearly define when derivatives may be used?
- Has senior management approved procedures and controls to implement these policies?
- Does the board make timely, corrective action on audit recommendations?

5. Market Risk

- Are derivatives periodically marked-to-market?
- Is the mark-to-market adjusted for expected future costs, including administrative costs?
- Does the risk management plan have a market risk limit?
- Is the method of measuring market risk consistent?

EXHIBIT 4-7
CHECKLIST FOR MANAGING DERIVATIVES RISK, *Cont'd*

6. Credit Risk

- Is credit risk measured by calculating current exposure, that is, by the current replacement cost of derivatives?
- Is credit risk measured by calculating potential exposure, that is, by the likely future replacement cost of derivatives?
- Is credit exposure on both derivatives and to all counter-parties aggregated?
- Does the risk management plan set a credit risk limit?
- Is the credit risk limit adhered to?
- Is there a credit risk manager with clear independence and authority?
- Does the credit risk manager approve credit exposure standards, set credit limits, monitor the use of credit limits, review credits and concentrations of credit risk, and monitor credit risk execution?
- Is there a master agreement with each counter-party, and is it used? If there is no master agreement, are other attempts made to reduce credit exposure with that party?
- Does the firm use credit rating agencies?

7. Operational Risk

- Do personnel handling derivatives have appropriate training, skills, and degrees of specialization?
- Are supervisors qualified?
- Are support staff qualified?
- Is EDP support adequate? If not, is there a plan in motion to secure adequate EDP support?
- Do the systems used make it easy to measure and compare various risks?
- Is the authority to commit the company to derivative transactions clear?
- Is the designated authority complied with?
- Are periodic reports of risks accurate?
- Does management use the reports?
- Have "panic values" that require immediate reporting been set?
- When "panic values" are reached, are they reported immediately?

EXHIBIT 4-7
CHECKLIST FOR MANAGING DERIVATIVES RISK, *Cont'd*

  8. Legal Risk

  • Does trained legal counsel regularly review the law in all jurisdictions where these transactions occur?
  • Does legal counsel periodically review derivative instruments to make sure they are legally enforceable?
  • Does counsel periodically review the capacity of all parties to enter into derivative transactions?

  9. Systems Risk

  • Is a large percentage of derivatives activity with a small number of customers?
  • Is a large percentage of derivatives activity with a small number of dealers?
  • Do authorities monitor currency-related derivatives activity in the appropriate countries?

Purpose: To provide a checklist for managing risk in the use of derivatives

Distribution: Directors, chief investment officer, treasurer, CFO, CEO

Use: To analyze options for using futures contracts to hedge

Action to be taken: Establish a derivative management policy to minimize currency, interest rate, and market risk.

CHAPTER 5

Sales Efficiency Reporting

The reports in this chapter are designed to help you evaluate how well the sales function is being performed.

- Exhibits 5-1 and 5-2 help you monitor expenses for the entire sales department and expenses by product.

- Exhibits 5-3 through 5-6 trace sources of backlogs and possible reasons why sales were lost.

EXHIBIT 5-1
SALES DEPARTMENT EXPENSES

Actual			Better (Worse) than Budget	
Current Month	Year-to-Date		Current Month	Year-to-Date
$5,000	$20,000	Salaries–management	$0	$0
16,250	67,500	Salaries–reps	265	(1,450)
8,910	41,244	Commissions	(654)	2,059
2,105	9,204	Allowances	351	(849)
4,256	15,487	Traveling	422	218
3,525	11,893	Advertising	(1,101)	618
1,575	6,300	Occupancy	0	876
1,988	8,029	Telephone	(326)	698
685	3,074	Other expenses	(98)	326
$44,294	$182,731	TOTAL	($1,141)	$2,496
4.80%	4.95%	Sales Department Expenses/Net Sales	-0.20%	0.80%

Purpose: To monitor expenses of the sales department

Distribution: Sales manager

Use: To compare actual and budgeted departmental expenses for month and year-to-date

Action to be taken: Investigate unfavorable variances and take steps to reduce unproductive costs.

EXHIBIT 5-2
SALES EXPENSE REPORT

Month				Year-to-Date		
Actual	**Budget**	**Difference**		**Actual**	**Budget**	**Difference**
			Net Sales			
11,254	12,500	(1,246)	Product A	35,924	39,600	(3,676)
21,362	18,250	3,112	Product B	59,142	52,800	6,342
8,965	9,450	(485)	Product C	29,586	28,600	986
15,672	14,600	1,072	Product D	46,821	43,000	3,821
			Sales Expense/			
			Net Sales			
0.0026	0.0025	0.0001	Product A	0.0027	0.0024	0.0003
0.0021	0.0015	0.0006	Product B	0.0021	0.0016	0.0005
0.0026	0.0033	(0.0007)	Product C	o.0022	0.0026	(0.0004)
0.0020	0.0019	0.0001	Product D	0.0014	0.0017	(0.0003)

Purpose: To monitor sales expense and net sales by product

Distribution: Sales manager

Use: To track actual and budgeted net sales for each product and compare with sales expense for the same period

Action to be taken: Investigate unfavorable variances and reasons for higher sales expense relative to net sales.

EXHIBIT 5-3
BACKLOG—MONTHLY

	Jan.	Feb.	March	April	May	June	July	Aug.	Sept.	Oct.	Nov.	Dec.
Beginning Backlog	$55,000	$36,031	$14,070	$5,436								
Add: New orders	42,500	23,470	65,897	49,521								
Less: Shipments	61,250	45,620	76,542	39,845								
Adjustments	(219)	189	2,011	1,087								
Ending backlog	$36,031	$14,070	$5,436	$16,199								
Backlog by Customer												
U.S. govt. (defense)	$9,167	$1,961	$1,019	$3,795								
U.S. govt. (non-defense)	14,358	5,239	2,497	4,986								
Commercial (domestic)	6,895	4,859	1,055	3,354								
Commercial (foreign)	5,611	2,011	865	4,064								
	$36,031	$14,070	$5,436	$16,199								

Purpose: To monitor the status of sales backlog

Distribution: Sales manager

Use: To calculate changes in backlog for the month, and determine backlog by customer

Action to be taken: Identify the largest backlogs and take corrective action.

EXHIBIT 5-4
END-OF-MONTH BACKLOG—ACTUAL VERSUS BUDGET (in Thousands)

	Jan.	Feb.	March	April	May	June	July	Aug.	Sept.	Oct.	Nov.	Dec.
Product A												
Actual	$782	$597	$271	$462	$314	$351	1,000	1,250	600	425	1,250	200
Budget	725	500	410	500	375	400						
Difference	57	97	(139)	(38)	(61)	(49)						
Product B												
Actual	395	370	498	702	615	839	925	1,150	850	625	950	325
Budget	410	340	425	625	510	725						
Difference	(15)	30	73	77	105	114						

Purpose: To monitor end-of-month backlog compared with budget

Distribution: Sales manager, production planning manager

Use: To compare actual performance against budget amount

Action to be taken: Where backlogs continue to grow (as with Product B), corrective action may be necessary.

EXHIBIT 5-5
LOST SALES REPORT

Date	Product	Customer	Amount of Lost Sale	Reason(s) for Lost Sale
1-Nov	Motors	Phillips	$32,450	Price
12-Nov	Bearings	Merthna's	3,456	Credit terms/freight
23-Nov	Sheatings	Joyce's Automotive	8,563	Delivery terms
6-Dec	Motors	Carruther's Brothers	49,563	Price
10-Dec	Steel Drums	Packwood Supplies	4,291	Credit terms/promotional allowance
19-Dec	Casings	Diamond, Inc.	12,489	Freight/delivery terms

Purpose: To track specific reason why sales were lost

Distribution: Sales manager

Use: To document why customers do not buy an item from us

Action to be taken: First, reevaluate motor pricing, because in the above example, motor sales were lost twice because of price.

EXHIBIT 5-6
DIVISION SALES EXPENSE

Division	Net Sales Actual	Budget	% of Plan	Sales Exp/Net Sales Actual %	Planned %
A	$623,498	$705,000	88.44	3.3233	3.3220
B	519,463	493,500	105.26	2.9581	3.2160
C	227,865	205,000	111.15	3.4116	3.3500
D	825,854	954,500	86.52	3.1125	3.1350

Purpose: To monitor whether sales expense is a steady and reasonable percentage of net sales

Distribution: Sales manager, division manager

Use: To calculate actual sales made compared with plan and determine actual and planned sales expense percentage for each division

Action to be taken: Investigate unfavorable trends to improve profitability and cut excessive costs.

CHAPTER 6

Reporting on Sales and Service Revenue

Essential to good reporting of sales and service revenue is the continuous monitoring of product sales performance.

- The Exhibits 6-1 through 6-8 will help you monitor product performance by product line, territory, and channel of distribution, among others.

- Finally, Exhibit 6-9 will help you assess the performance of new products.

EXHIBIT 6-1
SALES REPORT BY PRODUCT

| | Current Month | | | | Year-to-Date | | | |
| | Budget | | Actual | | Budget | | Actual | |
Product	Units	Amount	Units	Actual	Units	Amount	Units	Amount
Division A:								
Housewares	12,000	$264,000	11,524	$253,548	39,500	$869,000	37,529	$825,638
Furniture	6,250	343,750	7,392	406,560	19,500	1,072,500	20,922	1,150,710
Apparel	4,500	15,750	4,291	15,019	13,000	45,500	14,344	50,204
Subtotal	22,750	623,500	23,207	675,127	72,000	1,987,000	72,795	2,026,552
Division B:								
Housewares	8,500	170,000	9,044	181,882	26,750	535,200	31,521	630,487
Furniture	4,550	236,600	5,975	310,749	14,500	754,225	12,941	689,938
Apparel	12,700	34,925	10,989	30,218	36,750	101,060	34,639	97,257
Subtotal	25,750	441,525	26,008	522,849	78,000	1,390,485	79,101	1,417,682

Purpose: To assess monthly and year-to-date actual and budgeted sales by product group

Distribution: Sales manager

Use: To accumulate budgeted and actual sale units and amounts by product within division

Action to be taken: In conjunction with other reports, evaluate divisional performance.

EXHIBIT 6-2
CHANNEL PROFITABILITY ANALYSIS

Channel	Sales			Manufacturing Margin	Total Expenses	Gross Earnings		Last Year's Earnings	% Sales to New Cust.
	Product A	Product B	Total			$	%		
Wholesale									
Special	$2,422	$1,540	$3,962	$1,531	$330	$1,201	30.3	$1,104	13.0
General	417	731	1,148	386	322	64	5.6	21	26.4
Total	2,839	2,271	5,110	1,917	652	1,265	24.8	1,125	15.0
Retail									
Appliance	5,920	2,566	8,486	4,296	822	3,474	40.9	3,515	29.4
Department	2,488	1,282	3,770	1,873	595	1,278	33.9	1,301	0
Discount	2,821	3,871	6,692	3,375	735	2,640	39.3	2,372	41.0
Furniture	631	226	857	415	177	238	27.7	240	25.8
Supermarket	286	8	294	140	164	(24)	(8.1)	0	100.0
Trading Stamps	542	46	588	266	171	95	16.1	15	0
Variety	299	2	301	150	130	20	6.6	(2)	0
Total	12,987	8,001	20,988	10,515	2,794	7,721	36.8	7,441	27.2
Other	1,828	1,319	3,147	1,643	340	1,303	41.4	1,298	24.8
Grand Total	$17,654	$11,591	$29,245	$14,075	$3,786	$10,289	35.2	$9,864	23.1

Purpose: To determine which outlets for merchandise are most profitable and are growing

Distribution: Sales manager, top management

Use: To accumulate returns by channel of distribution, compare with last year, and separate out sales to new customers

Action to be taken: Decide where sales effort should be focused and where expenses can be reduced.

EXHIBIT 6-3
FORECAST BY TERRITORY (in thousands)

Territory	Previous Year Actual	Current Year Forecast Half			Next Year Forecast Quarter				
		1st	2nd	Total	1st	2nd	3rd	4th	Total
New England									
Net sales	$1,875,126	$950,250	$1,110,500	$2,060,750	$511,000	$515,250	$525,600	$540,100	$2,091,950
GP%	19.70	20.10	20.10	20.10	19.50	20.80	20.50	21.00	20.75
Contribution margin %	10.90	11.20	11.25	11.23	11.40	11.35	11.25	11.40	11.32
Northeast									
Net sales	$2,150,232	$1,275,000	$1,350,000	$2,625,000	$835,000	$841,250	$826,300	$852,500	$3,355,050
GP%	16.80	17.00	16.90	16.96	17.25	17.50	16.90	17.30	17.28
Contribution margin %	12.15	13.20	13.10	13.15	14.20	13.80	14.15	14.10	14.13
Southeast									
Net sales	$920,576	$515,000	$525,500	$1,040,500	$280,000	$295,560	$315,600	$287,600	$1,178,760
GP%	21.56	22.00	22.10	22.00	22.0	22.50	22.25	22.45	22.35
Contribution margin %	13.48	13.50	13.85	13.70	13.40	13.60	13.50	13.60	13.50

Purpose: To provide forecasts by territory

Distribution: Top management, territory manager

Use: To accumulate last year actual and forecasts for this year and next by territory

Action to be taken: Correct unfavorable trends in each of the territories.

EXHIBIT 6-4
PRODUCT LINE PERFORMANCE—YEAR-TO-DATE

	Total	Products A	B	C
Net Sales	$100,000	$50,000	$20,000	$30,000
Less: Variable cost of sales	43.000	20,000	13,000	10,000
Manufacturing margin	57,000	30,000	7,000	20,000
Less: Variable distribution costs	20,000	15,000	2,000	3,000
Contribution margin	$37,000	$15,000	$5,000	$17,000
Less: Fixed and allocated costs				
Manufacturing	3,000	1,000	1,000	1,000
Selling	5,000	2,000	2,000	1,000
Advertising	5,000	2,000	2,000	1,000
Administration	2,200	1,000	500	700
Total	15,200	6,000	5,500	3,700
Operating income (or loss)	$21,800	$9,000	$(500)	$13,300
Contribution margin/net sales	37.00%	30.00%	25.00%	56.67%
Operating income/net sales	21.80%	18.00%	-2.50%	44.33%

Purpose: To track performance of various products

Distribution: Sales manager, product managers

Use: To determine contribution and operating income by product

Action to be taken: Investigate reasons for poorly performing products (e.g., Product B).

EXHIBIT 6-5

SUMMARY DIVISIONAL PERFORMANCE (Thousands of dollars)

	Actual ($)	Plan ($)	% of Plan
Net Sales			
Western Division			
Month	1,870	1,800	104%
Year-to-date	14,981	14,000	107%
Southwestern Division			
Month	1,412	1,500	94%
Year-to-date	11,967	14,000	85%
Southern Division			
Month	882	700	126%
Year-to-date	6,781	4,120	165%
Consolidated			
Month	4,164	4,000	104%
Year-to-date	33,729	32,120	105%
Net Income			
Western Division			
Month	76	72	106%
Year-to-date	679	600	113%
Southwestern Division			
Month	71	75	95%
Year-to-date	657	700	94%
Southern Division			
Month	40	35	114%
Year-to-date	439	200	220%
Consolidated			
Month	187	182	103%
Year-to-date	1,775	1,500	118%

Purpose: To summarize performance by division

Distribution: Sales manager, division managers

Use: To compare divisional actual and budgeted sales and net income for month and year-to-date to determine how well budget is being met

Action to be taken: Investigate areas that are not at 100% of plans.

EXHIBIT 6-6
ACTUAL PERFORMANCE BY TERRITORY

	Month			Year-to-Date		
	Current	Last Year	Variance	Current	Last Year	Variance
New England						
Net sales	$15,221	$19,785	$ (4,564)	$33,020	$39,026	$ (6,006)
Gross profit	11,099	12,254	(1,155)	21,512	25,041	(3,529)
Contribution margin	8,655	9,654	(999)	17,041	20,236	(3,195)
Northeast						
Net sales	9,586	10,566	(980)	19,245	22,056	(2,811)
Gross profit	3,562	4,514	(952)	7,055	9,002	(1,947)
Contribution margin	2,042	3,652	(1,610)	4,083	6,943	(2,860)
Southeast						
Net sales	26,566	22,055	4,511	52,522	43,452	9,070
Gross profit	15,923	13,548	2,375	31,214	26,357	4,857
Contribution margin	6,052	4,502	1,550	14,560	9,031	5,529

Purpose: To track performance by territory

Distribution: Sales manager, territory managers

Use: To compare current dollar volumes with last year's by territory

Action to be taken: In conjunction with other reports, investigate unfavorable variances.

EXHIBIT 6-7
SALES BY TERRITORY

	Month				Year-to-Date			
	Actual	Budget	Variance	LY Actual	Actual	Budget	Variance	LY Actual
New England	$218,450	$279,000	$ (60,550)	$258,289	$793,482	$842,000	$ (48,518)	$837,124
Mid-Atlantic	335,129	324,000	11,129	319,541	992,896	976,000	16,896	952,394
Southeast	207,412	218,000	(10,588)	211,088	642,521	657,000	(14,479)	639,215
Central	182,741	176,000	6,741	154,221	573,624	531,000	42,624	502,842
Rocky Mountain	104,944	117,000	(12,056)	90,212	384,987	352,000	32,987	349,864
Far West	108,577	97,500	11,077	80,544	287,623	293,500	(5,877)	224,818
Total	$1,157,253	$1,211,500	$ (54,247)	$1,113,895	$3,675,133	$3,651,500	$23,633	$3,506,257

Purpose: To monitor sales activity by territory

Distribution: Sales manager, territory managers

Use: To accumulate monthly and YTD actual vs. budget vs. last-year (LY) sales for each territory

Action to be taken: Decide where to concentrate activities to improve profitability.

EXHIBIT 6-8
SALES AND GROSS PROFIT BY PRODUCT LINE
(Thousands of dollars)

Product: _____

	Month			Year-to-Date		
	Actual	Budget	Difference	Actual	Budget	Difference
Net sales	$15,900	$14,275	$1,625	$62,925	$58,250	$4,675
Gross profit (GP)	$5,250	$4,950	$300	$20,570	$19,800	$770
% GP to net sales	33.02	34.68	(1.66)	32.69	33.99	(1.30)
Net profit	$2,310	$2,200	$110	$7,256	$8,750	$ (1,494)
% Net profit to net sales	14.53	15.41	(0.88)	11.53	15.02	(3.49)

Purpose: To monitor how well a particular product is performing

Distribution: Sales manager, product manager

Use: To compare actual sales, gross profit, and net profit with budget for month and year-to-date

Action to be taken: Although sales for this product are greater than budget, gross and net profit percentages are below budget; find out why.

EXHIBIT 6-9
NEW PRODUCT SALES

	Month				Year-to-Date			
	Actual	Budget	Difference	%	Actual	Budget	Difference	%
Product A	$21,276	$22,500	$ (1,224)	(5.44)	$89,451	$92,750	$ (3,299)	(3.56)
Product B	14,824	12,250	2,574	21.01	52,142	65,275	(13,133)	(20.12)
Product C*	6,027	8,250	(2,223)	(26.95)	6,027	8,250	(2,223)	(26.95)

*Product introduced in current month

Purpose: To assess sales of new products

Distribution: Sales manager, top management

Use: To compare actual sales with budget for month and year-to-date

Action to be taken: Decide whether a new product introduction is successful, or how it should be modified.

CHAPTER 7

Reporting on Salespersons

The reports in this chapter help you gauge the performance of your sales force. The statistics they provide are a basis for measuring a salesperson's performance against prior year and against budget or quota for sales and profit. Crucial statistics for analysis are calls made, sales-to-calls, number of orders, and average order size.

EXHIBIT 7-1
SALES AND PROFIT ACTIVITY

Salesperson_____

	Current Month		Year-to-Date		
	Forecast	Actual	Forecast	Actual	Actual Last Year
Gross sales	$13,750	$14,200	$55,000	$57,700	$54,250
Gross profit (GP)	$4,950	$5,250	$19,800	$20,570	$19,286
% GP to gross sales	36.00%	36.97%	36.00%	35.65%	35.55%
Net Profit	$2,200	$2,310	$8,800	$9,151	$8,577
% Net profit to gross sales	16.00%	16.27%	16.00%	15.86%	15.81%

Purpose: To monitor actual performance for sales and profit by salesperson

Distribution: Sales manager

Use: To compare actual and forecasted sales and profit data for each salesperson

Action to be taken: Here, although YTD sales are above forecast, the GP % and net profit % are below, indicating lower margin items are being sold.

EXHIBIT 7-2
ANALYSIS OF CALLS AND ORDERS (Thousands of dollars)

Salesperson _____

		Call Analysis						Order Analysis			
		Calls		Sales/Call		No. New Custom.		Orders		Sales/Order	
Week	Sales	Act	Var	Act	Var	Act	Var	Act	Var	Act	Var
7-Apr	4.9	20	0	0.24	(0.14)	6	0	15	(1)	0.33	(0.07)
14-Apr	6.8	18	(3)	0.38	0.08	7	1	12	(5)	0.56	0.18
21-Apr	7.4	20	2	0.37	0.01	3	(3)	19	5	0.39	(0.07)
28-Apr	3.0	19	(3)	0.16	(0.13)	0	(6)	14	(4)	0.21	(0.17)
Total April	22.1	77	(4)	0.29	(0.03)	16	(8)	60	(5)	0.39	(0.02)

Purpose: To monitor performance against plan for each salesperson

Distribution: Sales manager

Use: To determine how well salespeople are meeting targets

Action to be taken: If number of calls or orders are above plan but sales/calls or sales/orders are below plan, salesperson may be making smaller sales.

EXHIBIT 7-3
SALES QUOTA

	Month			Year to Date		
		Over(Under) Quota			Over(Under) Quota	
Salesperson	Actual	Amount	Percentage	Actual	Amount	Percentage
Abbott	$25,325	$3,225	12.73%	$105,398	$4,198	3.98%
Baker	19,480	(2,920)	-14.99%	84322	(1,822)	-2.16%
Jamison	22,975	275	1.20%	94233	3,033	3.22%
Zigler	14,022	1,322	9.43%	69876	(1,024)	-1.47%

Purpose: To monitor each salesperson's performance against quota

Distribution: Sales manager

Use: To compare actual sales quota by each salesperson both dollar amount and percentage

Action to be taken: Investigate reasons for unfavorable performance.

EXHIBIT 7-4
QUARTERLY PROJECTED SALES BY SALESPERSON

Salesperson	FIRST QUARTER				QUARTERS			Total Year	Actual Last Year	Difference
	January	February	March	Total	Second	Third	Fourth			
A	$2,250	$2,125	$2,325	$6,700	$6,925	$6,500	$7,150	$27,275	$25,722	1,553
B	3,500	3,225	3,600	10,325	11,250	9,075	12,500	43,150	39,062	4,088
C	2,925	2,750	3,125	8,800	9,150	7,950	9,950	35,850	31,950	3,900
D	3,825	3,650	3,975	11,450	12,575	10,750	13,200	47,975	42,999	4,976
TOTAL	$12,500	$11,750	$13,025	$37,275	$39,900	$34,275	$42,800	$154,250	$139,733	$14,517

Purpose: To cumulate budgeted sales by salesperson

Distribution: Sales manager

Use: To set goals and measure against sales last year

Action to be taken: In conjunction with other data, decide whether goals are feasible.

EXHIBIT 7-5
PLANNED VS. ACTUAL SALES BY QUARTER

Salesperson	First Quarter			Second Quarter			Third Quarter			Fourth Quarter			Total Actual	
	Actual	Forecast	Variance	Actual	Forecast	Variance	Actual	Forecast	Variance	Actual	Forecast	Variance	Current Year	Last Year
A	$67,522	$62,500	$5,022	$92,496	$89,750	$2,746	$71,287	$76,500	($5,213)	$82,544	$91,525	($8,981)	$313,849	$259,344
B	43,698	49,275	(5,577)	63,019	54,025	8,994	52,841	51,250	1,591	51,024	57,550	(6,526)	210,582	233,814
C	82,826	76,800	6,026	80,159	82,500	(2,341)	82,412	80,525	1,887	94,087	83,275	10,812	339,484	298,631
D	56,247	58,200	(1,953)	60,253	61,250	(997)	60,545	60,925	(380)	65,029	64,500	529	242,074	198,456
GRAND TOTALS	$250,293	$246,775	$3,518	$295,927	$287,525	$8,402	$267,085	$269,200	($2,115)	$292,684	$296,850	($4,166)	$1,105,989	$990,245

Purpose: To monitor salesperson's performance against budgeted sales

Distribution: Sales manager

Use: To compare actual sales against budget

Action to be taken: Investigate reasons for unfavorable variances.

EXHIBIT 7-6
SALESPERSON PERFORMANCE

	Total # of Orders		Amount		Average Order Size	
Salesperson	This Year	Last Year	This Year	Last Year	This Year	Last Year
Andersen	177	207	$93,200	$109,920	$527	$531
Feinstein	152	146	77,045	89,270	507	611
Morrone	665	759	297,650	311,220	448	410
Phillips	448	415	228,560	212,410	510	512
Torres	316	330	197,300	214,395	624	650
TOTAL	1,758	1,857	$893,755	$937,215	$508	$505

Purpose: To monitor each salesperson's orders compared with last year

Distribution: Sales manager

Use: To accumulate year-to-date number of orders and dollar volume to determine average order size; compare to same period last year

Action to be taken: Determine why Feinstein's average order size, which was well above average for the firm last year, decreased significantly this year to below the firm's average.

EXHIBIT 7-7
SALES CALLS AND ACCOUNTS ACTIVITY

Salesperson _____

	1st Quarter Actual	1st Quarter Budget	2nd Quarter Actual	2nd Quarter Budget	3rd Quarter Actual	3rd Quarter Budget	4th Quarter Actual	4th Quarter Budget	Total Year Actual	Total Year Budget
Number of sales calls	308	310		325		345		360		1,340
Number of orders										
From existing accounts	77	70		78		85		96		329
From new accounts	11	10		12		15		20		57
Number of accounts										
Gained	4									
Lost	2									
Potential	7									
At end of quarter	43	40		47		54		64		64
Total Sales	$418,247	$435,000		$460,000		$483,000		$505,000		$1,883,000
Less:										
Variable expenses	$257,356	$246,000		$258,000		$271,000		$285,000		$1,060,000
Contribution	$160,891	$189,000		$198,000		$209,000		$219,000		$815,000

Purpose: To monitor orders and account activity

Distribution: Sales manager

Use: To record actual sales calls, number of orders, and accounts as well as contribution data and compare with budget for each salesperson

Action to be taken: Here, investigate why although more orders were written than budgeted the first quarter, total actual sales were *less*, yet variable expenses are *greater* than budget.

EXHIBIT 7-8

SALESPERSON PROFITABILITY ANALYSIS (Thousands of dollars)

| | | Salesperson's Contribution | | | | | |
| | | Sales | This Year | | | | |
Salesperson	% Fulfill	Actual	Amount	%	LY Amount	No. of Calls	Ave $ Contri per Call
Baker	99	$395	$166.7	42.3	$164.2	3,100	$54
Caplan	102	404	171.8	42.6	159.4	3,270	54
Navarro	82	328	139.6	42.3	152.7	2,761	50
Evert	99	394	167.7	42.6	151.3	3,081	55
French	104	415	174.7	42.2	168.5	3,268	53

Purpose: To track contribution by salesperson

Distribution: Sales manager

Use: To record actual sale, contribution, and percentages and compare with previous year

Action to be taken: In conjunction with other data, investigate reasons for unfavorable trends.

CHAPTER 8

Customer Service Reporting

Good sales reporting requires the continuous monitoring of sales performance of each customer. Even more information should be reported for major customers. The reports in this chapter will help you track the amount, gross profit, contribution margin, and average order size for sales made to individual customers, as well as billings and collection by customers.

EXHIBIT 8-1
CUSTOMER CONTRIBUTION ANALYSIS (in thousands)

District _____

Customer Name	Sales	Gross Margin	Variable Customer Expenses							Contribution		
			Comm	Sales Exp	Price Conc	Advtg	Frt & Deliv	Order Handl	Total Variable	$	%	Last Year
Ardsley	$64.9	33.1	1.7	1.5	3.6	1.0	1.6	0.8	10.2	22.9	35.3%	23.2
Barton	71.0	36.3	1.9	1.8	3.3	1.5	1.7	0.7	10.9	25.4	35.8%	21.7
Cronen	84.3	43.5	2.2	2.4	4.4	1.6	1.9	1.1	13.6	29.9	35.5%	28.7
Dannon	58.2	28.0	1.4	1.3	3.6	1.0	1.2	0.5	9.0	19.0	32.6%	25.4
Equis	45.3	22.5	1.1	0.8	1.5	0.9	1.0	1.6	6.9	15.6	34.4%	17.8
Fernstein*	38.2	17.8	0.9	1.4	3.6	1.3	0.9	0.7	8.8	9.0	23.6%	0.0
Granger	61.7	32.1	1.6	1.3	1.2	1.4	1.7	1.5	8.7	23.4	37.9%	19.7
Holland	75.8	39.8	2.0	2.4	3.4	1.6	2.1	0.3	11.8	28.0	36.9%	23.4
Intep	68.4	35.5	1.8	0.9	1.4	1.1	1.6	1.1	7.9	27.6	40.4%	27.0
Jupiter	65.3	34.7	1.8	1.3	1.3	1.0	1.5	1.8	8.7	26.0	39.8%	24.2

*New Customer

Purpose: To show the details of variable customer expenses

Distribution: Sales manager, district manager

Use: To accumulate sales and variable expenses by customer within districts

Action to be taken: Minimize variances in gross margin by endeavoring to control variable costs.

EXHIBIT 8-2
MAJOR SALES ACCOUNTS

	Number of Orders		Dollar Sales		Average Order Size	
Customer	This Year	Last Year	This Year	Last Year	This Year	Last Year
Banks	395	419	$418,095	$455,000	$1,058.47	$1,085.92
Ferdiner	210	156	215,455	193,450	1,025.98	1,240.06
Jones	322	372	322,451	325,020	1,001.40	873.71
Schaeffer	212	228	227,525	295,452	1,073.23	1,295.84
Turner	151	82	195,385	93,450	1,293.94	1,139.63

Purpose: To monitor sales performance of major customers

Distribution: Sales manager

Use: To compare current and previous year sales volume, number of orders, and average order size of major customers

Action to be taken: In conjunction with other reports, investigate negative trends.

EXHIBIT 8-3
CUSTOMER GROSS PROFIT PERFORMANCE

	Sales			Gross Profit	
Customers	Actual	Budget	% 0f Plan	Actual %	Planned %
A	$623,498	$705,000	88.4394	33.23	33.00
B	519,463	493,500	105.2610	29.58	32.00
C	227,865	205,000	111.1537	30.41	33.50
D	825,854	954,500	86.5222	31.12	31.00

Purpose: To monitor whether customer gross profit is being maintained

Distribution: Sales manager

Use: To calculate actual sales made compared to plan and determine actual and planned Gross Profit % for each customer

Action to be taken: Here, investigate why, although sales to B and C are above plan, the actual Gross Profit % is significantly under plan.

EXHIBIT 8-4
CUSTOMER CONTRIBUTION (000s)

| | Year-to-Date | | |
Customers	Actual	Prior Year	Variance
Applebaum			
Net Sales	$18,526	$19,025	($499)
GP	$3,983	$4,186	($202)
GP%	21.50	22.00	(0.50)
Baker			
Net Sales	$24,523	$23,500	$1,023
GP	$5,792	$5,405	$387
GP%	23.62	23.00	0.62
Dennisville			
Net Sales	$21,055	$24,100	($3,045)
GP	$4,834	$5,483	($649)
GP%	22.96	22.75	0.21

Purpose: Toonitor customer gross profit contribution

Distribution: Sales manager

Use: For each customer, to compare year-to-date actual versus prior-year for net sales, gross profit, and percentage

Action to be taken: Investigate unfavorable trends with a goal of improving customer profitability.

EXHIBIT 8-5
MAJOR CUSTOMER CONTRIBUTION—YEAR-TO-DATE

| | Total | Customers | | |
		A	B	C
Net Sales	$100,000	$50,000	$20,000	$30,000
Less: Variable cost of sales	43,000	21,000	13,500	12,000
Manufacturing contribution	57,000	29,000	6,500	18,000
Less: Variable distribution costs	20,000	15,000	2,000	3,500
Contribution margin	37,000	14,000	4,500	14,500
Less: Fixed costs				
Manufacturing	3,000	1,000	1,000	1,000
Advertising	5,000	2,000	2,000	2,000
Selling	5,000	2,000	2,000	2,000
Administrative	2,200	1,500	725	750
Total	15,200	6,500	5,725	5,750
Operating income (or loss)	$21,800	$7,500	($1,225)	$8,750
Contribution margin/net sales	37.00%	28.00%	22.50%	48.33%
Operating income/net sales	21.80%	15.00%	-6.13%	29.17%

Purpose: To monitor contribution of sales made to major customers

Distribution: Sales manager

Use: To calculate contribution and operating income for each major customer

Action to be taken: Decide where to place more sales effort (e.g., here, sales to C are extremely profitable, while those to B produce a loss).

EXHIBIT 8-6
CUSTOMER ANALYSIS

Annual Volume	Customers No.	Customers %	Sales Amount	Sales %	Calls No.	Calls %
$500,000 and above	7	4.70	$4,900,000	25.92	27	7.89
$400,000 to $499,000	12	8.05	5,275,000	27.90	39	11.40
$300,000 to $399,000	6	4.03	2,125,000	11.24	21	6.14
$200,000 to $299,000	16	10.74	3,423,000	18.10	28	8.19
$100,000 to $199,000	12	8.05	1,656,000	8.76	32	9.36
$50,000 to $99,000	9	6.04	571,700	3.02	27	7.89
Under $50,000	87	58.39	957,000	5.06	168	49.12
	149	100.00	$18,907,700	100.00	342	100.00

Purpose: To analyze sales and sales effort by customer volume

Distribution: Sales manager

Use: To accumulate by annual sales volume the number of customers, as well as the amount of sales and number of calls to those customers

Action to be taken: Determine at which level the sales effort is most productive. In this case, almost 50% of the sales calls result in only about 5% of sales.

EXHIBIT 8-7
CUSTOMER BILLING AND COLLECTION REPORT

Customer	Budgeted Sales	Actual Sales to Date	% Billings to Date	Cash Receipts
A	$93,000	$63,240	0.68	$49,350
B	38,000	20,140	0.53	16,588
C	30,000	14,400	0.48	13,955
D	42,000	25,210	0.60	22,546
E	85,000	52,700	0.62	45,988

Purpose: To track billings and collections by customer

Distribution: Sales, billing, and collections managers

Use: To accumulate actual and budgeted sales, % billings, and cash received to date

Action to be taken: In conjunction with other reports, identify potential problem customers.

CHAPTER 9

Geographic Area Reporting

Managers of a business want to know which geographic areas provide the greatest sales dollars and profit, so they can decide where to concentrate their resources and activity in terms of bottom line, risk, and growth potential.

- Exhibit 9-1 shows quarterly revenue, costs, and earnings by major territory.

- Exhibits 9-2 and 9-3 help you analyze variances by geographic area. Variance analysis identifies areas of strength or weakness. An unfavorable variance means a problem with either budgeted figures or actual performance. If actual results are a problem, immediate corrective action is needed.

- Exhibit 9-4 breaks down contribution margin earned by sales territory.

- Exhibits 9-5, 9-6, and 9-7 compare actual quarterly costs and sales compared with budget. In Exhibit 9-8, there is a quarterly variance report by product to identify those products doing or not doing well in the marketplace in the various states.

EXHIBIT 9-1
QUARTERLY REVENUE, COSTS, AND PROFIT BY TERRITORY

	Iowa	Florida	Georgia	Alabama	Total
Gross sales	$800,000	$900,000	$700,000	$600,000	$3,000,000
Less: Sales returns					
and allowances	20,000	50,000	10,000	2,000	82,000
Net sales	780,000	850,000	690,000	598,000	2,918,000
Less: Costs:					
Manufacturing costs	400,000	420,000	300,000	250,000	1,370,000
Administrative costs	100,000	90,000	60,000	40,000	290,000
Selling costs	80,000	60,000	40,000	30,000	210,000
Other costs	15,000	12,000	5,000	2,000	34,000
Total costs	595,000	582,000	405,000	322,000	1,904,000
Profit	185,000	268,000	285,000	276,000	1,014,000

Purpose: To assess revenue, product returns, costs, and profit by region

Distribution: Product manager, service manager, chief financial officer, sales manager, marketing manager, territory manager

Use: To determine which geographic areas are doing well or poorly financially and to compare areas

Action to be taken: Increase promotion and cost reduction efforts in areas experiencing low earnings.

EXHIBIT 9-2
QUARTERLY SALES DOLLARS AND VOLUME BY
GEOGRAPHIC AREA

Territory	Current Quarter Sales Dollars	Current Quarter Units Sold	Prior Quarter Sales Dollars	Prior Quarter Units Sold	Variance Sales Dollars	Variance Units Sold
North America	$280,000	10,000	$240,000	9,800	$40,000	200
South America	300,000	10,500	330,000	11,000	(30,000)	(500)
Europe	500,000	16,000	460,000	15,200	40,000	800
Asia	600,000	20,100	525,000	19,000	75,000	1,100
Africa	50,000	2,000	60,000	2,500	(10,000)	(500)
Middle East	70,000	2,400	120,000	4,000	(50,000)	(1,600)

Purpose: To analyze sales contributions of different areas

Distribution: International manager, sales manager, marketing manager, chief financial officer, product manager

Use: To compare the trend in sales of the company's product by major foreign area; to identify why sales increased or decreased from the prior period

Action to be taken: Improve advertising and promotion in weak areas.

EXHIBIT 9-3
QUARTERLY PROFIT BY GEOGRAPHIC REGION

Area	First Quarter			Second Quarter		
	Actual	Budget	Variance	Actual	Budget	Variance
Rocky Mountain	$95,000	$80,000	$15,000F	$86,000	$70,000	$16,000F
Northeast	100,000	70,000	30,000F	90,000	85,000	5,000F
Northwest	80,000	90,000	10,000U	89,000	88,000	1,000F
Southeast	160,000	140,000	20,000F	118,000	120,000	(2,000)U
Southwest	20,000	60,000	40,000U	46,000	50,000	(4,000)U
Total	$455,000	$440,000	$15,000F	$429,000	$413,000	$16,000F

Purpose: To identify areas of the country in which the company has been successful in achieving profitability

Distribution: Regional manager, chief financial officer, chief executive officer, budget analyst, controller

Use: To determine the deviation between expected and actual profit; to identify regions requiring attention so as to improve profitability

Action to be taken: Emphasize sales of products or services in areas generating the greatest profit return.

EXHIBIT 9-4
QUARTERLY CONTRIBUTION BY SALES TERRITORY

	California	New Mexico	Oregon	Wisconsin
Sales	$800,000	$900,000	$650,000	$780,000
Less: Variable cost of sales	300,000	250,000	170,000	430,000
Manufacturing contribution margin	500,000	650,000	480,000	350,000
Less: Variable selling expenses	150,000	200,000	180,000	100,000
Contribution margin	350,000	450,000	300,000	250,000
Less: Fixed costs	75,000	100,000	60,000	80,000
Net Income	$275,000	$350,000	$240,000	$170,000

Purpose: To determine the financial success of the company in major states

Distribution: Sales manager, regional managers, marketing manager, chief financial officer

Use: To identify geographic markets where the company is doing well or poorly; to highlight states in which more attention is needed to improve sales

Action to be taken: Give more attention to areas where sales are weak.

EXHIBIT 9-5
QUARTERLY COST PER TERRITORY REPORT

| | Current Quarter | | | | Year-to-Date | | | |
	Actual	Budget	Dollar Variance	% Variance	Actual	Budget	Dollar Variance	% Variance
Northeast:								
New York	60,000	55,000	(5,000)	9	140,000	132,000	(8,000)	6
New Jersey	70,000	80,000	10,000	1	190,000	200,000	10,000	5
Massachusetts	89,000	90,000	1000	1	236,000	240,000	4,000	2
Connecticut	68,000	65,000	(3,000)	5	184,000	183,000	(1,000)	1
Pennsylvania	52,000	50,000	(2,000)	4	157,000	158,000	1,000	1
Delaware	80,000	95,000	15,000	16	270,000	310,000	40,000	13
Total	410,000	435,000	16,000	4	1,177,000	1,223,000	46,000	4

Purpose: To determine costs expected and incurred in major states

Distribution: Chief financial officer, regional manager, planning analyst

Use: To determine the cost experience relative to expectations by territory; to compute the variance in costs in percentage and dollars terms so as to identify areas in which costs are excessive, necessitating cost control

Action to be taken: Improve budgeting for costs.

EXHIBIT 9-6
QUARTERLY VARIANCE BETWEEN ACTUAL SALES AND ESTIMATED SALES BY AREA

Regions	Current Year Quarter ending 3/31/19X5				Prior Year Quarter ending 3/31/19X4			
	Actual	Budget	Dollar Variance	% Variance	Actual	Budget	Dollar Variance	% Variance
Northern	500,000	480,000	20,000	4	470,000	490,000	(20,000)	4
Eastern	660,000	600,000	60,000	10	610,000	600,000	10,000	2
Southern	450,000	500,000	(50,000)	10	430,000	415,000	15,000	4
Western	720,000	710,000	10,000	1	750,000	700,000	50,000	7
Midwest	315,000	350,000	(35,000)	10	300,000	325,000	(25,000)	8
Total	$2,645,000	$2,640,000	5,000F	0	$2,560,000	$2,530,000	30,000F	3

Purpose: To track sales by region, comparing expectations with actual results

Distribution: Marketing manager, sales manager, regional manager, budget analyst, CFO

Use: To determine actual sales by major domestic region and compare those sales with budgeted amounts, computing trend in variances of sales in dollars and percentages

Action to be taken: Improve revenue generation by region, emphasizing regions providing the most revenue growth.

EXHIBIT 9-7
QUARTERLY VARIANCE BY TERRITORY

	Actual Units Sold	Budgeted Units Sold	Variance in Units	Average Actual Selling Price	Budgeted Average Selling Price	Variance in Selling Price	Average Actual Cost/Unit	Budgeted Cost/Unit	Variance in Cost/Unit
New York:									
Manhattan	25,000	23,000	2,000	$11	$10	$1	5	4	$(1)
Queens	30,000	25,000	5,000	7	8	(1)	4	3	(1)
Staten Island	42,000	45,000	(3,000)	15	12	3	8	6	(2)
Brooklyn	15,000	18,000	(3,000)	8	6	2	5	4	(1)
Bronx	20,000	15,000	5,000	3	5	(2)	1	2	1
Nassau County	40,000	39,000	1,000	25	20	5	11	10	(1)
Suffolk County	16,000	20,000	(4,000)	13	13	0	6	5	1
Westchester County	10,000	12,000	(2,000)	19	16	3	9	7	(2)

Purpose: To determine how well a company is doing financially within a particular state

Distribution: Regional manager, sales manager, controller, marketing manager

Use: To examine the success of a company's pricing structure including its adequacy relative to unit cost; to compute the variance in units, sales, selling price, and cost per unit as a basis to judge either the adequacy of budgeted figures or the financial success of the company by major territory

Action to be taken: Improve the relationship between costing and pricing of products to reach a good balance.

EXHIBIT 9-8
QUARTERLY VARIANCE BY PRODUCT

	Cost Variance	Price Variance	Volume Variance	Mix Variance
Territory:				
Texas				
Product A	20,000	35,000	15,000	25,000
Product B	15,000	20,000	10,000	35,000
Product C	12,000	5,000	18,000	7,000
Utah				
Product A	16,000	20,000	15,000	40,000
Product B	11,000	14,000	12,000	20,000
Product C	5,000	13,000	14,000	19,000

Purpose: To determine the variances associated with various products in major states

Distribution: Product manager, sales manager, regional manager, marketing manager, CFO

Use: To gauge financial performance, adequacy of pricing structure, sales planning, and cost control

Action to be taken: Find ways to minimize variances in volume, cost, and selling price of products in each state.

CHAPTER 10

Analysis and Reporting of Purchasing

Since purchases make up such a large portion of commercial costs, controlling them will significantly improve performance.

- Exhibit 10-1 documents the physical receipt of materials.
- Exhibits 10-2 and 10-3 monitor orders.
- Exhibits 10-4 through 10-6 track purchase needs and variances with vendors and from standard costs.

EXHIBIT 10-1
DAILY RECEIVING REPORT

Received From	Via	No. Packages	Weight (lbs)	Goods	P.O. or Req. No.	Charges Paid/ Delivered To	Comments
FJ Reynolds, Pittsburgh, PA	Truck	12	1,625	Bags of Gravel	125698	$125 Storeroom	
FJ Reynolds, Pittsburgh, PA	Truck	25	5,250	Bags of Sand	125722	203 Storeroom	
Phillips, Cleveland, OH	Rail	1	2,060	Paver	PO1855	718 Garage	
Jacobs Bros., Chicago, IL	Truck	18	1,018	Cement Blocks	125422	188 Storeroom	Damaged

Purpose: To document receipt of items as they are delivered

Distribution: Purchasing manager, materials manager

Use: To record required information as material is received

Action to be taken: Since goods received are damaged (as were the cement blocks), not in accordance with packing slip, etc., contact shipper immediately.

EXHIBIT 10-2
PURCHASE ORDER STATUS

Item	Opening Balance, POs	This Period Add: New POs	This Period Less: Goods Received	Ending Balance, POs
Part # 12556	$24,000	$8,200	$12,500	$19,700
Part # 25466	12,500	3,250	5,700	10,050
Part # 15424	4,500	1,700	2,450	3,750
Part # 21566	19,750	6,750	4,500	22,000
Part # 18852	9,750	575	1,450	8,875

Purpose: To track outstanding purchase orders and related liabilities

Distribution: Purchasing manager, production manager

Use: To monitor performance of vendors and emerging liabilities

Action to be taken: Use with other reports to determine if PO balance is appropriate.

EXHIBIT 10-3
OPEN PURCHASE ORDERS

	January	February	March	April	May	June	July	August	September	October	November	December
PO, opening balance	$1,250	$1,505	$2,227	$3,796								
Purchase orders placed	12,500	8,950	14,250	12,750								
Subtotal	13,750	10,455	16,477	16,546								
Materials received	12,245	8,228	12,681	13,376								
PO, Ending balance	1,505	2,227	3,796	3,170								
Inventory, ending balance	4,029	3,388	4,496	2,496								

Purpose: To track open purchase orders for items used in manufacturing

Distribution: Purchasing manager

Use: To assist in maintaining appropriate inventory levels

Action to be taken: If inventory balance is not sufficient to ensure continuous manufacturing, increase purchase orders placed and materials received.

EXHIBIT 10-4
MATERIALS PURCHASING PLAN

Department _____

	January	February	March	Second Qtr.	Third Qtr.	Fourth Qtr.
Units						
Planned production	650	540	725	1,725	2,050	2,690
Plus: Ending inventory	120	140	175	215	160	195
Less: Opening inventory	195	120	140	175	215	160
Required purchases	575	560	760	1,765	1,995	2,725
Cost per unit	$127.00	$127.00	$127.00	$127.00	$131.00	$131.00
Total Cost	$73,025	$71,120	$96,520	$224,155	$261,345	$356,975

Purpose: To determine materials required by department for planned production by quarter

Distribution: Purchasing manager, production manager

Use: To plan purchases to meet production needs

Action to be taken: An increase in planned production would require an increase in disbursements to purchase required materials.

EXHIBIT 10-5
VENDOR PURCHASE ANALYSIS

	Current Month			This Mon.- LY				Year-to-Date			YTD-LY	
	Gross Amount	Returns	Net Purchases	Net Purchases	Difference	Vendor Name	Gross Purchases	Returns	Net Purchases	Net Purchases	Difference
	$21,150	$845	$20,305	$20,986	($681)	Abbott Electric	$68,351	$2,857	$65,494	$72,483	($6,989)
	35,245	1,254	$33,991	32,471	$1,520	Bentley Supplies	105,540	6,350	$99,190	124,560	($25,370)
	28,541	524	$28,017	21,841	$6,176	Demerest Chemicals	77,245	1,203	$76,042	114,562	($38,520)
	12,041	619	$11,422	12,588	($1,166)	Genetic Supply	39,564	1,563	$38,001	31,521	$6,480

Purpose: To track purchases from each vendor

Distribution: Purchasing manager

Use: To review vendor relationships; analyze variances

Action to be taken: Investigate variances from prior year.

EXHIBIT 10-6
YEAR-TO-DATE PURCHASE VARIANCES

Item Description	Cost		
	Actual	Standard	Variance
Part # 12-847	$3,249	$3,220	($29)
Part # 14-654	13,524	14,568	1,044
Part # 23-219	25,589	25,956	367
Part # 28-529	18,524	16,956	(1,568)

Purpose: To determine if an item is being purchased at standard cost

Distribution: Purchasing manager

Use: To check for cost changes over time

Action to be taken: Investigate significant variances.

CHAPTER 11

Analysis and Reporting of Distribution

Careful monitoring of distribution costs can lead to improved decisions about distribution strategies and operations and thus to increased profits.

- Exhibits 11-1 and 11-4 are designed to track open orders and shipments.

- Developing a budget for the distribution department and comparing it with actual is another important control technique (Exhibits 11-2 and 11-3).

- Since transportation is the largest component of distribution costs, reports that monitor and control transportation costs (Exhibits 11-5 through 11-7) are integral to controlling distribution.

EXHIBIT 11-1
SHIPPING RECORD: ORDERS RECEIVED AND SHIPPED WEEKLY (Thousands of dollars)

Week Ended	New Orders Received Number	$	Open Orders from Prior Week Number	$	Orders Shipped Number	$	Open Orders End-of-Week Number	$
4-Mar	467	$5,612	22	$234	471	$5,651	18	$201
11-Mar	623	6,886	18	201	611	6,733	30	344
18-Mar	702	7,955	30	344	696	7,705	36	411
25-Mar	736	8,122	36	411	729	8,011	43	462

Purpose: To monitor changes in open orders for the week

Distribution: Distribution manager

Use: To see if deliveries are timely and consistent with past performance

Action to be taken: Improve shipping system, since orders open are rising steadily.

EXHIBIT 11-2
DISTRIBUTION DEPARTMENT BUDGET

	Prior Year Actual 10 Mos	Est 2 Mos	Total	Plan Year 1st Qtr	2nd Qtr	2nd Half	Total	Inc/ Dec
# of Staff	2	2	2	2	2	2	2	0
Expenses								
Salaries	$8,500	$1,750	$10,250	$2,550	$2,600	$5,250	$10,400	$150
Fringe Benefits	1,275	263	1,538	383	390	787	1,560	22
Occupancy	3,500	700	4,200	1,050	1,100	2,210	4,360	160
Repairs	4,250	850	5,100	1,275	1,300	2,250	4,825	(275)
Total	$17,525	$3,563	$21,088	$5,258	$5,390	$10,497	$21,145	$57
% of net sales	2.245%	2.265%	2.250%	2.250%	2.250%	2.250%	2.250%	0

Purpose: To monitor department costs

Distribution: Distribution manager

Use: To make sure expenses stay within targeted range

Action to be taken: Determine why planned expenses for repairs are expected to decrease $275 compared with last year, while all other expenses are expected to increase. (This could be due to the purchase of new equipment.)

EXHIBIT 11-3
ACTUAL PERFORMANCE

	Current Month			Year-to-Date			
			(Over)/ Under Budget	Budget		(Over)/ Under Budget	
	Budget	Actual	Budget	(Adjusted)	Actual	Amount	Percent
Salaries	$2,800	$2,770	$30	$11,500	$11,300	$200	1.7%
Wages	25,000	24,800	200	102,000	105,300	(3,300)	-3.2%
Fringe benefits	5,560	5,510	50	22,700	23,320	(620)	-2.7%
Subtotal	33,360	33,080	280	136,200	139,920	(3,720)	-2.7%
Supplies	1,000	1,240	(240)	4,800	4,680	120	2.5%
Gasoline and oil	1,940	1,860	80	7,360	7,810	(450)	-6.1%
Repairs:							
Regular-labor	920	950	(30)	3,480	3,220	260	7.5%
Regular-material	920	900	20	3,480	3,100	380	10.9%
Major-labor	0	0	0	12,300	12,000	300	2.4%
Major-material	0	0	0	15,700	16,800	(1,100)	-7.0%
Heat, light, power	620	600	20	2,280	2,090	190	8.3%
Miscellaneous	80	80	0	320	310	10	3.1%
Depreciation	900	900	0	3,600	3,600	0	-
Property taxes/Ins.	250	250	0	1,000	1,000	0	-
TOTAL	$39,990	$39,860	$130	$190,520	$194,530	($4,010)	-2.1%

Purpose: To control distribution department expenses

Distribution: Distribution manager

Use: To make sure actual expenses are in target range

Action to be taken: Take steps to reduce excessive and unproductive costs.

EXHIBIT 11-4
SHIPPING REPORT

Date	Time	Description of Contents	Ship Via	Destination City/State	Zone No.	# of Ctns.	Wght (lbs.)	Loaded by:
1-Oct	9:45AM	Transmissions	Truck	Cincinnati, OH	12	18	9,255	R. Randall
1-Oct	10:30AM	Filters	Truck	Chicago, IL	3	6	315	G. Brandeis
1-Oct	3:35PM	Engines	Air	San Francisco, CA	25	8	1,632	R. Randall
1-Oct	4:50PM	Transmissions	Truck	Cleveland, OH	7	11	5,624	F. Franks
1-Oct	5:40PM	Filters	Truck	Detroit, MI	14	5	257	G. Brandeis
2-Oct	9:25AM	Engines	Rail	New York, NY	4	35	7,117	F. Franks
2-Oct	11:25AM	Filters	Air	Seattle, WA	31	5	257	R. Randall

Purpose: To keep track of shipments

Distribution: Distribution manager

Use: To measure timely shipments; measure loader performance

Action to be taken: Find out whether the two shipments of transmissions to Ohio could have been combined at lower cost.

EXHIBIT 11-5
BUDGETED TRANSPORTATION COST PER UNIT

Origin	Destination	Product	Transportation Cost per Unit		
			Private Fleet	Car Load	Truck Load
Plant I	Dist Center 1	A	$5.25		
Plant I	Dist Center 1	B	7.50		
Plant I	Dist Center 2	A	5.25		
Plant I	Dist Center 2	B			$8.35
Plant II	Dist Center 1	C		$16.75	
Plant II	Dist Center 2	C		12.50	
Plant III	Dist Center 3	A			6.15

Purpose: To monitor transportation costs

Distribution: Distribution manager

Use: To benchmark actual transportation costs per unit

Action to be taken: Apply these rates to help determine the best way to ship them.

EXHIBIT 11-6
DRIVER COST ANALYSIS

Driver #	Driver Name	Total Miles Operated	Revenue/ Mile	Variable Costs/Mile	Contribution/ Mile	Total Costs/ Mile
282	Jones, T	9,321	$1.18	$0.96	$0.22	$1.06
368	Feng, F	6,782	1.11	0.95	0.16	1.08
552	Hermes, J	12,652	1.09	0.91	0.18	1.02
589	Frankel, M	4,533	1.13	0.94	0.19	1.05
633	Marks, L	8,544	1.21	1.03	0.18	1.13

Purpose: To measure driver productivity and performance

Distribution: Distribution manager

Use: To see whether some drivers are more economical than others

Action to be taken: Investigate reasons for poorer performance.

EXHIBIT 11-7
DISTRIBUTION FREIGHT ANALYSIS

Product	Via	Actual Freight	Weight (CWT)	Actual Freight/CWT	Budgeted Freight/CWT	Variance Rate	Variance Amount
Transmissions	Truck	$15,256	15,408.56	$1.0100	$0.9900	($0.0200)	($308)
Transmissions	Rail	6,022	7,346.84	1.2200	1.1700	(0.0500)	(367)
Engines	Truck	12,055	12,115.28	1.0050	0.9900	(0.0150)	(182)
Engines	Rail	5,042	5,798.30	1.1500	1.1700	0.0200	116

Purpose: To monitor freight charges

Distribution: Distribution manager

Use: To analyze efficiency of different modes of transportation

Action to be taken: Change mode of transportation to most efficient.

CHAPTER 12

Employee Performance Reporting

The reports in this chapter will help you monitor employee performance, which is extremely difficult to quantify accurately.

- Essential to tracking employee performance is the control of headcount. Exhibits 12-1 and 12-2 provide reports that can be used to help achieve this.

- Exhibits 12-3 to 12-5 track various measures of performance by employee.

- Exhibit 12-6 can help you analyze labor variance from standard.

EXHIBIT 12-1
QUARTERLY HEAD COUNT: BUDGET VS. ACTUAL

	Budget for Quarter	Actual (at End of Month)		
		January	February	March
Direct labor:				
Production department	14	13	13	14
Assembly department	22	23	22	22
Total direct	36	36	35	36
Indirect labor:				
Quality control	2	2	2	2
Materials management	1	1	1	1
Purchasing	3	2	3	3
Engineering	4	3	3	3
Maintenance	2	2	2	2
Total indirect	12	10	11	11

Purpose: To maintain budgeted headcount

Distribution: Top management, division managers

Use: To ensure appropriate staffing

Action to be taken: Find out why Engineering stays understaffed.

EXHIBIT 12-2
WORK FORCE REPORT

	1st Qtr	2nd Qtr	3rd Qtr	4th Qtr
Department A				
Opening work force	566	587	589	598
Additions	23	5	11	6
Deletions	2	3	2	1
Ending work force	587	589	598	603
Planned work force	595	595	608	608
Difference	(8)	(6)	(10)	(5)
Department B				
Opening work force	159	161	159	163
Additions	5	2	5	3
Deletions	3	4	1	3
Ending work force	161	159	163	163
Planned work force	162	162	164	164
Difference	(1)	(3)	(1)	(1)

Purpose: To monitor changes in work force for each department

Distribution: Top management, department managers

Use: To maintain required staff

Action to be taken: Investigate why Department B has consistently remained below its work force budget.

EXHIBIT 12-3
DIVISIONAL SALES PER EMPLOYEE

	January	February	March	April	May	June	July	August	September	October	November	December
Division A												
Sales per employee												
Actual	2,355	3,023	2,854	3,889								
Budget	2,450	3,150	3,050	4,250								
Difference	(95)	(127)	(196)	(361)								
% Difference	(4.03)	(4.20)	(6.87)	(9.28)								
Division B												
Sales per employee												
Actual	3,995	4,312	3,858	4,552								
Budget	3,775	4,125	4,050	4,350								
Difference	220	187	(192)	202								
% Difference	5.51	4.34	(4.98)	4.44								

Purpose: To monitor sales per employee by division

Distribution: Top management, division manager

Use: To maintain progress toward targeted goals

Action to be taken: Investigate why sales for Division A have been trending down.

EXHIBIT 12-4
SALES PER EMPLOYEE BY TERRITORY

	# of Employees		Net Sales		Net Sales/Employee		
Territory	This Year	Last Year	This Year	Last Year	This Year	Last Year	Variance
New England	195	207	$93,200	$109,920	$478	$531	($53)
Northeast	152	146	77,540	89,270	510	611	(101)
Southeast	665	759	297,650	311,220	448	410	38
North Central	312	304	228,560	212,410	733	699	34
South Central	316	398	197,300	214,395	624	539	85
Total	1,640	1,814	$894,250	$937,215			
Company Average					$545	$517	$28

Purpose: To monitor sales per employee by territory

Distribution: Top management, territory managers

Use: To keep territories moving toward budgeted goals

Action to be taken: Investigate unfavorable trends.

EXHIBIT 12-5
CONTRIBUTION PER EMPLOYEE

	Departments			
	X	Y	Z	Total
Net sales	$123,600	$166,500	$202,600	$492,700
Less: Variable costs				
Variable cost of sales	30,000	35,000	40,000	105,000
Variable selling expenses	10,000	5,000	15,000	30,000
Variable administrative expenses	6,000	8,000	7,000	21,000
Total variable costs	46,000	48,000	62,000	156,000
Contribution margin	77,600	118,500	140,600	336,700
Less: Fixed costs				
Fixed manufacturing costs	7,000	10,000	11,000	28,000
Fixed selling expenses	4,000	6,000	9,000	19,000
Fixed administrative expenses	3,000	5,000	12,000	20,000
Total fixed costs	14,000	21,000	32,000	67,000
Departmental profit	$63,600	$97,500	$108,600	$269,700
Contribution margin/employee	$242.50	$348.53	$312.44	$303.33
Profit/employee	$198.75	$286.76	$241.33	$242.97

Purpose: To monitor contribution per employee by department

Distribution: Top management, department managers

Use: To calculate contribution by department

Action to be taken: Investigate whether to improve profitability.

EXHIBIT 12-6
EMPLOYEE VARIANCE REPORT

Department	Actual Direct Labor	Standard Direct Labor	Variance Week %	Variance Month to-Date %	Variance Year-to-Date $	Variance Year-to-Date %
A	$15,384	$16,250	2.10	(4.52)	(866)	(5.33)
B	22,049	21,245	(4.50)	4.01	804	3.78
C	35,456	38,500	2.25	(6.52)	(3,044)	(7.91)
D	29,566	28,456	4.50	4.10	1,110	3.90

Purpose: To help control labor costs in each department

Distribution: Top management, department managers

Use: To determine actual and standard labor costs by department and calculate variances

Action to be taken: Investigate unfavorable trends.

CHAPTER 13

Manager Performance Reports

Manager performance must be evaluated to identify which managers are doing well and which are not. These reports highlight managerial strengths and weaknesses, and identify areas where corrective action is needed to improve performance. Managers may be appraised in terms of many measures, including sales in units and dollars, cost control, productivity, and resource management.

- Exhibit 13-1 looks at quarterly revenue generation by manager.
- Exhibit 13-2 presents billing experience and profit thereon by manager.
- Exhibit 13-3 is a comprehensive analysis of manager performance in terms of revenue, cost, profit, assets, return on investment (ROI), residual income (RI), quality control, stockouts, and complaints.
- Exhibit 13-4 analyzes useful profitability measures for managers.
- Ratios that deal with profit generation, rate of return, and productivity by manager can be found in Exhibit 13-5.
- Exhibit 13-6 measures accountability in terms of such gauges as cost, production, machine hours, idle time, quality defects, and backlog.
- Exhibit 13-7 shows the effectiveness of managers in controlling costs.
- Exhibit 13-8 compares department manager accomplishments with targeted goals.

- Semi-annual manager efficiency is measured by Exhibit 13-9.
- Exhibit 13-10 looks at manager performance in fulfilling jobs and contracts.
- Exhibit 13-11 presents a semi-annual manager assessment and workload report.
- To determine a manager's quality control success, use Exhibit 13-12.
- How a manager handles personnel and customers is noted in Exhibits 13-13 and 13-14.

EXHIBIT 13-1
QUARTERLY REVENUE BY DIVISIONAL MANAGER

	Blake	Klemer	Akel
Units sold:			
Product A	20,000	15,000	24,000
Product B	30,000	18,000	17,000
Product C	10,000	16,000	22,000
Dollar sales–U.S.			
Product A	$290, 000	$225,000	$346,000
Product B	380,000	234,000	221,000
Product C	140,000	228,000	318,000
Dollar sales–Foreign			
Product A	312,000	253,000	361,000
Product B	400,000	270,000	245,000
Product C	168,000	268,000	334,000

Purpose: To determine by manager the revenue generated by product domestically and in foreign markets

Distribution: Division manager, sales manager, chief financial officer, marketing manager

Use: To ascertain which products are selling well or poorly in volume and dollar terms; to monitor manager performance

Action to be taken: Reward managers doing well and improve performance of managers doing poorly, emphasizing successful products.

EXHIBIT 13-2
MONTHLY MANAGER BILLABLE REPORT

Manager	Budgeted Hours	Actual Hours	Hours Charged to Clients	Unbillable Hours	Hourly Rate	Service Revenue	Manager Salary	Profit	Profit/ Billable Hour	Manager Salary/ Billable Hour
Mesa	250	270	240	30	$90	$21,600	$10,000	$11,600	$48	$42
Cohen	240	220	200	20	100	20,000	12,000	8,000	40	60
Palmiero	280	280	270	10	85	22,950	9,000	13,950	52	33
Davis	300	290	250	40	75	18,750	85,000	10,250	41	34
Fitzginons	260	275	230	45	110	25,300	13,000	12,300	53	57

Purpose: To ascertain the productivity of managers

Distribution: Department managers, controller's office, vice-president of operations, chief executive officer, service manager

Use: To determine how effective managers are in spending their time, maximizing revenue and profit, and justifying their salaries; to identify unbillable time and the reasons for it

Action to be taken: Take steps to make managers more productive and profitable.

EXHIBIT 13-3
QUARTERLY MANAGER PERFORMANCE REPORT

Manager	Divisional Revenue	Divisional Cost	Profit	Divisional Total Assets	ROI	Residual Income Based on 10% Cost Rate	Number of Quality Control Problems	Returns of Manufactured Goods	Number of Stockouts	Employee Complaints	Customer Complaints
Jones	$160,000	$120,000	$40,000	$200,000	20%	$20,000	15	6	3	0	2
Cohen	300,000	200,000	100,000	600,000	17	40,000	3	2	1	4	3
Groza	90,000	60,000	30,000	300,000	10	0	4	6	7	1	2
Dena	140,000	60,000	80,000	500,000	16	30,000	2	1	0	0	1
Harris	250,000	200,000	50,000	400,000	13	10,000	6	5	4	3	4

Purpose: To measure managers performance in conducting duties and achieving profitability

Distribution: Divisional manager, sales manager, service manager, vice-president of operations

Use: To evaluate the manager's ability to maximize rates of returns, assure high quality, minimize runs and stock-outs, and achieve good customer and employee relations

Action to be taken: Have managers performing poorly take appropriate training.

EXHIBIT 13-4
QUARTERLY PERFORMANCE BY DIVISION MANAGER

	Division A	Division B	Division C
Revenue	$1,600,000	$2,000,000	$1,900,000
Less: Variable manufacturing costs	400,000	900,000	600,000
Manufacturing Contribution Margin	1,200,000	1,100,000	1,300,000
Less: Variable selling and administrative costs	200,000	300,000	400,000
Contribution Margin	1,000,000	800,000	900,000
Less:			
Controllable fixed costs by manager	100,000	250,000	300,000
Short-run performance margin	900,000	650,000	600,000
Less: Uncontrollable fixed costs by manager	150,000	200,000	100,000
Segment Margin	$750,000	$450,000	$500,000

Purpose: To appraise the financial performance of managers

Distribution: Division manager, chief financial officer, vice-president of operations

Use: To express financially how the manager is doing

Action to be taken: Find ways to improve a division's profitability, perhaps by finding new sources of revenue or ways to reduce costs.

EXHIBIT 13-5
QUARTERLY DEPARTMENT MANAGER RATIO REPORT

Ratio	Dauber	Saft	Riggio
Profit margin(net income/sales)	25%	16%	30%
Gross profit margin(gross profit/sales)	47%	36%	42%
Employee productivity:			
Units produced/number of employees	315	428	514
Sales/number of employees	$94,615	$82,712	$100,105
Sales/factory salaries	5.6	7.2	9.1
Return on investment(operating profit/total assets)	20%	18%	32%
Gross profit/total assets	41%	32%	46%

Purpose: To determine how well a department manager is performing financially and operationally

Distribution: Department manager, financial analyst, chief financial officer, vice-president of operations

Use: To compute the return on sales and investment a manager has; to ascertain the manager's ability to spur worker productivity in volume and generate sales dollars

Action to be taken: Take steps to improve worker efficiency and effectiveness; search for ways to improve overall profitability.

EXHIBIT 13-6
SEMI-ANNUAL DEPARTMENT MANAGER ACCOUNTABILITY

Item	Levine	Chi	Morgan
Revenue	$550,000	$610,000	$740,000
Total cost	$300,000	$420,000	$512,000
Units produced	10000	11000	11800
Number of stockouts	25	30	36
Number of machine hours	40000	45000	52000
Number of employee hours	43000	47000	51000
Number of over time hours	400	430	450
Number of machine/equipment break-downs	0	2	3
Idle time in hours	150	160	180
Number of quality defects	3	4	6
Number of bottle/necks	1	2	10
Number of unfilled orders (backlog)	8	10	13

Purpose: To determine how effectively department managers generate revenue and control costs

Distribution: Department manager, vice-president of operations, service manager, production manager, plant manager

Use: To assess the success of a manager in handling operations, in terms of machine and employee productivity, smooth running of facilities, and quality control

Action to be taken: Instruct managers on ways to maximize profitability and units produced.

EXHIBIT 13-7
QUARTERLY MANAGER EFFECTIVENESS IN
CONTROLLING COSTS

	Actual	Budget	Dollar Variance	% Variance
Variable cost of sales				
Direct material	$60,000	$50,000	$(10,000)	20%
Direct labor	100,000	85,000	(15,000)	18
Factory overhead				
Insurance	10,000	10,000	0	0
Rent	6,000	5,500	$(500)	9
Electricity	2,600	3,000	400	13
Spoilage	1,700	1,800	100	6
Supervision	7,500	8,000	(500)	6
Repairs and maintenance	6,400	6,000	(400)	7

Purpose: To appraise a manager's ability to control department costs

Distribution: Budget analyst, department manager, chief financial officer, financial analyst

Use: To determine variances in budget versus actual costs; to evaluate how well specific cost items are being controlled and to identify cost areas requiring corrective action

Action to be taken: Improve planning and monitor costs.

EXHIBIT 13-8
ANNUAL SUMMARY COMPARISON: DEPARTMENT
MANAGER ACCOMPLISHMENT

Department	Actual	Budget	Dollar Variance	% Variance
Sales:				
Assembling	$80,000	$700,000	$100,000	14%
Polishing	550,000	600,000	(50,000)	8
Finishing	440,000	400,000	40,000	10
Costs:				
Assembling	410,000	425,000	14,000	4
Polishing	325,000	350,000	25,000	7
Finishing	230,000	170,000	(60,000)	35
Profit:				
Assembling	390,000	275,000	115,000	42
Polishing	225,000	250,000	(25,000)	10
Finishing	210,000	230,000	(20,000)	9

Purpose: To ascertain a department manager's ability to meet benchmarks or revenue generation, cost incurrence, and profit generation

Distribution: Department manager, budget analyst, financial analyst, CFO, top management

Use: To rate manager performance and identify unfavorable variances to uncover trouble spots requiring attention

Action to be taken: Investigate finishing cost overruns and low polishing department sales.

EXHIBIT 13-9
SEMI-ANNUAL MANAGER EFFICIENCY REPORT

Measure	Davis		Masters		Winston	
	1/1 - 6/30	7/1 - 12/31	1/1 - 6/30	7/1 - 12/31	1/1 - 6/30	7/1 - 12/31
Departmental revenue/manager's salary	5	4.8	7.2	6.1	8.3	6.4
Departmental revenue/manager's working hours	$1,212	$2,014	$1,632	$1,494	$1,835	$744
Employee complaints against manager	0	1	2	3	4	5
Departmental profit/manager's salary	3.2	2.6	5.1	4.9	6.6	4.3
Departmental profit/manager's working hours	$413	$2,415	$811	$1,614	$3,915	$3,416
Revenue per worker	46,512	49,500	32,814	34,914	41,316	38,219
Profit per worker	28,411	26,918	20,412	20,813	19,136	20,413
Cost savings	12,618	13,443	11,815	14,903	13,642	14,836
Units produced	10,000	11,614	12,040	12,653	9,438	9,810
Average number of workers per job	5	5	6	5	4	3
Average hours per worker	1040	1092	1115	1026	962	953
Number of completed jobs	103	110	97	122	146	158
Number of stockouts	0	1	3	4	5	7
Machine hours	952	1012	1014	960	861	903
Percentage of idle time	4%	5%	3%	6%	8%	7%
Number of production delays	6	7	8	5	7	6
Unfilled orders	1	0	3	4	6	5

Purpose: To determine the productivity of managers

Distribution: Department manager, vice-president of operations, financial analyst, production manager

Use: To determine the ability of managers to generate revenue, control costs, maximize profitability, motivate workers, complete jobs, and make efficient use of time and equipment

Action to be taken: Take appropriate steps to improve worker and supervisor productivity so as to lower costs.

EXHIBIT 13-10
QUARTERLY MANAGER PERFORMANCE IN
FULFILLING JOBS AND CONTRACTS

Performance Measures	Simon	Luster	Dienstag
Number of jobs/contracts completed	41	52	36
Number of jobs/contracts signed	38	58	41
Percentage of jobs/contracts completed on time	98%	95%	89%
Cost overruns on jobs/contracts	$41,212	$10,914	$60,178
Cost overruns as a percentage of total cost by job/contract	2%	1%	9%
Number of jobs/contracts in process at end of quarter	12	14	8
Number of jobs/contacts lost because of high bids	0	5	3
Average unit cost per job/contracts	$18,412	$19,610	$15,314

Purpose: To determine how well each manager completes jobs/contracts

Distribution: Vice-president of operations, contracts manager, department manager, production manager

Use: To determine how many contracts were lost due to poor bidding practices; to appraise the manager's ability to negotiate successfully with potential customers

Action to be taken: Work with Dienstag to improve scheduling of jobs and contracts to reduce costs and overruns and complete more contracts.

EXHIBIT 13-11
SEMI-ANNUAL MANAGER ASSIGNMENT AND WORK LOAD

Measure	Harris	Smith	Jones
Number of repeat projects	36	28	41
Cost of repeat projects	$295,000	$410,600	$382,100
Number of new projects	21	19	32
Cost of new projects	$183,000	$310,500	$286,000
Number of staff supervised	46	37	34
Number of hours worked	1,210	1,086	1,341
Number of new clients	28	31	32
Number of clients listed	0	1	5
Number of creative and innovative ideas	3	7	6
Number of jobs worked on	29	42	37
Percentage of reports delivered on time	100%	90%	93%
Number of employee complaints about manager	3	0	10
Number of customer complaints about manager	5	3	0
Number of units completed in department	12,000	11,600	13,500

Purpose: To determine how many projects are in process and how well the manager is handling client needs

Distribution: Department manager, vice-president of operations, personnel manager, plant manager

Use: To determine the manager's ability to complete jobs on time, to attract new accounts and retain old ones, and to supervise staff

Action to be taken: Improve how managers handle their projects.

EXHIBIT 13-12
QUARTERLY MANAGER QUALITY CONTROL PERFORMANCE

Measure	Russo	O'Leary	Anton
Sales returns/sales	8%	5%	3%
Sales allowances/sales	2%	1%	4%
Percentage defects to units produced	3%	2%	7%
Machine breakdowns	0	5	9
Rework time as a percentage of total manhours	4%	2%	8%
Number of employee injuries	1	3	7
Number of product liability lawsuits	2	0	6
Number of product awards	3	1	0
Number of new customers	48	33	2
Number of orders	163	152	107
Number of customer complaints	2	0	16

Purpose: To monitor quality control

Distribution: Product manager, quality control manager, vice-president of operations, plant manager, production manager

Use: To appraise the quality of goods produced and sold, identify problems in production, and ascertain incidence of injuries and product liability associated with manufacturing

Action to be taken: Improve inspection and monitoring of operations.

EXHIBIT 13-13
QUARTERLY REPORT ON MANAGER'S HANDLING OF PERSONNEL AND CUSTOMERS

Measure	Davis	Hartman	Minars
Number of employees being supervised	48	52	36
Average weekly hours worked per employee	36	43	48
Units produced per employee	643	821	912
Sales generated per employee	$61,400	$78,210	$86,514
Employee turnover percentage	5%	12%	13%
Number of customers serviced	21	17	28
Sales dollars per customer	$43,112	$30,615	$21,516
Number of customer complaints	6	2	0

Purpose: To determine how effective manager's interpersonal relations are

Distribution: Personnel manager, marketing manager, service manager, department manager, labor union

Use: To ascertain whether the manager can maximize employee productivity and revenue generation from customers; to make sure customers are properly serviced without undue complaints

Action to be taken: Improve training of managers; find out why Davis has low productivity and more complaints; and why the other two have high employee turnover.

EXHIBIT 13-14
ANNUAL DEPARTMENT MANAGER'S PERFORMANCE IN HANDLING STAFF

Evaluation Criteria	Lane	Drake	Smith
Units produced per factory workers	3,000	3,100	3,250
Sales per factory workers	$83,500	$91,000	$94,000
Sales per office employees	$98,000	$112,000	$128,000
Sales per factory salaries	5.3	6.1	7.2
Manufacturing costs per number of factory worker	$42,700	$43,000	$43,250
Employee turnover rate	3	2.5	4
Average number of days sickness per employee	2	4	6
Number of employee complaints	0	1	5
Sales/office salaries	7.2	8.3	9.1
Manufacturing costs/factory workers salaries	3.1	4	4.2

Purpose: To determine a manager's ability to motivate employees so as to maximize revenue and control costs

Distribution: Department manager, personnel manager, financial analyst, plant manager

Use: To assess a manager's effectiveness in accomplishing high employee productivity and job satisfaction

Action to be taken: Improve training and monitoring of managers.

CHAPTER 14

Segmental Reporting

Organizations often are structured in segments with managers that have control over specific activities. A key variable in analyzing managerial performance here is how much control the manager is allowed to exercise. Some companies believe that managers should not be charged with costs over which they have no control; other companies allocate all costs, controllable by the manager or not, to remind managers to keep the total picture in mind at all times.

- Exhibit 14-1 is useful for assessing performance week by week. It compares actual hours produced with standard hours allowed, giving a performance percentage.

- Exhibit 14-2 is a typical responsibility report for a single department; the performance of each level is incorporated into the level above. This report can be very long.

- Exhibit 14-3 compares budgeted gross profit with actual.

- The next three exhibits analyze gross profit by component. The variables are summarized in Exhibit 14-7.

EXHIBIT 14-1
WEEKLY PERFORMANCE REPORT BY DEPARTMENT

Department	Actual Hours Produced	Standard Hours Allowed	Performance Percentage
Dept. A	130	120	92
Dept. B	420	380	90
Dept. C	360	420	117
Dept. D	400	300	75
Dept. E	350	280	80
Dept. F	280	150	54
Dept. G	190	250	132
Dept. H	440	290	66
Dept. I	150	115	77
Dept. J	360	250	69

Weekly Department Performance

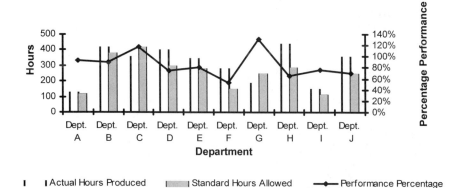

Actual Hours Produced   Standard Hours Allowed   Performance Percentage

Purpose: To compare actual hours with forecast hours

Distribution: Production manager, department managers

Use: To evaluate department performance; highlight departments with superior or inferior performance

Action to be taken: Investigate causes of low percentages, as in Departments F, H, and J.

EXHIBIT 14-2
ABC COMPANY RESPONSIBILITY REPORT
(for years ended 20X4)

	Budgeted	Actual	Variance
Level 4: President:			
President's office	$125,000	$130,000	$5,000
Vice-president–finance	115,000	140,000	25,000
Vice-president–marketing	200,000	250,000	50,000
Vice-president–manufacturing	857,700	842,700	(15,000)
Total controllable costs	1,297,700	1,362,700	65,000
Level 3: Vice-president–manufacturing:			
Vice president–manufacturing office	4,500	5,500	1,000
Plant A	135,000	145,000	10,000
Plant B	145,000	135,000	(10,000)
Plant C	273,200	252,200	(21,000)
Plant D	165,000	160,000	(5,000)
Plant E	135,000	145,000	10,000
Total controllable costs	857,700	842,700	(15,000)
Level 2: Plant manager–Plant C:			
Plant manager's salary	3,000	3,000	–
Cutting department	34,700	29,200	(5,500)
Painting department	125,500	120,000	(5,500)
Finishing department	110,000	100,000	(10,000)
Total controllable costs	273,200	252,200	(21,000)
Level 1: Cutting department–Plant C:			
Direct materials	13,000	7,000	(6,000)
Direct labor	15,000	16,000	1,000
Factory overhead	6,700	6,200	(500)
Total controllable costs	34,700	29,200	(5,500)

Purpose: To evaluate segment performance

Distribution: Senior management and department managers

Use: To compare budgeted against actual costs

Action to be taken: Investigate underperformance and find reasons for good performance.

EXHIBIT 14-3
COMPARATIVE GROSS PROFIT STATEMENT

Product 1	Budgeted	Actual	Variance	%
Volume	10,000	9,000	1,000	10%
Sales price per unit	$8.50	$10.85	$(2.35)	-28%
Cost per unit	3.15	4.60	(1.45)	-46%
Gross profit per unit	$5.35	$6.25	$(0.90)	-17%
Sales	$85,000	$97,650	$(12,650)	-14.88%
Cost of goods sold	31,500	41,400	(9,900)	-31.43%
Gross profit	$53,500	$56,250	$(2,750)	-5.14%
Cost of goods sold ratio	37.06%	42.40%		
Gross profit ratio	62.94%	57.60%		
Total	100.00%	100.00%		

Product 2				
Volume	16,000	14,000	2,000	13%
Sales price per unit	$6.75	$7.20	$(0.45)	-7%
Cost per unit	5.10	4.95	0.15	3%
Gross profit per unit	$1.65	$2.25	$(0.60)	-36%
Sales	$108,000	$100,800	$7,200	6.67%
Cost of goods sold	81,600	69,300	12,300	15.07%
Gross profit	$26,400	$31,500	$(5,100)	-19.32%
Cost of goods sold ratio	75.56%	68.75%		
Gross profit ratio	24.44%	31.25%		
Total	100.00%	100.00%		

Purpose: To show the gross profit for each division

Distribution: Divisional and senior management

Use: To evaluate a division's ability to meet its budgeted

Action to be taken: Conduct variance analysis, as in Exhibits 14-4 to 14-7, if there are significant deviations.

EXHIBIT 14-4
DIVISIONAL SALES PRICE VARIANCE

| | Sales Price | | Volume | Sales Price |
	Budgeted	Actual	Actual	Variance*
Product 1	$12.00	$13.10	12,000	$(13,200)
Product 2	10.00	12.80	1,400	(3,920)
Product 3	8.50	10.95	1,600	(3,920)
Product 4	9.25	8.40	17,000	14,450
Product 5	15.00	16.35	4,500	(6,075)
Product 6	19.00	18.15	6,750	5,738
Product 7	24.00	22.00	8,295	16,590
Product 8	16.00	17.65	6,000	(9,900)
Product 9	14.25	11.00	7,255	23,579
Product 10	18.65	16.70	9,300	18,135
Product 11	11.75	14.30	14,750	(37,613)
Product 12	13.55	12.10	12,600	18,270
Total				22,134

*Variances in parentheses are favorable.

Sales Price Variance

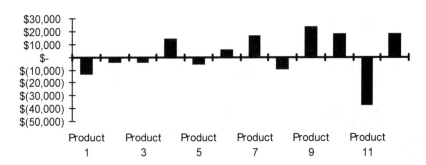

Purpose: To calculate sales price variance for several divisions

Distribution: Divisional and senior management, marketing department

Use: To evaluate the success of the marketing department in increasing sales price

Action to be taken: A higher price (favorable variance) may be offset by a lower volume (unfavorable variance). Look at each variance individually because the total variance may not be revealing.

EXHIBIT 14-5
DIVISIONAL COST VARIANCE

	Cost Budgeted	Actual	Volume Actual	Cost Variance*
Product 1	$8.00	$9.20	12,000	$(14,400)
Product 2	7.00	5.50	1,400	2,100
Product 3	6.50	8.00	1,600	(2,400)
Product 4	7.60	7.10	17,000	8,500
Product 5	12.35	14.00	4,500	(7,425)
Product 6	15.55	14.00	6,750	10,463
Product 7	21.00	23.00	8,295	(16,590)
Product 8	13.25	14.65	6,000	(8,400)
Product 9	11.00	12.00	7,255	(7,255)
Product 10	14.00	15.00	9,300	(9,300)
Product 11	9.20	8.00	14,750	17,700
Product 12	11.00	9.00	12,600	25,200
Total				(1,808)

*Figures in parentheses are unfavorable.

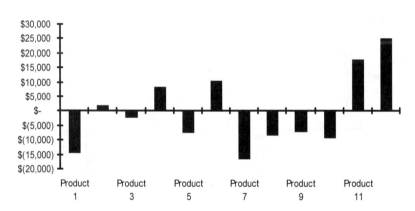

Cost Variance

Purpose: To calculate the cost variance for several divisions

Distribution: Divisional and senior management, purchasing department, production department

Use: To evaluate how well department is reducing costs

Action to be taken: Investigate cost variances that reflect the failure of the department to control costs.

EXHIBIT 14-6
DIVISIONAL VOLUME VARIANCE

	Volume		Budgeted Gross	Volume
	Budgeted	Actual	Profit	Variance*
Product 1	13,570	12,000	$4.00	$6,280
Product 2	1,600	1,400	3.00	600
Product 3	1,545	1,600	2.00	(110)
Product 4	14,250	17,000	1.65	(4,538)
Product 5	6,100	4,500	2.65	4,240
Product 6	6,600	6,750	3.45	(518)
Product 7	9,350	8,295	3.00	3,165
Product 8	7,265	6,000	2.75	3,479
Product 9	8,355	7,255	3.25	3,575
Product 10	8,200	9,300	4.65	(5,115)
Product 11	13,600	14,750	2.55	(2,933)
Product 12	13,540	12,600	2.55	2,397
Total				10,523

*Figures in parentheses are unfavorable.

Volume Variance

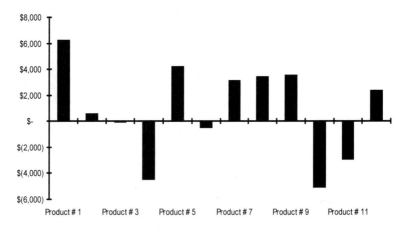

Purpose: To calculate sales volume variance for several divisions

Distribution: Divisional and senior management, marketing department

Use: To evaluate the success of the marketing department in increasing sales

Action to be taken: Investigate unfavorable volume variances. A higher volume (favorable variance) may be off-set by a lower price (unfavorable variance).

EXHIBIT 14-7
GRAPHS OF TOTAL DIVISIONAL VARIANCES

Pie Chart of Total Variances

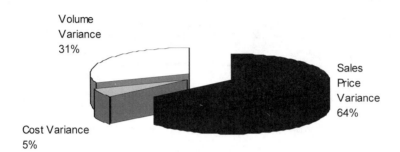

Volume
Variance
31%

Sales
Price
Variance
64%

Cost Variance
5%

Summary of Variances

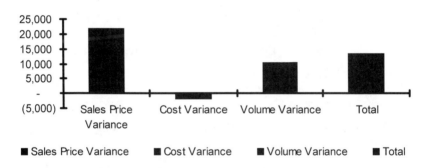

■ Sales Price Variance   ■ Cost Variance   ■ Volume Variance   ■ Total

Purpose: Summarizes combined variances

Distribution: Divisional and senior management, marketing department, production department

Use: To visually highlight the primary cause(s) of total variance

Action to be taken: Investigate unfavorable variances. Sales price variance and volume variance generally reflect on the efforts of the marketing department, cost variance on the work of a purchasing or production manager.

CHAPTER 15

Managerial Accounting and Reporting

Most organizations have several decentralized divisions, which may be:

- Cost Centers. These have control over costs only, not over revenues, sales, marketing, or investment activities.

- Profit Centers. These have control over both revenues and expenses, but not over investing or financing activities. Most decentralized units are profit centers; their managers are evaluated on the basis of divisional net income.

- Investment Centers. These have control over not only revenues and expenses but also investing. The greater level of control also means that much more is expected from their managers.

- Exhibit 15-1 shows return on investment (ROI) and its two components: the earnings ratio (ER) and investment turnover. It should be used by investment centers.

- Exhibit 15-2 is a typical report for a cost center; it emphasizes keeping costs within budget.

- Profit center performance is evaluated by Exhibit 15-3. Controllable income is a crucial measure.

- The graphs in Exhibit 15-4 highlight variances between budgeted and actual income components for a profit center.

- Exhibits 15-5 and 15-6 compared budgeted and actual ROI and residual income (RI).

- Exhibit 15-7 looks at the effect of a proposed investment on ROI and RI. Finally, Exhibits 15-8 and 15-9 show ROI and RI trend comparisons for multi-divisional organizations.

EXHIBIT 15-1
TREND ANALYSIS OF EARNINGS RATIO, INVESTMENT TURNOVER, AND RETURN ON INVESTMENT

Year	Revenue	Income	Assets	Earnings Ratio	Investment Turnover	Return on Investment
20X9	$250,000	$145,000	$1,150,000	58%	22%	12.6%
20X8	265,000	165,000	1,450,000	62%	18%	11.4%
20X7	300,000	135,000	1,300,000	45%	23%	10.4%
20X6	250,000	125,500	1,145,000	50%	22%	11.0%
20X5	325,000	120,000	1,325,000	37%	25%	9.1%
20X4	285,000	160,000	2,600,000	56%	11%	6.2%
20X3	325,000	155,000	1,800,000	48%	18%	8.6%
20X2	345,000	126,000	1,350,000	37%	26%	9.3%
20X1	350,000	145,000	1,250,000	41%	28%	11.6%
20X0	375,000	130,000	1,150,000	35%	33%	11.3%

Purpose: To analyze the direction of earnings

Distribution: Divisional and corporate controllers, top management

Use: To compare performance with prior years

Action to be taken: Investigate falling ratios. Earnings ratio shows income as a percentage of sales. Investment turnover shows sales as a percentage of assets. Return on investment shows income as a percentage of assets.

EXHIBIT 15-2
COST CENTER PERFORMANCE EVALUATION REPORT

Controllable Costs	Actual Cost	Budgeted Cost*	Variance
Variable controllable costs			
Indirect materials	$35,000	$33,000	$(2,000)
Indirect labor	65,000	68,000	3,000
Supplies	20,000	18,000	(2,000)
Payroll taxes	15,000	19,000	4,000
Fringe benefits	20,000	25,000	5,000
Repairs	40,000	30,000	(10,000)
Electric	12,000	10,000	(2,000)
Total	$207,000	$203,000	$(4,000)
Fixed controllable costs			
Depreciation	$45,000	$50,000	$5,000
Supervisor salaries	85,000	80,000	(5,000)
Insurance	30,000	28,000	(2,000)
Payroll taxes	4,000	5,000	1,000
Fringe benefits	6,000	3,000	(3,000)
Rent	17,000	20,000	3,000
Electric	3,500	6,000	2,500
Total	$190,500	$192,000	$1,500
Total controllable costs	$397,500	$395,000	$(2,500)

*Budgeted cost is based on 22,000 actual hours.

Purpose: To evaluate a cost center's performance using budgeted and actual controllable costs

Distribution: Cost center manager, senior management

Use: To identify variations from expectations for further investigation

Action to be taken: A flexible budget is prepared for comparison purposes; unfavorable variance does not necessarily mean poor cost center performance. Conduct variance analysis to identify specific causes for unfavorable variances.

EXHIBIT 15-3
PROFIT CENTER PERFORMANCE EVALUATION

	Budgeted Controllable Income		Actual Controllable Income		Unfavorable (Favorable) Variances
Sales	$1,850,000	100.00%	$1,900,000	100.00%	$(50,000)
Variable cost of goods sold	650,000	35.14%	685,200	36.06%	(35,200)
Manufacturing					
contribution margin	1,200,000	64.86%	1,214,800	63.94%	(14,800)
Variable operating expenses					
Selling	128,500	6.95%	104,350	5.49%	24,150
Administrative	104,590	5.65%	112,600	5.93%	(8,010)
Variable					
operating expenses	233,090	12.60%	216,950	11.42%	16,140
Contribution margin	966,910	52.27%	997,850	52.52%	(30,940)
Controllable fixed expenses					
Fixed factory overhead	140,500	7.59%	185,000	9.74%	(44,500)
Selling	125,600	6.79%	145,000	7.63%	(19,400)
Administrative	98,000	5.30%	112,800	5.94%	(14,800)
Controllable fixed expenses	364,100	19.68%	442,800	23.31%	(78,700)
Profit center controllable income	$602,810	32.58%	$555,050	29.21%	$47,760

Purpose: To evaluate a profit center's performance

Distribution: Profit center manager, senior management

Use: To identify variances between budgeted and actual controllable income

Action to be taken: Investigate unfavorable variances between budgeted and actual controllable income.

EXHIBIT 15-4
PROFIT CENTER EVALUATION GRAPHS

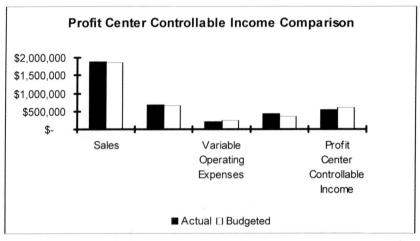

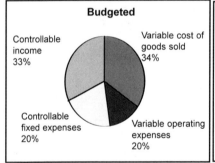

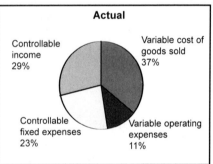

Purpose: To visually identify budgeted and actual income statement components

Distribution: Profit center manager, senior management

Use: To highlight the differences between budgeted and actual amounts

Action to be taken: Use the graphs to easily identify the percentage and dollar value of components of income statement.

EXHIBIT 15-5
DIVISION PERFORMANCE EVALUATION USING
RETURN ON INVESTMENT

	Controllable Income	Controllable Revenues	Controllable Assets
Budgeted Amount	$965,000	$16,500,000	$7,400,000
Actual Amount	890,000	17,000,000	8,365,000
Unfavorable (Favorable) Variances			
	$75,000	$(500,000)	$(965,000)

	Investment Turnover	X	Earnings Ratio	=	Return on Investment
Budgeted ROI at 850,000 units produced and sold:					
	$16,500,000 / $7,400,000	X	$ 965,000 / $16,500,000	=	13.04%
	2.23	X	5.85%	=	13.04%
Actual ROI at 850,000 units produced and sold:					
	$17,000,000 / $8,365,000	X	$ 890,000 / $17,000,000	=	10.64%
	2.03	X	5.24%	=	10.64%

Purpose: To calculate investment turnover, earnings ratio, and return on investment

Distribution: Investment center manager, senior management

Use: To compare budgeted and actual performance

Action to be taken: A return on investment lower than expectation can be caused by lower sales, lower income, higher assets, or a combination of factors. Find out the true cause.

EXHIBIT 15-6
DIVISION PERFORMANCE EVALUATION USING
RESIDUAL INCOME (RI)

	Controllable Income	– Controllable Assets	X	Minimum Rate of Return	=	Residual Income
Budgeted RI at 850,000 units produced and sold:	$2,250,000	– ($5,100,000	X	22%)	=	$1,128,000
Actual RI at 850,000 units produced and sold:	1,950,000	– (6,200,000	X	22%)	=	$586,000
Unfavorable (Favorable) Variances	$300,000	+ ($1,100,000	X	22%)	=	$542,000

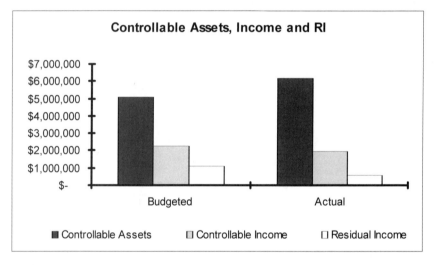

Controllable Assets, Income and RI

■ Controllable Assets   ▢ Controllable Income   ▢ Residual Income

Purpose: To calculate residual income

Distribution: Investment center manager, senior management

Use: To compare budgeted and actual performance

Action to be taken: Residual income shows income after deduction for a minimum required return on investment. Investigate variance between budgeted and actual.

EXHIBIT 15-7
ANALYZING AN INVESTMENT PROPOSAL

	Controllable Income	Controllable Revenues	Controllable Assets
After accepting an additional project	$1,875,550	$16,500,000	$9,875,000
Before accepting an additional project	1,562,000	14,260,000	7,400,000
Difference	$313,550	$2,240,000	$2,475,000

RETURN ON INVESTMENT

	Investment Turnover	X	Earnings Ratio	=	Return on Investment
Before	$14,260,000 / $7,400,000	X	$1,562,000 / $14,260,000	=	21.11%
	1.93	X	10.95%		
After	$16,500,000 / $9,875,000	X	$1,875,550 / $16,500,000	=	18.99%
	1.67	X	11.37%		
Difference					-2.12%

RESIDUAL INCOME

	Controllable Income	−	Controllable Assets	X	Minimum Rate of Return	=	Residual Income
Before	$1,562,000	−	$7,400,000	X	15%	=	$452,000
After	1,875,550	−	9,875,000	X	15%	=	$394,300
Difference							$(57,700)

EXHIBIT 15-7
ANALYZING AN INVESTMENT PROPOSAL, *Cont'd*

Purpose: To evaluate the desirability of accepting an additional investment

Distribution: Division manager

Use: To provide pre- and post-investment data on investment turnover, earnings ratio, return on investment, and residual income

Action to be taken: A lower post-return on investment does not necessarily mean that the investment proposal should be rejected. Compare the new project's ROI with the minimum required rate of return. Negative residual income, on the other hand, should trigger a rejection.

EXHIBIT 15-8
MULTI-YEAR RETURN ON INVESTMENT (ROI) BY DIVISION

Division	Year	Income	Assets	ROI
Division A	2005	$145,000	$1,150,000	12.6%
Division A	2004	165,000	1,450,000	11.4%
Division A	2003	135,000	1,300,000	10.4%
Division A	2002	125,500	1,145,000	11.0%
Division A	2001	120,000	1,325,000	9.1%
Division B	2005	160,000	2,600,000	6.2%
Division B	2004	155,000	1,800,000	8.6%
Division B	2003	126,000	1,350,000	9.3%
Division B	2002	145,000	1,250,000	11.6%
Division B	2001	130,000	1,150,000	11.3%
Division C	2005	335,000	1,500,000	22.3%
Division C	2004	265,000	1,250,000	21.2%
Division C	2003	220,000	1,300,000	16.9%
Division C	2002	180,000	1,355,000	13.3%
Division C	2001	167,000	1,100,000	15.2%

Purpose: Analyze the return on investment trend by division over a five year time period.

Distribution: Division manager and senior management

Use: To identify decreasing trends

Action to be taken: Improve ROI by increasing investment turnover, or earnings ratio, or both.

EXHIBIT 15-9
MULTI-YEAR RESIDUAL INCOME (RI) BY DIVISION

Division	Year	Income	Assets	Rate	RI
Division A	2005	$210,000	$1,150,000	10%	$95,000
Division A	2004	300,000	1,450,000	10%	155,000
Division A	2003	225,000	1,300,000	10%	95,000
Division A	2002	195,000	1,145,000	10%	80,500
Division A	2001	140,000	1,325,000	10%	7,500
Division B	2005	300,000	2,600,000	10%	40,000
Division B	2004	210,000	1,800,000	10%	30,000
Division B	2003	175,000	1,350,000	10%	40,000
Division B	2002	145,000	1,250,000	10%	20,000
Division B	2001	130,000	1,150,000	10%	15,000
Division C	2005	335,000	1,500,000	10%	185,000
Division C	2004	265,000	1,250,000	10%	140,000
Division C	2003	220,000	1,300,000	10%	90,000
Division C	2002	180,000	1,355,000	10%	44,500
Division C	2001	200,000	1,100,000	10%	90,000

Purpose: To analyze the residual income trend for the division over a reasonable period

Distribution: Division manager, senior management

Use: To identify decreasing trends

Action to be taken: Improve RI by increasing income, reducing assets, or lowering the required rate of return.

CHAPTER 16

Planning and Control Reports

Planning reports help managers structure their future activities. Once they set operational and financial goals, they can take steps to assure profit generation and operating productivity.

Planning reports may be used for marketing purposes, product development and analysis, and project appraisal. Control reports compare estimated costs with actual costs for variance analysis. By identifying excessive costs and implementing control measures, the firm can improve its bottom line.

- Exhibit 16-1 presents a profit plan for managers showing sales, variable costs, fixed costs, contribution margin, and departmental profit.

- In planning marketing efforts, Exhibit 16-2 would be useful.

- Product plans are shown in Exhibit 16-3.

- Exhibits 16-4, 16-5, and 16-8 are used for project plans.

- Exhibit 16-6 presents a quarterly operating service report showing service revenue, costs, and operating profit. This exhibit also highlights employee productivity, including idle time.

- Exhibit 16-7 is a variable profit report comparing estimated profit with actual profit. It takes into account selling price, selling volume, material and labor quantity and price, overhead, and administrative costs.

EXHIBIT 16-1
PROFIT PLAN FOR MANAGERS

	Dept. X Zweig	Dept. Y Davis	Dept. Z Okin
Net sales	$100,000	$150,000	$200,000
Less: Variable costs			
Variable cost of sales	30,000	35,000	40,000
Variable selling expenses	10,000	5,000	15,000
Variable administrative expenses	6,000	8,000	7,000
Total variable costs	46,000	48,000	62,000
Contribution margin	54,000	102,000	138,000
Less: Fixed costs			
Fixed manufacturing costs	7,000	10,000	11,000
Fixed selling expenses	4,000	6,000	9,000
Fixed administrative expenses	3,000	5,000	12,000
Total fixed costs	14,000	21,000	32,000
Departmental profit	$40,000	$81,000	$106,000
Contribution margin/net sales	54%	68%	69%
Profit/net sales	40%	54%	53%

Purpose: To estimate each manager's profit plan estimate for a forthcoming period

Distribution: Departmental managers, divisional managers, executive vice-presidents for operations

Use: To appraise whether the profit plan and its major components is realistic; to decide proper funding levels to accomplish goals

Action to be taken: Identify areas in which to control costs to improve profitability.

EXHIBIT 16-2
MARKETING PLAN REPORT

Product	Units	Average Selling Price	Total Sales	U.S. Sales				Overseas
				East	West	North	South	Sales
A	12000	$40	$480,000	$150,000	$70,000	$200,000	$30,000	$30,000
B	15000	42	630,000	140,000	210,000	80,000	60,000	140,000
C	18000	50	900,000	50,000	40,000	60,000	50,000	700,000
D	10000	13	130,000	20,000	60,000	10,000	40,000	-
E	13000	25	325,000	50,000	50,000	250,000	-	200,000
F	20000	60	1,200,000	200,000	-	110,000	90,000	800,000
Total	88000	$40	$3,665,000	$610,000	$430,000	$485,000	$270,000	$1,870,000

Purpose: To determine the revenue generated by product in total and by geographic locality

Distribution: Product manager, marketing manager, director of international operations, CFO

Use: To ascertain which products are selling where, and determine if sales of a product are significantly being influenced by its pricing

Action to be taken: Improve promotion of products in those areas having the most demand.

EXHIBIT 16-3
PRODUCT PLAN

	Dollars	Per Unit	Relative to Sales
Net units sold after returns = 10,000 units			
Net sales	$3,400,000	$340	100%
Variable costs:			
Variable cost of sales	1,600,000	160	47
Variable selling costs	250,000	25	7
Variable administrative costs	150,000	15	4
Total variable costs	2,000,000	200	58
Contribution margin	1,400,000	140	42%
Fixed costs:			
Fixed overhead	500,000	50	15
Fixed selling costs	100,000	10	3
Fixed administrative costs	220,000	22	7
Total fixed costs	820,000	82	25
Operating income	$580,000	$58	17

Purpose: To determine the financial success of the company's product line

Distribution: Chief executive officer, chief financial officer, financial officer, financial analyst, product manager, marketing manager

Use: To compute the contribution margin and profit earned in total, per unit, and on a relative basis so as to decide which products to emphasize or de-emphasize; to ascertain the revenue and costs associated with the entity's product mix

Action to be taken: Restructure product lines to achieve a combination of the most profitable products.

EXHIBIT 16-4
PROJECT BUDGETED COST

Budgeted Item	Annual Budget	Budget per Quarter			
		1	2	3	4
Supervision	$800,000	$100,000	$200,000	$400,000	$100,000
Worker salaries	900,000	150,000	300,000	400,000	50,000
Materials	100,000	20,000	30,000	40,000	10,000
Repairs and maintenance	60,000	15,000	10,000	25,000	10,000
Insurance	10,000	2,500	2,500	2,500	2,500
Inspection	7,000	2,000	3,000	1,500	500
Utilities	1,800	500	700	400	200
Supplies	600	150	250	100	100

Purpose: To allocate costs by major cost item

Distribution: Project manager, department manager, budget analyst, plant manager

Use: To plan for the forthcoming period

Action to be taken: Undertake a cost tracking and analysis program.

EXHIBIT 16-5
QUARTERLY APPRAISAL OF PROJECT: ACTUAL VS. BUDGET

Project	Actual Cost	Budgeted Cost	Variance	Actual Hours	Budgeted Hours	Variance
A	$80,000	$70,000	$10,000U	11000	10000	$1,000U
B	60,000	65,000	5,000F	8400	8000	400U
C	90,000	83,000	7,000U	13000	12000	1,000U
D	40,000	40,000	-	5050	5000	50U
E	50,000	65,000	15,000F	8000	9000	1,000F

U = Unfavorable; F = Favorable

Purpose: To assess if projects are performing in line with budgeted costs and time

Distribution: Project manager, department manager, budget analyst, plant manager

Use: To determine if projects are experiencing cost overruns or excessive hours, and the reasons why

Action to be taken: Prioritize and take steps to reduce the time and costs for project completion.

EXHIBIT 16-6
QUARTERLY OPERATING SERVICE REPORT

	Current Quarter			Prior Year Quarter		
	Budget	Actual	Difference	Budget	Actual	Difference
Service revenue in dollars	$800,000	$850,000	$50,000F	$700,000	$725,000	$25,000F
Service revenue in hours	20,000	21,250	1,250F	20,000	18,125	(1,875)U
Average billing rate per hour	40	40	-	35	40	5F
Service costs:						
Employee salaries	280,000	300,000	20,000U	250,000	240,000	(10,000)F
Tools and supplies used	60,000	55,000	(5,000)F	50,000	46,000	(4,000)F
Unassigned time	35,000	40,000	5,000U	30,000	28,000	(2,000)F
Training	20,000	20,000	-	20,000	22,000	2,000U
Professional development	15,000	19,000	4,000U	15,000	16,000	1,000U
Total service costs	410,000	434,000	24,000U	365,000	352,000	(13,000)F
Operating profit	390,000	416,000	26,000F	335,000	373,000	38,000F
Operating profit/service revenue in $	49%	49%	-	48%	51%	3%F
Total service costs/service revenue in $	51%	51%	-	52%	49%	-3%F
Service revenue in dollars/ employee salaries	2%	3%	0%U	3%	3%	0%F
Unassigned time/service revenue in $	4%	5%	1%U	4%	4%	-

U = Unfavorable; F = Favorable

Purpose: To identify variances between budget and actual for operating activities; to compute ratios showing staff productivity

Distribution: Vice-president of operations, financial analyst, chief executive officer

Use: To ascertain how well services are being performed, identify unproductive time, and analyze and control costs

Action to be taken: Identify problems and ways to improve the service function and control service costs.

EXHIBIT 16-7
VARIANCE PROFIT REPORT

Divisional profit:

Actual	$860,000
Budget	700,000
Favorable variance	160,000

Reasons for variance:

Sales price	40,000 F
Sales volume	30,000 F
Product mix	5,000 U
Material quantity	10,000 F
Material price	6,000 U
Labor quantity	25,000 F
Labor price	15,000 F
Overhead	18,000 F
Administration	33,000 F
Total favorable variance	$160,000

Purpose: To compare expected versus actual profit by division

Distribution: Division manager, budget manager, vice-president of operations, financial analyst, chief financial officer

Use: To identify reasons for profit variances for control and corrective purpose

Action to be taken: Improve budget process and action performance.

EXHIBIT 16-8
PROJECT PLAN

	Project A	Project B	Project C
Expected revenue	$550,000	$620,000	$680,000
Anticipated cost	310,000	340,000	350,000
Expected time in days	100	84	75
Risk	High	Low	Moderate
Number of workers required	5	4	6
Skill level	High	Moderate	Low
Dependence with another project?	No	Yes	No

Purpose: To determine the benefit, cost, time, and difficulty level associated with a project

Distribution: Project manager, vice-president of operations, planning analyst, production manager

Use: To ascertain the financial and operational feasibility of undertaking

Action to be taken: Reduce project cost and time to completion.

CHAPTER 17

Budget Reporting and Control

Budgets quantify management goals and objectives. They help managers control operations. Significant deviations of actual from projected figures alert managers to take corrective action.

A year is the typical planning period for budgets. Most budgets represented in the exhibits in this chapter are for three months; modify the period to suit your needs.

Some companies use continuous budgeting: a month or quarter is added whenever the current month or quarter ends. This approach forces managers to think continuously about their targets.

- Exhibits 17-1, 17-2, and 17-3 project income statements, balance sheets, and cash flow. Other schedules would add details to the lines in these plans.

- Exhibit 17-4 is a typical cash budget projecting receipts and disbursements for the first quarter. This information is essential for managing cash.

- Exhibits 17-5 through 17-8 detail the major components of an income statement by region.

- The unit product budget and its components are modeled in Exhibits 17-9 through 17-12.

- Exhibit 17-13 shows budgeted inventory unit cost and its percentage components.

EXHIBIT 17-1
QUARTERLY BUDGETED INCOME STATEMENT

	January	February	March	Quarter
Sales	$125,000	$145,000	$160,000	$430,000
Cost of goods sold	37,500	43,500	48,000	129,000
Gross profit	87,500	101,500	112,000	301,000
Selling expenses	25,000	29,000	32,000	86,000
Administrative expenses	18,750	21,750	24,000	64,500
Income before taxes	43,750	50,750	56,000	150,500
Taxes	15,313	17,763	19,600	52,675
Net income after taxes	$ 28,438	$ 32,988	$ 36,400	$ 97,825

Purpose: To estimate income using gross profit, selling and administrative expenses, and taxes.

Distribution: Divisional and corporate controllers, top management

Use: To estimate monthly income

Action to be taken: If income is inadequate, increase sales or cut expenses.

EXHIBIT 17-2
QUARTERLY BUDGETED BALANCE SHEET (as of March 31, 20X1)

Assets		
Cash		$300,000
Accounts receivable	$450,000	
Less: Allowance for doubtful accounts	15,000	435,000
Inventories		
Finished goods	125,000	
Materials	35,000	160,000
Property, plant, and equipment	1,785,000	
Less: Accumulated depreciation	315,000	1,470,000
Other assets		255,000
Total assets		$2,620,000
Liabilities and Equity		
Accounts payable		$250,000
Notes payable		375,000
Other current liabilities		85,000
Long-term debt		650,000
Common stock		425,000
Retained earnings		835,000
Total liabilities and equity		$2,620,000

Purpose: To estimate assets, liabilities, and stockholders' equity

Distribution: Divisional and corporate controllers, and top management

Use: To set benchmarks for amounts and ratios

Action to be taken: Unfavorable performance against budget could lower credit ratings. An inadequate ROI may suggest a need to modify budgets.

EXHIBIT 17-3
QUARTERLY BUDGET OF CASH FLOWS—DIRECT METHOD
(for quarter ended March 31, 20X1)

CASH FLOWS FROM OPERATING ACTIVITIES		
Cash received from customers	$1,347,000	
Dividends received	6,600	
Cash paid to suppliers	(860,000)	
Cash paid for operating expenses	(296,500)	
Taxes paid	(38,980)	
Interest paid	(90,000)	
Net cash from operating activities		$ 68,120
CASH FLOWS FROM INVESTING ACTIVITIES		
Sale of short-term investment	45,000	
Sale of land	210,000	
Purchase of equipment	(250,000)	
Net cash from investing activities		5,000
CASH FLOWS FROM FINANCING ACTIVITIES		
Issuance of common stock	110,000	
Payment of principal on long-term debt	(20,000)	
Payment of dividends	95,000	
Net cash from financing activities		185,000
Net change in cash		258,120
Beginning cash balance		10,000
Ending cash balance		$268,120

Purpose: To estimate cash flow from operating, investing, and financing activities

Distribution: Divisional and corporate controllers, top management

Use: To plan for cash flow requirements

Action to be taken: If cash is inadequate to pay dividends or obligations or finance plant expansion, budgets may need to be modified.

EXHIBIT 17-4
QUARTERLY CASH BUDGET

	January	February	March	Quarter
Beginning cash balance	$10,700	$17,000	$18,100	$10,700
Cash receipts				
Cash sales	15,000	18,000	22,000	55,000
Collections on accounts receivable	35,000	65,000	58,000	158,000
Interest received	6,000	6,200	5,900	18,100
Cash proceeds from sale of equipment	13,000	-	83,000	96,000
Total cash receipts	69,000	89,200	168,900	327,100
Total cash available	79,700	106,200	187,000	337,800
Cash disbursements				
Cash expenses	8,700	9,900	13,000	31,600
Payment on accounts payable	23,000	29,000	35,000	87,000
Purchase of land	108,000	-	45,000	153,000
Income taxes	11,000	13,000	22,000	46,000
Total cash disbursements	150,700	51,900	115,000	317,600
Cash flow	(71,000)	54,300	72,000	20,200
Financing				
Borrowing, beginning of month	$80,000	-	-	80,000
Repayment, end of month	-	45,000	20,000	65,000
Interest	8,000	8,800	3,000	19,800
Net financing	88,000	(36,200)	(17,000)	34,800
Ending cash balance	$ 17,000	$ 18,100	$55,000	$55,000

Purpose: To estimate future cash receipts, cash disbursements, and financing requirements

Distribution: Divisional and corporate controllers, treasurers

Use: To stabilize cash balances by keeping cash close to requirements

Action to be taken: Time loan repayments to match cash flows.

EXHIBIT 17-5
QUARTERLY SALES BUDGET

	January	February	March	Quarter
Northeastern Region				
Sales units	25,000	35,000	40,000	100,000
Sales price ($)	10	$ 12	$ 14	$ 12.30
Sales revenue	$250,000	$420,000	$560,000	$1,230,000
Southeastern Region				
Sales units	40,000	28,000	35,000	103,000
Sales price ($)	11	11.50	13	11.82
Sales revenue	$440,000	$322,000	$455,000	$1,217,000
Northwestern Region				
Sales units	35,000	37,000	36,000	108,000
Sales price ($)	10.50	12.00	13.00	11.85
Sales revenue	$367,500	$444,000	$468,000	$1,279,500
Southwestern Region				
Sales units	22,000	33,000	38,000	93,000
Sales price ($)	12	14	13.50	13.32
Sales revenue	$264,000	$462,000	$513,000	$1,239,000
Company				
Sales units	122,000	133,000	149,000	404,000
Average sales price ($)	10.83	12.39	13.40	12.29
Sales revenue	$1,321,500	$1,648,000	$1,996,000	$4,965,500

Purpose: To estimate monthly and quarterly sales

Distribution: Sales manager, controller, top management

Use: To forecast sales revenue

Action to be taken: Modify budget if revenues are lower than forcasted. If the company has several products or the sales are from different geographic regions, a separate schedule can be prepared for each region and each product to support the master sales budget.

EXHIBIT 17-6
QUARTERLY MANUFACTURING EXPENSE BUDGET

	January		February		March		Quarter	
Depreciation	$40,000	12%	$40,000	13%	$40,000	8%	$120,000	11%
Electricity	10,000	3%	12,000	4%	14,000	3%	36,000	3%
Equipment lease	35,000	11%	35,000	11%	35,000	7%	105,000	9%
Fuel	15,000	5%	18,000	6%	23,000	5%	56,000	5%
Insurance	18,000	5%	18,000	6%	18,000	4%	54,000	5%
Labor fringe benefits	36,000	11%	35,000	11%	38,000	8%	109,000	10%
Payroll taxes	12,000	4%	11,000	4%	13,000	3%	36,000	3%
Real estate taxes	8,000	2%	8,000	3%	8,000	2%	24,000	2%
Rent	10,000	3%	10,000	3%	10,000	2%	30,000	3%
Repairs	22,000	7%	8,000	3%	25,000	5%	55,000	5%
Salaries	85,000	26%	75,000	24%	90,000	19%	250,000	22%
Supplies	9,500	3%	11,500	4%	120,000	25%	141,000	13%
Telephone	2,500	1%	2,000	1%	3,000	1%	7,500	1%
Travel	6,500	2%	4,000	1%	8,000	2%	18,500	2%
Utilities	20,000	6%	25,000	8%	30,000	6%	75,000	7%
Total	$329,500	100%	$312,500	100%	$475,000	100%	$1,117,002	100%

Purpose: To estimate manufacturing expense

Distribution: Plant manager, controller, top management

Use: To plan manufacturing expenses by month for the quarter

Action to be taken: Modify budget if expenses in any category are excessive.

EXHIBIT 17-7
QUARTERLY ADMINISTRATIVE EXPENSE BUDGET

	Variable	Fixed	Total
January			
Office salaries	$12,000	$20,000	$32,000
Legal fees	15,000	-	15,000
Utilities	10,000	6,000	16,000
Insurance	-	5,000	5,000
Supplies	2,500	-	2,500
Depreciation	-	8,500	8,500
Miscellaneous office expense	8,500	6,500	15,000
Total	$48,000	$46,000	$94,000
February			
Office salaries	$17,000	$22,000	$39,000
Legal fees	12,000	-	12,000
Utilities	9,000	7,500	16,500
Insurance	-	5,000	5,000
Supplies	3,500	-	3,500
Depreciation	-	8,500	8,500
Miscellaneous office expense	4,000	6,000	10,000
Total	$45,500	$49,000	$94,500
March			
Office salaries	$14,000	$17,000	$31,000
Legal fees	22,000	-	22,000
Utilities	20,000	5,000	25,000
Insurance	-	5,000	5,000
Supplies	2,800	-	2,800
Depreciation	-	8,500	8,500
Miscellaneous office expense	3,700	4,500	8,200
Total	$62,500	$40,000	$102,500
Quarter			
Office salaries	$43,000	$59,000	$102,000
Legal fees	49,000	-	49,000
Utilities	39,000	18,500	57,500
Insurance	-	15,000	15,000
Supplies	8,800	-	8,800
Depreciation	-	25,500	25,500
Miscellaneous office expense	16,200	17,000	33,200
Total	$156,000	$135,000	$291,000

Purpose: To plan for administrative expenses

Distribution: Office manager, controller

Use: To monitor both fixed and variable administrative costs

Action to be taken: Modify schedule if variable and/or fixed administrative costs change.

EXHIBIT 17-8
QUARTERLY SELLING EXPENSE BUDGET

	Variable	Fixed	Total
January			
Wages	$-	$20,000	$20,000
Commission	15,000	-	15,000
Advertising	-	5,000	5,000
Bad Debts	5,000	-	5,000
Travel	2,500	-	2,500
Depreciation	-	8,000	8,000
Miscellaneous	7,500	7,000	14,500
Total	$30,000	$40,000	$70,000
February			
Wages	$-	$25,000	$25,000
Commission	18,000	-	18,000
Advertising	-	5,000	5,000
Bad debts	6,000	-	6,000
Travel	3,000	-	3,000
Depreciation	-	8,000	8,000
Miscellaneous	8,000	12,000	20,000
Total	$35,000	$50,000	$85,000
March			
Wages	$-	$30,000	$30,000
Commission	30,000	-	30,000
Advertising	-	10,000	10,000
Bad debts	10,000	-	10,000
Travel	5,000	-	5,000
Depreciation	-	8,000	8,000
Miscellaneous	5,000	17,000	22,000
Total	$50,000	$65,000	$115,000
Quarter			
Wages	$-	$75,000	$75,000
Commission	63,000	-	63,000
Advertising	-	20,000	20,000
Bad debts	21,000	-	21,000
Travel	10,500	-	10,500
Depreciation	-	24,000	24,000
Miscellaneous	20,500	36,000	56,500
Total	$115,000	$155,000	$270,000

Purpose: To plan for selling expenses

Distribution: Sales manager, controller

Use: To monitor fixed and variable selling costs

Action to be taken: Modify schedule if variable and/or fixed selling costs change.

EXHIBIT 17-9
QUARTERLY PRODUCTION BUDGET

	January	February	March	Quarter
Product X				
Sales units	25,000	35,000	40,000	100,000
+ Desired ending inventory	20,000	27,000	30,000	30,000
- Beginning inventory	10,000	20,000	27,000	10,000
Production units required	35,000	42,000	43,000	120,000
Product Y				
Sales units	15,000	30,000	35,000	80,000
+ Desired ending inventory	18,000	22,000	25,000	25,000
- Beginning inventory	12,000	18,000	22,000	12,000
Production units required	21,000	34,000	38,000	93,000
Product Z				
Sales units	40,000	25,000	15,000	80,000
+ Desired ending inventory	35,000	12,000	35,000	35,000
- Beginning inventory	15,000	35,000	12,000	15,000
Production units required	60,000	2,000	38,000	100,000

Purpose: To plan for production by adjusting production to changes in inventories

Distribution: Production manager, inventory supervisor

Use: To determine monthly production units required

Action to be taken: Adjust production to match sales and inventory levels.

EXHIBIT 17-10
QUARTERLY DIRECT MATERIALS BUDGET

Product X	January	February	March	Quarter
Production units required	35,000	42,000	43,000	120,000
Direct material needed per unit				
of finished goods	2	2	2	2
Direct materials required for production	70,000	84,000	86,000	240,000
+Desired direct material ending inventory	15,000	18,000	10,000	10,000
-Direct material beginning inventory	12,000	15,000	18,000	12,000
Direct materials units to be purchased	73,000	87,000	78,000	238,000
Material price per unit	$10.00	$11.00	$11.50	$10.86
Total direct materials cost	$730,000	$957,000	$897,000	$2,584,000
Product Y				
Production units required	20,000	25,000	35,000	80,000
Direct material needed per unit				
of finished goods	4	4	4	4
Direct materials required for production	80,000	100,000	140,000	320,000
+Desired direct material ending inventory	16,000	17,000	11,000	11,000
-Direct material beginning inventory	13,000	16,000	17,000	13,000
Direct materials units to be purchased	83,000	101,000	134,000	318,000
Material price per unit	$5.00	$5.50	$5.20	$5.24
Total direct materials cost	$415,000	$555,500	$696,800	$1,667,300
Product Z				
Production units required	45,000	50,000	35,000	130,000
Direct material needed per unit				
of finished goods	1	1	1	1
Direct materials required for production	45,000	50,000	35,000	130,000
+Desired direct material ending inventory	25,000	20,000	15,000	15,000
-Direct material beginning inventory	15,000	25,000	20,000	15,000
Direct materials units to be purchased	55,000	45,000	30,000	130,000
Material price per unit	$8.00	$8.75	$9.00	$8.49
Total direct materials cost	$440,000	$393,750	$270,000	$1,103,750
Total Direct Materials Cost				
Product X	$730,000	$957,000	$897,000	$2,584,000
Product Y	415,000	555,500	696,800	1,667,300
Product Z	440,000	393,750	270,000	1,103,750
Total	$1,585,000	$1,906,250	$1,863,800	$5,355,050

Purpose: To plan for direct material purchases

Distribution: Product manager

Use: To match materials purchases to needs, given inventory

Action to be taken: Use Economic Order Quantity (EOQ) models to ensure that inventory costs are kept to a minimum.

EXHIBIT 17-11
QUARTERLY DIRECT LABOR BUDGET

Product A	January	February	March	Quarter
Production units required	35,000	42,000	43,000	120,000
Direct labor hours per unit	3	3	3	3
Direct labor hours required	105,000	126,000	129,000	360,000
Rate per direct labor hour	$15.00	$15.00	$15.00	$15.00
Total direct labor cost	$1,575,000	$1,890,000	$1,935,000	$5,400,000
Product B				
Production units required	50,000	80,000	95,000	225,000
Direct labor hours per unit	2	2	2	2
Direct labor hours required	100,000	160,000	190,000	450,000
Rate per direct labor hour	$25.00	$25.00	$25.00	$25.00
Total direct labor cost	$2,500,000	$4,000,000	$4,750,000	$11,250,000
Product C				
Production units required	15,000	35,000	20,000	70,000
Direct labor hours per unit	5	5	5	5
Direct labor hours required	75,000	175,000	100,000	350,000
Rate per direct labor hour	$12.00	$12.00	$12.00	$12.00
Total direct labor cost	$900,000	$2,100,000	$1,200,000	$4,200,000
Total Direct Labor Cost				
Product A	$1,575,000	$1,890,000	$1,935,000	$5,400,000
Product B	2,500,000	4,000,000	4,750,000	11,250,000
Product C	900,000	2,100,000	1,200,000	4,200,000
Total	$4,975,000	$7,990,000	$7,885,000	$20,850,000

Purpose: To plan for direct labor requirements

Distribution: Product manager

Use: To budget for direct labor costs

Action to be taken: Monitor and adjust budget if direct labor skill levels/pay rates change.

EXHIBIT 17-12
QUARTERLY FACTORY OVERHEAD BUDGET

	Variable	Fixed	Total
January			
Indirect material	$35,000	$42,000	$77,000
Indirect labor	40,000	13,000	53,000
Utilities	15,000	4,000	19,000
Insurance	-	8,000	8,000
Rent	-	25,000	25,000
Depreciation	-	15,000	15,000
Taxes	-	7,000	7,000
Miscellaneous	25,000	11,000	36,000
Total	$115,000	$125,000	$240,000
February			
Indirect material	$25,000	$40,000	$65,000
Indirect labor	28,000	11,000	39,000
Utilities	12,000	4,000	16,000
Insurance	-	8,000	8,000
Rent	-	25,000	25,000
Depreciation	-	15,000	15,000
Taxes	-	7,000	7,000
Miscellaneous	30,000	20,000	50,000
Total	$95,000	$130,000	$225,000
March			
Indirect material	$40,000	$45,000	$85,000
Indirect labor	36,000	18,000	54,000
Utilities	17,000	4,000	21,000
Insurance	-	8,000	8,000
Rent	-	25,000	25,000
Depreciation	-	15,000	15,000
Taxes	-	7,000	7,000
Miscellaneous	32,000	18,000	50,000
Total	$125,000	$140,000	$265,000
Quarter			
Indirect material	$100,000	$127,000	$227,000
Indirect labor	104,000	42,000	146,000
Utilities	44,000	12,000	56,000
Insurance	-	24,000	24,000
Rent	-	75,000	75,000
Depreciation	-	45,000	45,000
Taxes	-	21,000	21,000
Miscellaneous	87,000	49,000	136,000
Total	$335,000	$395,000	$730,000

Purpose: To plan for factory overhead expenditure

Distribution: Product manager

Use: To monitor fixed and variable factory overhead

Action to be taken: Adjust budget if fixed and variable factory overhead change.

EXHIBIT 17-13
BUDGETED INVENTORY UNIT COST

Inventory Number	Dollars			Percentage		
	Direct Materials	Direct Labor	Overhead	Direct Materials	Direct Labor	Overhead
A4	$73	$500	$450	7%	49%	44%
B5	570	770	210	37%	50%	14%
C4	915	85	300	70%	7%	23%
C5	57	130	270	12%	28%	59%
D2	64	40	75	36%	22%	42%
D3	74	355	500	8%	38%	54%
G7	473	92	82	73%	14%	13%
G8	30	76	50	19%	49%	32%
Q4	227	140	300	34%	21%	45%
T8	81	50	75	39%	24%	36%
W9	62	15	90	37%	9%	54%
X2	10	67	20	10%	69%	21%
Z3	90	20	80	47%	11%	42%
Z4	55	45	65	33%	27%	39%

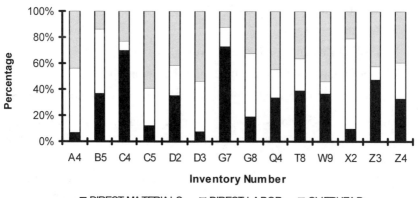

Budgeted Direct Material, Direct Labor & Overhead Costs as a Percentage of Unit Price

Purpose: To estimate per-unit manufacturing costs

Distribution: Production manager, plant manager, controller, top management

Use: To monitor the material, labor, and overhead components of each unit

Action to be taken: Modify budgeted material, labor, and overhead costs as necessary. For example, if the cost of direct materials increases, the per-unit manufacturing cost needs to be adjusted.

CHAPTER 18

Capital Budgeting Analysis and Reporting

Capital budgeting is the process of long-term planning for alternative investment opportunities. A company may have to make many investment decisions in order to grow.

Methods of evaluating investment projects include:

- Payback period
- Accounting rate of return (ARR)
- Internal rate of return (IRR)
- Net present value (NPV)
- Profitability index (or present value index).

To help you work through the capital budgeting process:

- Exhibits 18-1 through 18-4 illustrate project evaluation methods.

- Exhibit 18-5 shows how to compute after-tax cash inflow for a project. Income taxes make a difference in many capital budgeting decisions.

A project that seems attractive on a before-tax basis may have to be rejected on an after-tax basis and vice versa. Income taxes typically affect both the amount and the timing of cash flows. Since net income, not cash inflows, is subject to tax, after-tax cash inflows are not usually the same as after-tax net income.

The chapter closes with several important documents used for project application, change, and appropriation request (Exhibits 18-6 through 18-8), and a report describing the capital budgeting decision making process (Exhibit 18-9).

EXHIBIT 18-1
ACCOUNTING RATE OF RETURN

	Project		
	A	B	C
(a) Annual cash inflow	$35,000	$25,000	$62,000
(b) Useful life (in years)	5	7	6
(c) Depreciation	20,000	11,714	26,667
(d) Annual net income after taxes (a) - (c)	15,000	13,286	35,333
(e) Initial investment	100,000	82,000	160,000
(f) Average investment (e)/2	50,000	41,000	80,000
(g) Accounting rate of return (d)/(f)	0.30	0.32	0.44

Purpose: To guide selection among alternative investment proposals

Distribution: Project analyst, treasurer, cash manager, controller, CFO, CEO

Use: To evaluate a project's likely profitability

Action to be taken: Give priority to the project with the highest accounting rate of return—but use the accounting rate of return with caution because it fails to (1) consider cash flows and (2) incorporate the time value of money.

EXHIBIT 18-2
PAYBACK PERIOD

	Project			
	A	B	C	D
Annual cash inflow	$35,000	$25,000	$62,000	$50,000
Initial investment	75,000	82,000	120,000	60,000
Payback period in years	2.14	3.28	1.94	1.20

Purpose: To guide selection among alternative investment proposals

Distribution: Project analyst, treasurer, cash manager, controller, CFO, CEO

Use: To evaluate a project's likely risk and liquidity

Action to be taken: Give priority to the one with the shortest payback period because that indicates least risk, the best liquidity, and the fastest rate of return.

EXHIBIT 18-3
DISCOUNTED CASH FLOW (DCF) ANALYSIS

	0	1	2	3	4
			Years		
Initial investment (I)	$(140,000)				
Annual savings		48,000	48,000	48,000	48,000
Repairs and maintenance		(2,500)	(5,000)	(7,500)	(10,000)
Salvage value					20,000
Annual cash flow	$(140,000)	$45,500	$43,000	$40,500	$58,000
Present value of $1					
(T1 at 12%)	1	0.8929	0.7972	0.7118	0.6355
Present value (P)	$(140,000)	$40,627	$34,280	$28,828	$36,859
Net present value (NPV = P - I) 593.45		NPV (rate, value1,value2, ...)$528.11			
IRR (values, guess)	12.19%				

Purpose: To calculate net present value (NPV) and internal rate of return (IRR) for a capital investment project

Distribution: Project analyst, treasurer, cash manager, controller, CFO, CEO

Use: To estimate profitability of a capital expenditure project

Action to be taken: If NPV is greater than zero, the project is profitable. If IRR is greater than the cost of capital, accept the project.

EXHIBIT 18-4
CAPITAL RATIONING REPORT

Projects	Cost (1)	Present Value (2)	Profitability Index (2)/(1)	Ranking
A	$70,000	$112,000	1.6	1
B	100,000	145,000	1.45	2
C	110,000	126.500	1.15	5
D	60,000	79,000	1.32	3
E	40,000	38,000	0.95	6
F	80,000	95,000	1.19	4

Purpose: To rank projects competing for limited funds

Distribution: Project analyst, treasurer, cash manager, controller, CFO, CEO

Use: To select the mix of projects that provides the highest overall NPV

Action to be taken: Accept one project at a time from the highest ranked to the next until budget is exhausted.

EXHIBIT 18-5
NET CASH FLOW AFTER TAXES

Year	Cash Inflow (1)	Cash Outflow (2)	Net Cash Flow before Taxes (3)=(1) - (2)	Depreciation (Noncash Expense) (4)=.2 x 900,000	Net Income before Taxes (5)=(3) - (4)	Income Taxes (6)=.4 x (5)	Net Income after Taxes (7)=(5) - (6)	Cash Flow after Taxes (8)=(3) - (6) or (7) + (4)
1	$900,000	$600,000	$300,000	$180,000	$120,000	$48,000	$72,000	$252,000
2	950,000	625,000	325,000	180,000	145,000	58,000	87,000	267,000
3	950,000	625,000	325,000	180,000	145,000	58,000	87,000	267,000
4	825,000	575,000	250,000	180,000	70,000	28,000	42,000	222,000
5	750,000	550,000	200,000	180,000	20,000	8,000	12,000	192,000

Net Present Value (NPV) Calculation

Year	Net Cash Flow after Taxes	Present Value Table Value at 10%	Present Value
0	$(900,000)	$1.00	$(900,000)
1	252,000	0.909	229,068
2	267,000	0.826	220,542
3	267,000	0.751	200,517
4	222,000	0.683	151,626
5	192,000	0.621	119,232
		NPV =	$ 20,985

Purpose: To calculate the NPV of a capital investment project

Distribution: Project analyst, treasurer, cash manager, controller, CFO, CEO

Use: To project the profitability of a capital expenditure project

Action to be taken: If NPV is greater than zero, the project is profitable and should be undertaken.

EXHIBIT 18-6
APPROPRIATION REQUEST

Original Department Name	Department Code	Appropriation No.
Budget Capitalized ( ) Expensed ( )	Project Applic. No.	
Accounting Code	Project Appl. Total Exp. $	Appropriation Total $

Description

Purpose

Current Facilities

Proposed Facilities

Cost Justification (Savings/Benefits)

PROPOSED EXPENDITURES		APPROVALS	DATE
Equipment Cost	_____	Originator _____	
Material Cost	_____		_____ _____
Installation Costs:	_____		_____ _____
External Services	_____	Dept/Area Suprv. _____	_____
Internal Services	_____	V. President	_____ _____
Miscellaneous Costs	_____	Controller	_____ _____
Freight	_____	Division Head	_____ _____
Taxes	_____	CEO	_____ _____
Total	_____	Bd. of Dir.	_____ _____

Purpose: To provide description, purpose, cost justification, and proposed expenditures of a project

Distribution: Project analyst, executive vice president for operations, treasurer, controller, CFO, CEO

Use: To justify an appropriation request

Action to be taken: Make sure proposed expenditures are justified and within the company's overall capital budget.

EXHIBIT 18-7
PROJECT APPLICATION

Department Name	Application No.
Department Code _____	Offensive ____
Function Code _____	Defensive ____

Description Objectives

Expenditure Amounts

Fiscal Year	1st Qtr.	2nd Qtr.	3rd Qtr.	4th Qtr.	Total
20					
20					
20					
20					
20					
Total					
Date	Submitted by				

Comments

_____
For the Division

Purpose: To provide objectives and dollar amounts needed by quarter

Distribution: Project analyst, executive vice-president for operations, treasurer, controller, CFO, CEO

Use: To provide for longer-term capital expenditures

Action to be taken: Make sure scheduled expenditures are within the company's overall capital budget.

EXHIBIT 18-8
ADVICE OF PROJECT CHANGE

Department Name	Date
Department Code	Appropriation Request No.

Project Title

Expenditure Amounts

	Original Authorized	Latest Estimate	Increase (Decrease)
Capital			
Expense			
Total			

Amount spent to date $ _____   Amount committed to date $_____

WHAT IS THIS NEW AMOUNT BEING REQUESTED?

_____   _____
Project Sponsor   Department Area Supervisor

Project to be continued _____

Revised request required _____

See comment on reverse side _____

Final Approver _____   Date _____

Purpose: To describe project changes, reason for change request, and dollar amounts involved

Distribution: Project analyst, executive vice-president for operations, treasurer, controller, CFO, CEO

Use: To determine all the justifications for making a project change

Action to be taken: Determine if the proposed project change is justified on a cost-benefit basis.

EXHIBIT 18-9
CAPITAL RATIONING DECISION PROCESS

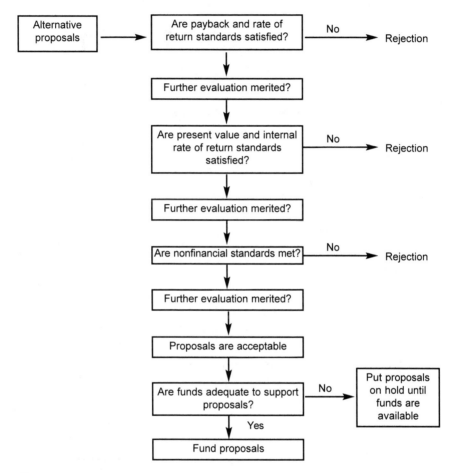

Purpose: To show, step by step, a decision making process for capital budgeting

Distribution: Project analyst, treasurer, controller, CFO, CEO

Use: To help management form an optimal mix of investment projects

Action to be taken: Make sure capital expenditures are within the company's overall capital budget.

CHAPTER 19

Analysis of Capital Expenditures

To plan for capital expenditures, you must find the optimal proposal and decide how much to spend and how long it will take for completion. You must appraise current programs, evaluate new proposals, and decide how to coordinate related proposals.

- Exhibits 19-1 and 19-2 deal with appraisal of make-or buy and buy-or-lease decisions.

- Exhibits 19-3 through 19-8 demonstrate capital expenditures reporting on (a) a spending plan for capital expenditures, with projected return on investment, (b) capital spending compared to budget, (c) planned financing methods, (d) activities for fixed asset acquisitions and disposals, (e) approved cost estimates and money spent/committed to date, and (f) dollar amounts authorized, spent, or committed and balance by project.

- Exhibit 19-9 assesses sources of funds available for capital addition.

- Exhibit 19-10 determines the amount of initial investment in a replacement decision.

EXHIBIT 19-1
BUY VERSUS MAKE APPRAISAL REPORT

Purchasing:

Purchase price of machine	$110,650	
Freight in	3,569	
Other costs:		
Installation	1,200	
Training	1,120	
Warranty agreement	3,500	
Total purchase price	120,039	(a)

Production:

Variable costs:		
Machine shop–material	27,500	
–direct labor	21,560	
–overhead	34,000	
Electronics	17,500	
Total	$100,560	
Fixed costs:		
Machine shop	17,500	
Electronics	6,500	
Total	24,000	
Total production costs	124,560	(b)
Excess of buy over make	$ (4,521)	(a) - (b)

Purpose: To analyze production costs versus purchase costs for a capital project

Distribution: Industrial engineer, project analyst, treasurer, cash manager, controller, CFO, CEO

Use: To guide the choice between buying and making a machine

Action to be taken: Purchase the machine since it is cheaper than making it.

EXHIBIT 19-2
BUY VERSUS LEASE EVALUATION REPORT

	Leasing		Purchase/Borrow					Discounted Cash Flow	
Year	Lease Payments	Net After-Tax Cash Flow	Loan Payments	Interest Expense	Depreciation Expense	Net After-Tax Cash Flow	Present Value Factor	Leasing	Purchase
0	$23,216	$23,216					1.000	$23,216	$10,538
1	23,216	11,608	$26,381	$10,000	$20,000	$11,381	0.9259	10,748	$10,538
2	23,216	11,608	26,381	8,362	20,000	12,200	0.8573	9,952	10,459
3	23,216	11,608	26,381	6,500	20,000	13,101	0.7938	9,214	10,400
4	23,216	11,608	26,381	4,578	20,000	14,092	0.7350	8,532	10,358
5	23,216	(11,608)	26,381	2,398	20,000	15,182	0.6806	(7,900)	10,333
	$92,864	$58,040	$131,905	$31,898	$100,000	$65,956		$53,761	$52,087

	Lease Proposal	Purchase Proposal
Cost of machine	$100,000	$100,000
Terms of payment	5 years	5 years
Interest rate	12%	10%
Down payment		
Monthly lease payment at the end of the year	$23,216	
Monthly loan payment		$26,381
Depreciation		Straight line
Residual purchase price	0%	0%
Corporate tax bracket	50%	50%
After-tax cost of capital	8%	8%

Purpose: To analyze purchase compared with leasing costs for a capital project

Distribution: Project analyst, treasurer, cash manager, controller, CFO, CEO

Use: To guide the choice between leasing and borrowing to purchase

Action to be taken: Buy, because the present value of borrowing $52,087 is less than the discounted value of leasing ($53,761).

EXHIBIT 19-3
QUARTERLY BUDGETING OF CAPITAL EXPENDITURES

Location	Project Description	Return on Investment	Total Appropriation	Current Year's Budget					Expended in Prior Years
				1st Quarter	2nd Quarter	3rd Quarter	4th Quarter	Total	
Detroit Plant	Replacement								
	Coolant press	5.40%	$6,785			$6,785		$6,785	
	Expansion								
	Thickness gauge	6.80%	19,870				$19,870	19,870	
Chicago Plant	Expansion								
	Thickness gauge	6.70%	7,890		$7,890			7,890	
	20" shears	11.20%	2,100		300	1,800		2,100	
	Replacement								
	Hydraulic press	15.0%	34,700	$14,300		15,400		29,700	$5,000
	Coolant system	11.0%	2,375			2,375		2,375	
	Tool block	8.0%	1,235				1,235	1,235	
			$48,300	$14,300	$8,190	$19,575	$1,235	$43,300	$5,000

Purpose: To project capital expenditures by quarter and projected return on investment

Distribution: Project analyst, controller, CFO, CEO

Use: To monitor capital spending as it occurs

Action to be taken: Make sure capital expenditures approved for the year fit within the cash budget limit.

EXHIBIT 19-4
CAPITAL PROJECT FLASH REPORT

Project:	Remodel Stockroom Conveying System	Approved Cost Estimate	Spent/ Committed	Balance
	Capital expenditures:			
	Slides	$7,750	$6,000	$1,750
	Neutral picker	32,450	16,500	15,950
	Automatic rollers	35,000	35,600	(600)
	Other expenditures:			
	Rearrangement of machinery	6,750	3,450	3,300
	Preparation of site	5,670	4,500	1,170
		$47,420	$43,550	$3,870

Purpose: To compare approved cost estimates with money committed to date

Distribution: Project manager, treasurer, controller, CFO, CEO

Use: To keep management informed of the status of capital projects

Action to be taken: Ensure commitments are in line with approved cost estimates so as to prevent cost overruns.

EXHIBIT 19-5
YEARLY PROJECTED MANAGEMENT REPORTING

	Current Year	2001	2002	2003	2004
Buildings	$180,000	$367,000			
Building improvements	88,000	61,000	25,000		
Machinery & equipment	134,000	56,000	71,000	79,000	81,000
Office equipment	9,700	5,100	5,200	14,500	4,000
Automobiles		245,000		34,000	15,000
	$411,700	$734,100	$101,200	$127,500	$100,000
Projected net income	435,000	540,000	497,000	540,000	600,000
Add: depreciation	150,000	200,000	220,000	175,000	158,000
Cash flow from operations	$585,000	$740,000	$717,000	$715,000	$758,000
Capital expenditure as a % of operational cash flow	70%	99%	14%	18%	13%
Planned financing:					
Internal operations	65%	45%	100%	80%	100%
External debt	35%	55%		20%	
External equity	100%	100%	100%	100%	100%

Purpose: To project five-year capital planning, capital expenditure as a percentage of operating cash flow, and planned financing methods

Distribution: Treasurer, controller, CFO, CEO

Use: To determine capital expenditure needs for the next five years

Action to be taken: Detail exactly how all capital additions will be financed.

EXHIBIT 19-6
QUARTERLY SUMMARY OF FIXED ASSET TRANSACTIONS

Acct. No.	Description	Asset				Reserve			
		Balance 6/30/_	Addition	(Disposals)	Balance 6/30/_	Balance 6/30/_	Depreciation Expense	(Disposals)	Balance 6/30/_
14251	Land	$52,300			$52,300				-
14252	Land improvements	23,450	$3,100		26,550	$3,400	$2,185		$5,585
14253	Machinery & equipment	345,670	45,000	$(5,600)	385,070	7,800	15,100	$(3,050)	19,850
14254	Office furniture	67,000	4,800		71,800	30,000	6,500		36,500
14255	Buildings	54,300			54,300	16,700	33,000		49,700
14256	Automobiles	31,000	12,400	10,789	54,189	15,425	5,625	(10,770)	10,280
14257	Equipment deposits	21,000	3,200	(15,000)	9,200				-
		$518,970	$65,400	$(9,811)	$574,559	$69,925	$60,225	$(13,820)	$116,330

Purpose: To show current financial status of fixed assets by account code

Distribution: Treasurer, controller, CFO, CEO

Use: To describe fixed asset activity for management review and to help financial officers manage cash flows

Action to be taken: Detail how capital additions will be financed.

EXHIBIT 19-7
QUARTERLY VARIANCE BETWEEN BUDGET AND ACTUAL CAPITAL EXPENDITURES

Property Description	Expenditures					
	Month			Year-to-date		
	Actual	Budget	Variance +(-)	Actual	Budget	Variance +(-)
Buildings	$76,800	$80,000	$3,200	$876,500	$850,000	
Building improvements		10,000	10,000	21,890	25,500	3,610
Leasehold improvements	9,760	13,200	3,440	22,340	23,400	1,060
Tooling	6,660	5,800	(860)	6,789	16,000	9,211
Equipment	24,350	27,500	3,150	145,679	156,000	10,321
Furniture & fixtures	4,567	3,450	(1,117)	6,730	5,800	(930)
Automobiles	12,300		(12,300)	15,600	19,000	3,400
Total	$134,437	$139,950	$5,513	$1,095,528	$1,095,700	$26,672

Purpose: To analyze capital spending by month and year-to-date compared with budget

Distribution: Treasurer, controller, CFO, CEO

Use: To monitor capital expenditures and check variances

Action to be taken: Take actions to remedy unfavorable variances.

EXHIBIT 19-8
CAPITAL PROJECT STATUS REPORT

Project	Date Authorized	Amount Authorized	Spent or Committed	Balance	
Conveying system	4/45/1999	$76,300	$67,000	$9,300	(b)
Line No. 4	8/1/1999	154,000	125,000	29,000	(a)
Line No. 7	8/1/1999	68,790	45,000	23,790	(a)
Line No. 9	9/1/1999	67,000	78,000	(11,000)	(a)
Modulators	8/10/1999	4,500	5,100	(600)	
Winder No. 5	8/1/1999	14,570	5,600	(20,170)	(a)
Winder No. 3	10/12/1999	7,890	4,300	3,590	(a)
Rail siding installation	3/7/1999	56,000	47,000	9,000	(a)
Cement slabs	6/15/1999	45,000	45,000	-	
Silos	6/15/1999	17,890	17,890	-	

Note: (a) On plant at this stage; (b) Additional work authorized

Purpose: To detail the financial status of each project

Distribution: Treasurer, controller, vice-president of production/operations CFO, CEO

Use: To keep management informed of progress on capital projects

Action to be taken: Monitor plans for capital additions and disposals. Determine variance between amount authorized and amount over committed.

EXHIBIT 19-9
INITIAL INVESTMENT REPORT

Cost of new equipment (per invoice)		$345,600
Add:	Freight	3,150
	Installation costs	1,750
	Other	1,250
	Total cost	351,750 (a)
Less:	Trade-in allowance	27,600
	Salvage recovery net of income taxes	4,320
	Costs avoided on old equipment, net of income taxes:	
	Savings in wages	6,700
	Repairs	2,100
	Maintenance	1,500
	Other	3,100
		45,320 (b)
Add:	Additional working capital needed	
	Cash	7,500
	Receivables	15,800
	Inventory	20,000
		23,300 (c)
Net investment for capital budgeting decision (a) - (b) + (c)		$329,730

Purpose: To determine how much must be invested in a piece of replacement equipment

Distribution: Project analyst, treasurer, cash manager, controller, CFO, CEO

Use: To estimate the profitability of a capital expenditure project

Action to be taken: If the present value of a projected purchase is greater than the initial investment, it is profitable to buy the new equipment.

EXHIBIT 19-10
CAPITAL FUNDING CAPACITY REPORT

Operating cash flow:	
Net income	$560,000
Plus depreciation	99,000
Less (investment) in noncash working capital	(75,000)
	584,000 (a)
Fixed funding sources and uses:	
Debt service	145,000
Dividends	35,000
	180,000 (b)
Other funding sources and uses:	
Cash on hand, beginning of period	78,000
Borrowing capacity	235,000
New equity capacity	500,000
Sale of fixed assets	34,000
	847,000 (c)
Total capital funding capacity (a) - (b) + (c)	$1,251,000

Purpose: To assess sources of funds for capital additions

Distribution: Project analyst, treasurer, cash manager, controller, CFO, CEO

Use: To identify funding sources, which is critical for constructing the capital budget

Action to be taken: Adjust projected investments to fit within funding capacity.

CHAPTER 20

Manufacturing Cost Reports: Material

Careful management of materials is essential to producing units at the lowest cost with the greatest efficiency. This requires detailed analysis of sales forecast, production, purchasing, storage, and distribution.

- Exhibits 20-1 through 20-4 deal with materials requirements, starting with inventory levels through quarterly materials requirements to number of units required in each quarter.

- Exhibits 20-5 and 20-6 contain materials utilization reports, providing specific inventory details for several parts and highlighting defect problems.

- Exhibits 20-7 and 20-8 show material price and efficiency variances.

EXHIBIT 20-1
MATERIALS REQUIREMENT FORECAST

Month	Monthly Requirement	Cumulative Requirement	Desired Ending Inventory Level
January	7,365,000	7,365,000	2,808,650
February	4,321,000	11,686,000	4,095,000
March	6,300,000	17,986,000	2,925,000
April	4,500,000	22,486,000	2,275,000
May	3,500,000	25,986,000	1,430,000
June	2,200,000	28,186,000	1,040,000
July	1,600,000	29,786,000	1,755,000
August	2,700,000	32,486,000	2,990,000
September	4,600,000	37,086,000	4,420,000
October	6,800,000	43,886,000	6,175,000
November	9,500,000	53,386,000	4,615,000
December	7,100,000	60,486,000	4,787,250

Materials Forecast

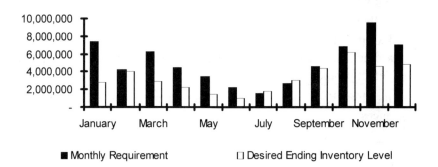

Purpose: To forecast materials requirements

Distribution: Production manager, purchasing manager

Use: To plan monthly production to meet desired ending inventory levels

Action to be taken: Adjust production to maintain desired inventory.

EXHIBIT 20-2
QUARTERLY MATERIALS REQUIREMENTS

Material	First Quarter			Quarter				Total
	Jan	Feb	Mar	1st Quarter	2nd Quarter	3rd Quarter	4th Quarter	Annual
Material 1	1,700	3,500	9,825	15,025	24,350	21,000	28,000	88,375
Material 2	2,400	4,200	4,525	11,125	8,250	13,000	17,500	49,875
Material 3	3,500	4,100	3,525	11,125	14,300	12,500	15,000	52,925
Material 4	4,800	6,300	5,550	16,650	28,000	24,365	20,000	89,015
Material 5	3,200	2,500	4,550	10,250	12,000	13,550	16,500	52,300
Material 6	4,500	2,200	3,750	10,450	9,800	11,000	13,500	44,750
Material 7	6,300	2,300	3,700	12,300	7,500	10,500	10,000	40,300
Material 8	2,200	4,950	3,000	10,150	9,000	10,000	9,500	38,650
Material 9	1,400	3,250	2,500	7,150	8,500	9,250	1,375	26,275
Material 10	1,600	1,675	2,275	5,550	6,500	7,500	12,000	31,550
Material 11	4,100	1,725	4,400	10,225	12,500	13,500	16,550	52,775
Material 12	2,200	1,500	3,275	6,975	12,550	8,550	14,365	42,440

Purpose: To forecast materials requirements

Distribution: Production manager, materials manager, purchasing manager

Use: To monitor inventories and purchases of materials monthly and quarterly

Action to be taken: Update each quarter in light of production needs.

EXHIBIT 20-3

GRAPH OF QUARTERLY MATERIALS REQUIREMENTS IN PERCENTAGE

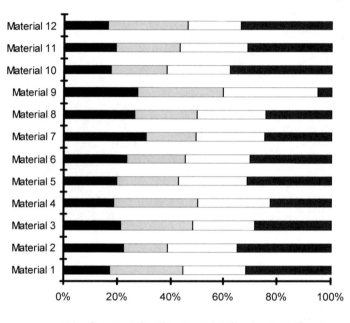

Material Requirements By Quarter - Percentage

■ 1st Quarter ▨ 2nd Quarter ☐ 3rd Quarter ▪ 4th Quarter

Purpose: To display visually how much material is required in each quarter

Distribution: Production manager, materials manager, purchasing manager

Use: To monitor fluctuations in units needed in each quarter

Action to be taken: Adjust production inventory at least quarterly to meet projections.

EXHIBIT 20-4
GRAPH OF QUARTERLY MATERIALS REQUIREMENTS
IN UNITS

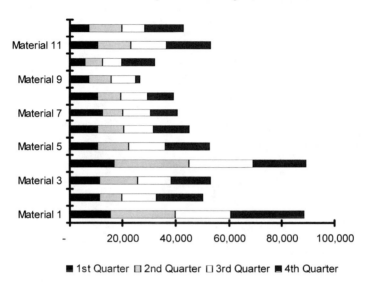

Material Requirements By Quarter - Units

■ 1st Quarter ▣ 2nd Quarter ☐ 3rd Quarter ■ 4th Quarter

Purpose: To detail the material requirements by quarter

Distribution: Production manager, materials manager, purchasing manager

Use: To monitor materials needs monthly and quarterly

Action to be taken: Time material purchases to match production needs.

EXHIBIT 20-5
RAW MATERIALS UTILIZATION REPORT

Part Description	Beginning Inventory	Issued to Floor	Received from Floor	Ending Inventory	Parts Used in Production	Defective Production	Defect Rate
Part # 1	35,000	20,000	5,000	22,000	28,000	2,400	8.6%
Part # 2	85,000	65,000	8,000	47,000	95,000	4,600	4.8%
Part # 3	22,000	30,000	10,000	32,000	10,000	800	8.0%
Part # 4	45,000	35,000	12,000	17,000	51,000	3,300	6.5%
Part # 5	95,000	60,000	14,000	74,000	67,000	3,100	4.6%
Part # 6	65,000	75,000	5,000	48,000	87,000	6,000	6.9%
Part # 7	40,000	55,000	15,000	42,400	37,600	1,600	4.3%
Part # 8	20,000	40,000	6,500	5,100	48,400	1,750	3.6%
Part # 9	15,000	25,000	2,500	24,000	13,500	420	3.1%

Purpose: To maintain a perpetual record of inventory usage for each part

Distribution: Production manager, materials manager

Use: To track inventory usage, including defect rate

Action to be taken: If ending inventory level is high, reduce investment in inventory; investigate causes of production defects.

EXHIBIT 20-6
MATERIALS UTILIZATION REPORT

Product	Machine Hours Available	Units per Hours	Production Budgeted	Production Actual	% Efficiency	Pounds per Unit	Material Utilization Budgeted	Material Utilization Actual	% Utilization
Item # 1	4,000	100	400,000	360,000	90%	2.0	720,000	700,000	97%
Item # 2	5,500	80	440,000	425,000	97%	0.5	212,500	215,000	101%
Item # 3	8,000	95	760,000	640,000	84%	3.0	1,920,000	2,200,000	115%
Item # 4	2,000	480	960,000	800,000	83%	4.0	3,200,000	3,100,000	97%
Item # 5	3,000	110	330,000	250,000	76%	0.2	50,000	75,000	150%
Item # 6	4,500	75	337,500	335,000	99%	10.0	3,350,000	4,000,000	119%
Item # 7	6,800	50	340,000	320,000	94%	1.0	320,000	325,000	102%
Item # 8	2,600	150	390,000	300,000	77%	0.1	30,000	35,000	117%
Item # 9	4,400	40	176,000	140,000	80%	6.0	840,000	800,000	95%
Item # 10	6,000	150	900,000	775,000	86%	0.2	155,000	135,000	87%

Purpose: To check on the efficiency of the production process

Distribution: Production manager, materials manager, plant manager

Use: To compare budgeted with actual production efficiency for a variety of items

Action to be taken: Adjust production processes where material utilization is below or above expectations.

EXHIBIT 20-7
DIRECT MATERIALS PRICE VARIANCE

Part Number	Actual Unit Price	Standard Unit Price	Actual Quantity Purchased	Variance*	Reasons for Variance				
					Lower Quality Material	Higher Quality Material	Material Shortage	Material Excess	Different Supplier
Part # 1	$15	$16	15,000	$(15,000)	$(10,000)	$-	$-	$(5,000)	$-
Part # 2	6	3	25,000	75,000	-	25,000	30,000	-	20,000
Part # 3	18	20	12,000	(24,000)	-	-	-	(14,000)	(10,000)
Part # 4	25	22	33,000	99,000	-	-	99,000	-	-
Part # 5	4	3	40,000	40,000	-	40,000	-	-	-
Part # 6	28	25	28,000	84,000	-	-	(1,400)	-	85,400
Part # 7	35	30	35,000	175,000	-	75,000	35,000	-	65,000
Part # 8	12	10	18,000	36,000	(20,000)	-	56,000	-	-

*Parentheses indicate a favorable variance.

Purpose: To identify causes of favorable or unfavorable price variances

Distribution: Production manager, purchasing manager, materials manager

Use: To determine if actual prices are the same as standard prices

Action to be taken: Adjust purchasing policies to respond to reasons for price variance. Even a favorable price variance may require corrective action as when lower quality material is being purchased.

EXHIBIT 20-8
DIRECT MATERIALS EFFICIENCY VARIANCE

Part Number	Actual Quantity Used	Standard Quantity Allowed	Standard Unit Price	Variance*	Reasons for Variance				
					Material Quality	Workmanship	Machine Efficiency	Theft/Pilferage	Misc.
Part # 1	12,500	14,000	$2.00	$(3,000)	$(1,500)	$(2,000)	$-	$500	$-
Part # 2	8,500	6,500	3.50	7,000	-	3,000	4,000	-	-
Part # 3	4,500	4,000	1.50	750	-	-	-	750	-
Part # 4	15,600	15,000	6.00	3,600	-	-	2,400	-	1,200
Part # 5	2,400	2,500	8.00	(800)	-	-	(800)	-	-
Part # 6	6,500	6,500	9.00	-	1,400	-	(1,400)	-	-
Part # 7	9,200	9,000	8.75	1,750	-	1,500	-	-	250
Part # 8	17,500	17,000	3.25	1,625	(1,500)	2,500	-	-	625

Parentheses indicate a favorable variance.

Purpose: To identify causes of favorable or unfavorable variances in efficiency

Distribution: Production manager, purchasing manager, materials manager

Use: To determine if actual quantity used is the same as standard quantity allowed

Action to be taken: Adjust policies to respond to reasons for efficiency variance. Even a favorable efficiency variance may require corrective action as when higher priced material is being purchased.

CHAPTER 21

Manufacturing Cost Reports: Labor

Though labor is often a significant portion of total product cost, it can be complex to measure and control. The requirements of each job need to be analyzed and an equitable pay rate determined. A base rate should be established for each operation or group of activities.

Worker productivity can be affected by planning, control, and motivation, among other factors. It can be enhanced by an efficient production process that includes better training and newer technology.

- Exhibit 21-1 shows employees' daily performance, which can be used to highlight potential problems.
- Exhibit 21-2 deals with employees whose performance is slipping significantly below their average performance; it compares their own current performance against their own past performance.
- Exhibit 21-3 summarizes a group of 21-2s into a report on all employees with chronically low performance.
- Exhibits 21-4 and 21-5 show labor rate and efficiency variances, with reasons.
- Exhibit 21-6 analyzes the degree of efficiency for all employees, making it easy to compare performance among employees and over time.
- Exhibit 21-7 is the monthly labor budget of both direct and indirect costs; it is graphed in Exhibit 21-8.
- Actual monthly labor cost for a project is shown in Exhibit 21-9.
- Exhibit 21-10 shows the learning curve for a new production process.

EXHIBIT 21-1
DAILY EMPLOYEE PERFORMANCE REPORT

Employee	Actual Hours Produced	Standard Hours Allowed	Performance Percentage
R. Murphy	5	7	140%
S. Adam	5	6	120%
T. Diaz	8	8	100%
G. Lucas	9	8	89%
M. Mann	7	6	86%
F. Clinton	6	5	83%
C. Bush	5	4	80%
J. Angel	9	6	67%
B. Tanaka	7	4	57%
L. Wood	4	2	50%

Purpose: To evaluate employee performance

Distribution: Department supervisor, production manager

Use: To compare actual hours produced with hours budgeted

Action to be taken: Evaluate employee performance and reward or penalize employees accordingly.

EXHIBIT 21-2
DAILY REPORT ON ADVERSE CHANGES IN EMPLOYEE PERFORMANCE

Employee	% Efficiency Today	% Efficiency Last Month			Times Reported in Last 30 Days
		Low	High	Average	
S. Adam	64%	55%	83%	78%	4
T. Diaz	45%	40%	77%	65%	3
G. Lucas	73%	75%	97%	91%	0
C. Bush	24%	40%	69%	55%	1
J. Angel	35%	35%	74%	48%	1
M. Mann	80%	72%	94%	90%	3
R. Murphy	85%	75%	98%	93%	2
L. Wood	34%	30%	84%	55%	4
B. Tanaka	55%	60%	79%	72%	0
F. Clinton	65%	66%	87%	80%	2

Purpose: To find adverse changes in employee performance

Distribution: Production manager

Use: To compare daily performance with previous average performance

Action to be taken: Only employees whose performance has deteriorated significantly are listed on this report; the criterion is not absolute low performance, but low performance related to an employee's own prior performance.

EXHIBIT 21-3
CHRONICALLY LOW EMPLOYEE PERFORMANCE

Employee	% Efficiency Current Month	% Efficiency Last 12 Months		
		Low	High	Average
S. Adam	34%	32%	65%	42%
T. Diaz	28%	35%	77%	53%
G. Lucas	45%	45%	62%	52%
C. Bush	24%	40%	55%	45%
J. Angel	32%	50%	74%	60%

Employees with Chronically Low Performance

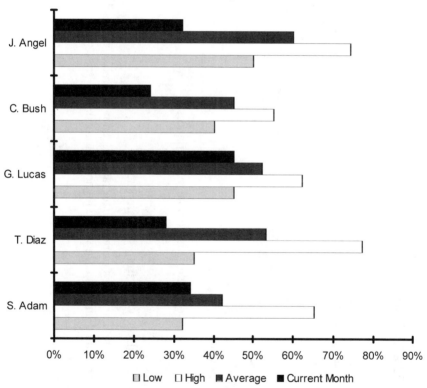

Purpose: To monitor employees whose performance is chronically not up to par

Distribution: Production manager

Use: To evaluate and penalize employees with low efficiency

Action to be taken: Retrain or terminate employees listed.

EXHIBIT 21-4
DIRECT LABOR RATE VARIANCE

Department	Actual Hourly Rate	Standard Hourly Rate	Actual Hours Worked	Variance*	Reasons for Variance			
					Lower Skilled Labor	Higher Skilled Labor	Labor Shortage	Misc.
Dept. # 1	$9.00	$8.00	4,500	$4,500	-	$4,500	-	-
Dept. # 2	5.00	4.00	30,000	30,000	-	-	$30,000	-
Dept. # 3	12.00	10.00	6,000	12,000	-	10,000	-	$2,000
Dept. # 4	20.00	15.00	8,000	40,000	-	25,000	15,000	-
Dept. # 5	10.00	12.00	4,000	(8,000)	$(8,000)	-	-	-
Dept. # 6	8.00	9.00	2,500	(2,500)	(2,000)	-	-	$(500)
Dept. # 7	9.00	8.75	3,000	750	-	750	-	-
Dept. # 8	15.00	14.00	9,000	9,000	(4,000)	-	13,000	-

*Parentheses indicate a favorable variance.

Purpose: To identify causes of favorable or unfavorable rate variances

Distribution: Production manager

Use: To determine why actual rate varies from standard rate

Action to be taken: Either redefine jobs or reevaluate rates. Even a favorable rate variance may require correction action, such as when lower skilled labor is used where higher is needed.

EXHIBIT 21-5
DIRECT LABOR EFFICIENCY VARIANCE

Department	Actual Hours Worked	Standard Hours Allowed	Standard Hourly Rate	Variance*	Reasons for Variance			
					Material Quality	Labor Skill Level	Machine Efficiency	Misc.
Dept. # 1	4,500	4,000	$8.00	$4,000	$4,000	-	-	-
Dept. # 2	2,500	2,000	5.50	2,750	-	-	$2,000	$750
Dept. # 3	6,000	5,800	10.00	2,000	-	$2,000	-	-
Dept. # 4	8,000	7,500	15.00	7,500	5,100	-	2,400	-
Dept. # 5	4,000	4,000	12.00	-	-	-	(800)	$800
Dept. # 6	2,500	2,800	9.00	(2,700)	-	(1,500)	(1,200)	-
Dept. # 7	3,000	3,500	8.75	(4,375)	(5,875)	1,500	-	-
Dept. # 8	9,000	8,000	14.00	14,000	3,500	2,500	8,000	-

*Parentheses indicate a favorable variance.

Purpose: To identify causes of variations in efficiency

Distribution: Production manager

Use: To monitor actual hours worked against hours budgeted

Action to be taken: Correct reasons for efficiency variances.

EXHIBIT 21-6
MONTHLY DIRECT LABOR EFFICIENCY PERFORMANCE

Employee	% Efficiency		
	Low	High	Average
S. Adam	55%	83%	78%
T. Diaz	40%	77%	65%
G. Lucas	75%	97%	91%
C. Bush	40%	69%	55%
J. Angel	35%	74%	48%
M. Mann	72%	94%	90%
R. Murphy	75%	98%	93%
L. Wood	30%	84%	55%
B. Tanaka	60%	79%	72%
F. Clinton	66%	87%	80%

Purpose: To evaluate monthly how well employees are performing

Distribution: Production manager

Use: To know what to expect of employees

Action to be taken: Reward employees with high efficiency; penalize those with lower efficiency.

EXHIBIT 21-7
MONTHLY LABOR BUDGET

JANUARY Estimated Production: 22,000

Department	Total Hours	Average Rate	Total Cost	Labor Hours per Unit	Direct Labor Hours	%	Direct Labor Cost	Indirect Labor Hours	%
Department 1	1,250	$15.00	$18,750	0.0568	1,175	94%	17,625	75	6%
Department 2	2,485	12.25	30,441	0.1130	2,400	97%	29,400	85	3%
Department 3	1,650	9.00	14,850	0.0750	1,575	95%	14,175	75	5%
Department 4	1,800	16.00	28,800	0.0818	1,785	99%	28,560	15	1%
Department 5	1,900	8.50	16,150	0.0864	1,635	86%	13,898	265	14%
Department 6	1,250	16.35	20,438	0.0568	1,220	98%	19,947	30	2%
Department 7	1,800	7.65	13,770	0.0818	1,650	92%	12,623	150	8%
Department 8	1,650	9.90	16,335	0.0750	1,545	94%	15,296	105	6%
Department 9	3,250	4.75	15,438	0.1477	3,100	95%	14,725	150	5%
Department 10	2,200	6.85	15,070	0.1000	2,165	98%	14,830	35	2%
Department 11	2,400	11.10	26,640	0.1091	2,285	95%	25,364	115	5%
Department 12	3,600	7.25	26,100	0.1636	3,250	90%	23,563	350	10%
	25,235	$9.62	$242,781	1.1470	23,785	94%	$230,004	1,450	6%

Purpose: To estimate monthly labor costs

Distribution: Product manager, plant manager, senior management

Use: To monitor total hours as well as dollar cost of direct labor and indirect labor in order to estimate and control labor cost

Action to be taken: Adjust procedures to meet budgeted costs.

EXHIBIT 21-8
GRAPHS OF MONTHLY LABOR BUDGET

Total Hours by Department

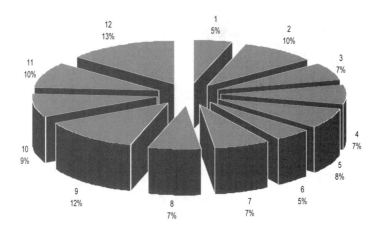

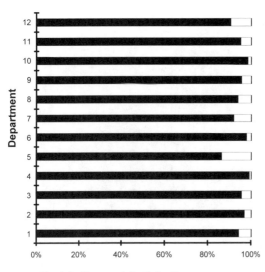

Percentage of Direct Labor and Indirect Labor Hours

■ Direct Labor Hours   □ Indirect Labor Hours

Purpose: To display visually direct labor and indirect labor hour requirements by department

Distribution: Product manager, plant manager, senior management

Use: To monitor the percentage of labor required by each department to maintain budgeted proportions

Action to be taken: Adjust procedures as needed to maintain balance, or revise budget to match actual needs.

EXHIBIT 21-9
PROJECT LABOR COST REPORT (for month ended July 31, 20--)

Job No.: *J47-2*
Project Manager: *J. Smith*

Project Phases	To Date				Total				To Complete	
	Regular Hours	OT Hours	Total Hours	Actual Cost	Est. Hours	Avail. Hours	Est. Cost	Bal. Avail.	Hours Needed	Amount Needed
Phase I	150	35	185	$4,100	220	35	$3,520	$(580)	$25	$325
Phase II	225	40	265	6,025	250	(15)	4,000	(2,025)	-	-
Phase III	25	55	80	1,175	175	95	2,800	1,625	50	650
Phase IV	95	80	175	3,175	270	95	4,320	1,145	20	260
Phase V	85	20	105	2,325	85	(20)	1,360	(965)	-	-
Phase VI	65	45	110	2,075	120	10	1,920	(155)	40	520
Phase VII	145	30	175	3,925	225	50	3,600	(325)	35	455
Total Labor	790	305	1,095	22,800	1,345	250	21,520	(1,280)	170	2,210

Purpose: To monitor labor cost for a project

Distribution: Project manager

Use: To monitor actual versus budgeted performance

Action to be taken: Evaluate progress and profitability of a project; identify and correct reasons for unfavorable variances.

EXHIBIT 21-10
LEARNING CURVE IN PRODUCTION

70% Learning Curve

Cumulative Units of Production	Average Units per Hour	Total Time in Hours	Unit Output per Hour
1	18.00	18.00	0.06
2	12.60	25.20	0.08
4	8.82	35.28	0.11
8	6.17	49.39	0.16
16	4.32	69.15	0.23
32	3.03	96.81	0.33
64	2.12	135.53	0.47
128	1.48	189.74	0.67
256	1.04	265.64	0.96
512	0.73	371.90	1.38

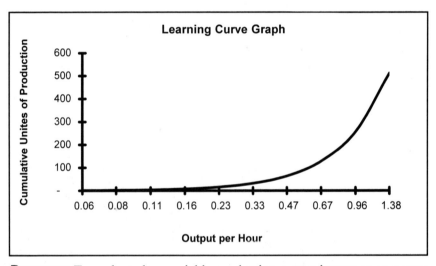

Purpose: To evaluate how quickly production output improves on a new product

Distribution: Production manager

Use: To identify how long it takes to double output in initial stages of production

Action to be taken: If the curve is not rising appropriately, retrain workers or remove bottlenecks. If it levels off or starts to fall, find ways to motivate workers who have become bored.

CHAPTER 22

Manufacturing Cost Reports: Overhead

Factory overhead consists of indirect materials, indirect labor, and all other factory items not easily or cost-effectively traced to a specific product. Because it is impossible to trace all factory overhead items to specific jobs or products, an arbitrary allocation must be made in an equitable and logical manner.

- Exhibit 22-1 shows how total factory overhead is allocated.

- Using the direct method, Exhibit 22-2 shows how service department costs may be allocated to the production department. Overhead rate calculation is also shown for production departments.

- Exhibit 22-3 contains the flexible overhead budget. This budget is prepared for different activity levels, such as theoretical capacity, practical capacity, expected actual capacity, or normal capacity.

- Exhibit 22-4 contains overhead breakdown by major cost centers.

- A report for calculating plant-wide overhead rate is shown in Exhibit 22-5.

- A comparison of budgeted and actual factory overhead—fixed and variable—is given in Exhibit 22-6. Bases, such as direct labor hours, machine hours, physical output, direct material cost, and direct labor cost can be used to allocate overhead.

- Exhibit 22-7 contains a survey report that can be used to determine factory overhead bases for overhead application purposes.

EXHIBIT 22-1
DEPARTMENTAL FACTORY OVERHEAD

Account	Total Overhead	Production Departments				Service Departments	
		Planning	Cutting	Assembling	Finishing	Inspection	EDP
Indirect material	$285,000	$25,000	$65,000	$85,000	$35,000	$30,000	$45,000
Fringe benefits	80,700	12,500	13,200	7,500	6,500	20,000	21,000
Supervisors	209,595	21,500	38,500	45,000	28,650	44,250	31,695
Indirect labor	181,500	20,000	31,250	68,750	21,500	15,000	25,000
Depreciation	79,600	10,700	14,000	18,750	15,500	8,750	11,900
Repairs	37,110	5,600	4,825	12,500	7,625	2,200	4,360
Maintenance	60,800	6,500	7,850	18,500	11,500	6,575	9,875
Utilities	92,830	15,000	16,800	22,000	19,800	8,000	11,230
Insurance	61,650	4,000	18,000	16,000	13,500	3,200	6,950
Total	$1,088,785	$120,800	$209,425	$294,000	$159,575	$137,975	$167,010

Purpose: To show actual factory overhead cost of production and service departments

Distribution: Production manager, plant manager, department supervisors

Use: To monitor overhead expenditures

Action to be taken: Compare actual with budgeted amounts to see if corrective action is needed.

EXHIBIT 22-2
CALCULATING DEPARTMENTAL OVERHEAD RATE

Account	Total Overhead	Production Departments				Service Departments	
		Planning	Cutting	Assembling	Finishing	Inspection	EDP
Total overhead	$1,088,785	$120,800	$209,425	$294,000	$159,575	$137,975	$167,010
Allocating service department overhead							
Inspection department (Allocated equally)			45,992	45,992	45,992	(137,975)	
						$ -	
EDP department (Based on processing hours)		33,402	50,103	66,804	16,701		(167,010)
							$ -
Total production overhead	$1,088,785	$154,202	$305,520	$406,796	$222,268		
Overhead Base							
Direct labor hours		18,500			14,000		
Direct labor cost				$685,000			
Machine hours			24,500				
Overhead rate		$8.34 per direct labor hour	$12.47 per machine hour	59% of direct labor cost	$15.88 per direct labor hour		

Purpose: Calculate components of the overhead rate

Distribution: Production manager, plant manager, department supervisors

Use: To monitor overhead allocations against budget

Action to be taken: Identify and correct causes of unbalanced allocations.

EXHIBIT 22-3
FLEXIBLE FACTORY OVERHEAD BUDGET

	Activity Level in Machine Hours		
	12,000	15,000	18,000
Fixed costs			
Indirect material	$25,000	$25,000	$25,000
Indirect labor	45,000	45,000	45,000
Utilities	30,000	30,000	30,000
Insurance	10,000	10,000	10,000
Rent	60,000	60,000	60,000
Depreciation	35,000	35,000	35,000
Payroll taxes	40,000	40,000	40,000
Miscellaneous	25,000	25,000	25,000
Total fixed costs	$270,000	$270,000	$270,000
Variable costs			
Indirect material	$32,000	$40,000	$48,000
Indirect labor	24,000	30,000	36,000
Utilities	40,000	50,000	60,000
Payroll taxes	48,000	60,000	72,000
Miscellaneous	16,000	20,000	24,000
Total variable costs	$160,000	$200,000	$240,000
Total overhead costs	$430,000	$470,000	$510,000

Purpose: To plan for factory overhead expenditure at different production levels

Distribution: Product manager

Use: To find the optimal level of production for your equipment

Action to be taken: Adjust production to make most efficient use of manufacturing facilities and capacities. Customize this schedule to the needs of your company.

EXHIBIT 22-4
OVERHEAD BREAKDOWN BY MAJOR COST CENTER

	Total Plant	Cutting	Assembling	Painting	Finishing
Indirect Labor					
Variable wages	$9,720	$1,325	$4,020	$875	$3,500
Fixed wages	9,950	2,500	4,800	1,450	1,200
Total	19,670	3,825	8,820	2,325	4,700
Non-Labor Variable Costs					
Supplies	9,850	1,500	2,500	1,650	4,200
Tools	12,050	2,800	3,650	2,100	3,500
Maintenance	8,250	3,750	1,200	1,100	2,200
Total	30,150	8,050	7,350	4,850	9,900
Non-Labor Fixed Costs					
Electrical	20,000	3,500	2,000	6,500	8,000
Telephone	17,000	2,500	3,500	8,000	3,000
Depreciation	21,300	3,800	4,000	7,000	6,500
Travel	15,000	6,500	2,500	2,000	4,000
Total	73,300	16,300	12,000	23,500	21,500
Total Overhead	$123,120	$28,175	$28,170	$30,675	$36,100

Purpose: To analyze overhead costs for the plant and various departments

Distribution: Plant manager, production manager, department supervisor

Use: To monitor actual versus budgeted amounts to maintain balance

Action to be taken: Identify reasons for cost imbalances and correct them.

EXHIBIT 22-5
CALCULATING PLANT-WIDE OVERHEAD

Factory Overhead

Description	Amount
Depreciation	$15,000
Electric	6,000
Gas	4,000
Insurance	25,000
Maintenance	12,000
Payroll Taxes	20,000
Rent	35,000
Supervision	30,000
Total Annual Overhead	147,000

Department A	4 operators @ 1,800 hours/year:	7,200 hours
Department B	2 operators @ 1,600 hours/year:	3,200 hours
Department C	5 operators @ 2,100 hours/year:	10,500 hours
Total direct labor hours		20,900 hours

$$\frac{\text{Total annual overhead}}{\text{Total direct labor hours}} = \frac{147,000}{20,900} = \$7.00 \text{ per direct labor hour}$$
(rounded to nearest dollar)

Department A	7,200 direct labor hours X $7.00 =	$50,400	35%
Department B	3,200 direct labor hours X $7.00 =	22,400	15%
Department C	10,500 direct labor hours X $7.00 =	73,500	50%
		146,300	100%

Purpose: To analyze components of overhead for the entire plant

Distribution: Plant manager, production manager

Use: To maintain direct labor/overhead balance

Action to be taken: If overhead costs get out of line, identify reasons and correct.

EXHIBIT 22-6
MANUFACTURING OVERHEAD VARIANCE REPORT

Department	Units Produced	Variable Rate Per Unit	Budgeted Variable Cost	Budgeted Fixed Cost	Actual Variable Cost	Actual Fixed Cost	Variance Variable Cost	Variance Fixed Cost
Department # 1	3,600	$3.00	$10,800	$15,000	$11,275	$14,500	$(475)	$500
Department # 2	4,525	4.75	21,494	25,000	20,450	22,000	1,044	3,000
Department # 3	2,895	6.00	17,370	15,850	17,650	18,050	(280)	(2,200)
Department # 4	3,200	4.20	13,440	12,500	1,400	13,500	12,040	(1,000)
Department # 5	4,115	12.50	51,438	35,000	55,000	37,500	(3,563)	(2,500)
Department # 6	5,300	8.00	42,400	80,000	45,500	84,050	(3,100)	(4,050)
Department # 7	2,820	7.65	21,573	65,500	18,700	60,000	2,873	5,500
Department # 8	2,960	5.00	14,800	25,300	15,250	23,000	(450)	2,300

Purpose: To monitor overhead

Distribution: Plant manager, production manager, department heads

Use: To compare actual with budgeted fixed and variable overhead to identify variances

Action to be taken: Investigate significant variations, whether favorable or unfavorable, and make any necessary adjustments.

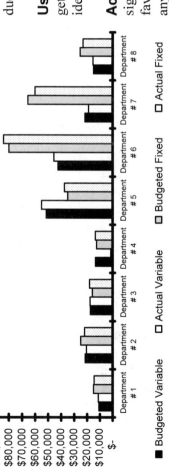

Budgeted and Actual Overhead Costs

EXHIBIT 22-7
FACTORY SURVEY TO DETERMINE OVERHEAD
COST ALLOCATION

Allocation Base	Planning	Cutting	Assembling	Finishing	Packaging	Total
Machine Hours	120	165	80	300	80	745
%	16%	22%	11%	40%	11%	100%
No. of Employees	25	40	75	90	35	265
%	9%	15%	28%	34%	13%	100%
Direct Labor Hours	1,625	1,000	4,125	2,700	1,750	11,200
%	15%	9%	37%	24%	16%	100%
Floor Area (sq. yd.)	12,000	35,000	60,000	50,000	70,000	227,000
%	5%	15%	26%	22%	31%	100%
Cost of Materials	$135,000	$365,000	$480,000	$300,000	$85,000	$1,365,000
%	10%	27%	35%	22%	6%	100%

Overhead Allocation Bases

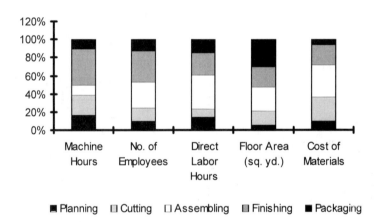

■ Planning   ▯ Cutting   ▯ Assembling   ▨ Finishing   ■ Packaging

Purpose: To identify components of factory overhead

Distribution: Plant manager, production manager, department supervisors

Use: To monitor components of factory overhead to maintain balance

Action to be taken: Identify and correct any imbalances.

CHAPTER 23

Manufacturing and Production Reports

The aim of the reports in this chapter is to enhance the production process.

- Exhibit 23-1, the product history report, shows the number of units produced each month and the number of machine hours needed. It is graphed in Exhibit 23-2.

- Exhibit 23-3, a production cost analysis report, shows the dollar and percentage breakdown of direct material, direct labor, and factory overhead.

- Exhibit 23-4 shows elements of costs for several products as a percentage of sales.

- Product costs are graphed in Exhibits 23-5 and 23-6.

- Exhibit 23-7 tracks changes in product cost; it is graphed in Exhibit 23-8.

- Exhibit 23-9, the daily yield report, shows how much material is used in production, and deviations from budgeted amounts.

- Exhibit 23-10 summarizes completed contracts through gross profit percentage.

- Exhibit 23-11 analyzes gross profit for completed contracts.

- Exhibit 23-12 summarizes contracts in progress; Exhibit 23-13 graphs them.

- Contracts in progress are shown, using the percentage of completion method, in Exhibit 23-14.

- Exhibit 23-15 analyzes over- and underbilling for contracts.
- Finally, Exhibit 23-16 uses the competed contract method to provide information for contracts in progress.

EXHIBIT 23-1
PRODUCTION HISTORY REPORT

Item number: CJ1145
Standard production per hour: 105 units
Standard maintenance percentage per hour: 5%

Product	Unit Production	Machine Hours	Units per Hour	Maintenance Hours	Maintenance %	Cumulative Unit Production	Cumulative Machine Hours	Cumulative Units per Hour	Cumulative Maintenance Hours	Cumulative Maintenance %
January	136,000	1,356	100.29	68	5%	136,000	1,356	100.29	68	5%
February	165,000	1,400	117.86	85	6%	301,000	2,756	109.22	153	6%
March	128,500	1,200	107.08	42	4%	429,500	3,956	108.57	195	5%
April	184,350	1,650	111.73	53	3%	613,850	5,606	109.50	248	4%
May	177,685	1,975	89.97	81	4%	791,535	7,581	104.41	329	4%
June	271,450	2,645	102.63	85	3%	1,062,985	10,226	103.95	414	4%
July	225,355	2,115	106.55	125	6%	1,288,340	12,341	104.40	539	4%
August	185,900	1,925	96.57	103	5%	1,474,240	14,266	103.34	642	5%
September	210,000	2,050	102.44	135	7%	1,684,240	16,316	103.23	777	5%
October	235,000	2,175	108.05	140	6%	1,919,240	18,491	103.79	917	5%
November	240,000	1,965	122.14	150	8%	2,159,240	20,456	105.56	1,067	5%
December	190,000	1,795	105.85	92	5%	2,349,240	22,251	105.58	1,159	5%

Purpose: To monitor monthly unit production and maintenance hours

Distribution: Production manager, plant manager

Use: To determine if production and maintenance are within budget

Action to be taken: If cumulative units per hour fall below budget, or if maintenance percentage rises above budget, take corrective action.

EXHIBIT 23-2
PRODUCTION HISTORY GRAPH

Item number: CJ1145
Standard production per hour: 105 units
Standard maintenance percentage per hour: 5%

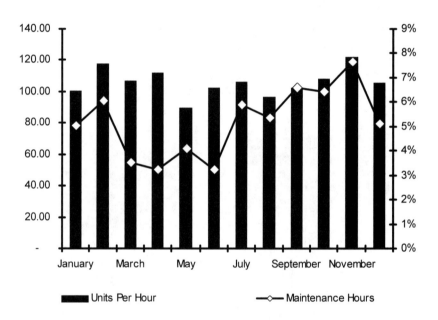

Purpose: To visually show actual units produced and maintenance hours

Distribution: Production manager, plant manager

Use: To analyze trends in unit production per hour and maintenance hours

Action to be taken: If units produced decrease or increase maintenance hours, take corrective action.

EXHIBIT 23-3
PRODUCTION COST ANALYSIS REPORT

	Dollars	Percent
Market value of production	$17,665,000	100%
Direct materials	2,395,000	14%
Direct labor	3,265,000	18%
Total prime costs	5,660,000	32%
Indirect material	485,000	3%
Indirect labor	875,000	5%
Fringe benefits	925,000	5%
Depreciation	1,365,000	8%
Utilities	745,000	4%
Other overhead	1,465,000	8%
Total factory overhead	5,860,000	33%
Total production cost	11,520,000	65%

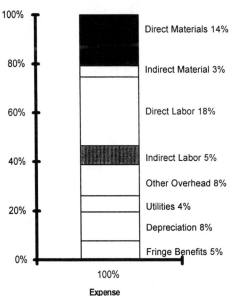

Production Cost Analysis Report

Purpose: To relate dollar and percentage amounts for direct material, direct labor, and overhead components of production

Distribution: Production manager

Use: To monitor actual direct materials, direct labor, and overhead as a percentage of market value to adhere to budget

Action to be taken: A higher than expected percentage for direct material, direct labor, or overhead requires close scrutiny and remedial action.

EXHIBIT 23-4
ELEMENTS OF PRODUCT COSTS AS A PERCENTAGE OF SALES

Product	Sales		Direct Material		Direct Labor		Variable Overhead		Total Variable		Contribution Margin		Fixed Overhead		Gross Profit	
A	$95,000	100%	$15,000	16%	$25,000	26%	$35,000	37%	$75,000	79%	$20,000	21%	$10,000	11%	$10,000	11%
B	125,000	100%	40,000	32%	35,000	28%	20,000	16%	95,000	76%	30,000	24%	5,000	4%	25,000	20%
C	250,000	100%	25,000	10%	15,000	6%	40,000	16%	80,000	32%	170,000	68%	95,000	38%	75,000	30%
D	85,000	100%	35,000	41%	10,000	12%	15,000	18%	60,000	71%	25,000	29%	12,500	15%	12,500	15%
E	195,000	100%	60,000	31%	50,000	26%	10,000	5%	120,000	62%	75,000	38%	5,000	3%	70,000	36%
F	278,000	100%	80,000	29%	85,000	31%	12,000	4%	177,000	64%	101,000	36%	25,000	9%	76,000	27%
G	345,000	100%	30,000	9%	45,000	13%	50,000	14%	125,000	36%	220,000	64%	60,000	17%	160,000	46%
H	457,000	100%	250,000	55%	65,000	14%	27,000	6%	342,000	75%	115,000	25%	35,000	8%	80,000	18%
I	192,000	100%	25,000	13%	85,000	44%	32,000	17%	142,000	74%	50,000	26%	30,000	16%	20,000	10%
J	65,000	100%	10,000	15%	30,000	46%	5,000	8%	45,000	69%	20,000	31%	10,000	15%	10,000	15%
K	165,000	100%	75,000	45%	25,000	15%	10,000	6%	110,000	67%	55,000	33%	20,000	12%	35,000	21%

Purpose: To show how overhead components relate to sales by product

Distribution: Production manager

Use: To monitor overhead component costs as a percentage of sales revenue against budget

Action to be taken: A higher than expected percentage for any component requires closer scrutiny and remedial action.

EXHIBIT 23-5
GRAPHIC ANALYSIS OF PRODUCT COSTS AS A PERCENTAGE OF SALES (Version 1)

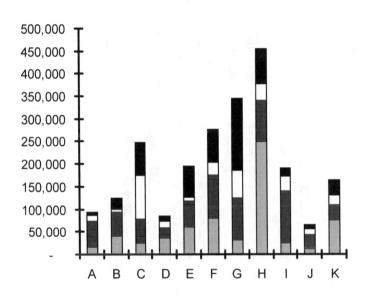

Dollar Analysis of Product Cost and Gross Profit

◫ Material ◼ Direct Labor ◼ Variable Overhead ◻ Fixed Overhead ◼ Gross Profit

Purpose: To visually represent proportionate shares of direct material, direct labor, variable overhead, fixed overhead, and gross profit

Distribution: Production manager

Use: To determine the dollar cost as related to gross profit for each product

Action to be taken: Identify and prioritize gross profit; consider eliminating less profitable items.

EXHIBIT 23-6

GRAPHIC ANALYSIS OF PRODUCT COST AS A
PERCENTAGE OF SALES (Version 2)

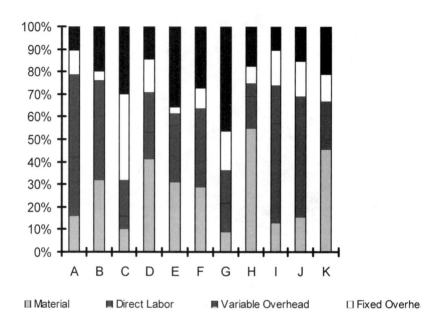

Percentage Analysis of Product Cost and Gross Profit

☐ Material   ▦ Direct Labor   ▦ Variable Overhead   ☐ Fixed Overhe

Purpose: To represent proportionate shares of direct material, direct labor, variable overhead, fixed overhead, and gross profit

Distribution: Production manager

Use: To determine the dollar cost as related to gross profit for each product

Action to be taken: Identify and prioritize gross profit; consider eliminating less profitable items.

EXHIBIT 23-7
COST CHANGE REPORT

Product	Current Sales Price	Cost		Change in Cost		Profit		Unit Sales	Effect on Total Profit
		Current	New	$	%	Current	New		
Product # 1	$4,250	$2,850	$3,225	$375	13.2%	$1,400	$1,025	200	$(75,000)
Product # 2	2,500	2,000	2,200	200	10.0%	500	300	175	(35,000)
Product # 3	6,500	5,000	5,450	450	9.0%	1,500	1,050	500	(225,000)
Product # 4	7,250	6,000	7,000	1,000	16.7%	1,250	250	1,500	(1,500,000)
Product # 5	12,550	11,000	10,000	(1,000)	-9.1%	1,550	2,550	100	100,000
Product # 6	6,575	5,500	5,250	(250)	-4.5%	1,075	1,325	375	93,750
Product # 7	1,800	1,400	1,200	(200)	-14.3%	400	600	400	80,000
Product # 8	1,250	850	1,000	150	17.6%	400	250	2,000	(300,000)
Product # 9	4,000	3,000	3,500	500	16.7%	1,000	500	50	(25,000)
Product # 10	5,500	4,000	5,000	1,000	25.0%	1,500	500	1,200	(1,200,000)
Product # 11	6,350	5,525	6,000	475	8.6%	825	350	1,425	(676,875)
Product # 12	8,825	6,150	5,800	(350)	-5.7%	2,675	3,025	2,600	910,000
Total									$(2,853,125)

Purpose: To show how changes in product cost affect profits

Distribution: Production manager, sales manager, senior management

Use: To identify changes in product cost

Action to be taken: Identify reasons for changes in cost and take any needed corrective action.

EXHIBIT 23-8
GRAPHIC ANALYSIS OF PRODUCT COST CHANGES

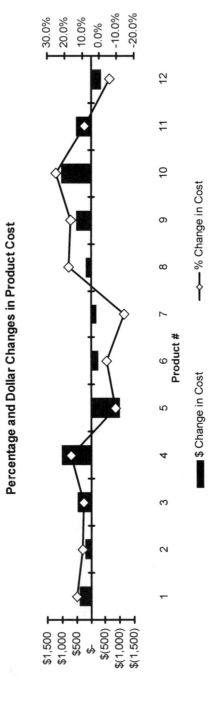

Percentage and Dollar Changes in Product Cost

Purpose: To see any dollar and percentage changes in product cost

Distribution: Production manager, sales manager, senior management

Use: To identify products whose costs have increased

Action to be taken: Investigate and correct any significant changes in cost.

EXHIBIT 23-9
DAILY YIELD REPORT

Assembly Line	Units of Production	Material Utilized (in Pounds) Actual	Material Utilized (in Pounds) Budgeted	Variance Units	Variance Percentage
Line #1	8,500	16,250	14,875	1,375	9.24%
Line #2	12,500	23,400	21,875	1,525	6.97%
Line #3	16,500	26,235	28,875	(2,640)	-9.14%
Line #4	12,425	19,855	21,744	(1,889)	-8.69%
Line #5	9,800	18,100	17,150	950	5.54%
Line #6	11,250	19,500	19,688	(188)	-0.95%
Line #7	15,300	28,365	26,775	1,590	5.94%
Line #8	14,825	24,000	25,944	(1,944)	-7.49%
Line #9	8,825	16,785	15,444	1,341	8.68%
Line #10	9,600	18,500	16,800	1,700	10.12%
Line #11	15,950	30,000	27,913	2,088	7.48%
Line #12	9,000	14,350	15,750	(1,400)	-8.89%

Percentage Variance in Material Utilization

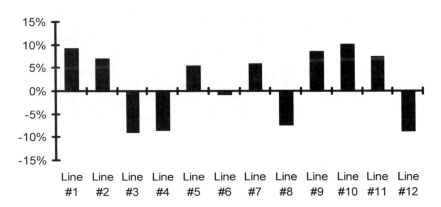

Purpose: To compare number of units produced with amount of material used

Distribution: Production manager, materials manager, line supervisor

Use: To monitor the efficiency of material utilization

Action to be taken: If more material was used in production than was budgeted, analyze the causes.

EXHIBIT 23-10
SUMMARY OF COMPLETED CONTRACTS

Job No.	Revenue	Expense	Gross Profit	GP %
Job # 1	$225,000	$165,000	$60,000	27%
Job # 2	295,000	280,000	15,000	5%
Job # 3	785,000	810,000	(25,000)	-3%
Job # 4	98,000	65,000	33,000	34%
Job # 5	74,000	60,000	14,000	19%
Job # 6	125,000	150,000	(25,000)	-20%
Job # 7	400,000	325,000	75,000	19%
Job # 8	285,000	310,000	(25,000)	-9%
Job # 9	325,000	300,000	25,000	8%
Job # 10	385,000	305,000	80,000	21%
Total	$2,997,000	$2,770,000	$227,000	8%

Summary of Completed Contracts

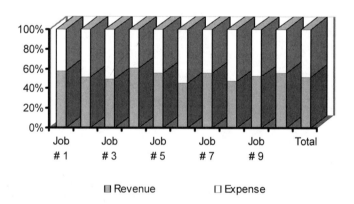

Purpose: To analyze and compare gross profit on several jobs

Distribution: Senior management

Use: To determine the profitability of completed jobs

Action to be taken: Use this data in preparing future bids.

EXHIBIT 23-11
GROSS PROFIT ANALYSIS OF COMPLETED CONTRACTS

Job No.	Revenue			Cost			Gross Profit		
	Budgeted	Actual	Variance	Budgeted	Actual	Variance	Budgeted	Actual	Variance
Job # 1	$180,000	$165,000	$15,000	$125,000	$145,000	$(20,000)	$55,000	$20,000	$35,000
Job # 2	250,000	280,000	(30,000)	250,000	250,000	-	-	30,000	(30,000)
Job # 3	600,000	705,000	(105,000)	400,000	480,000	(80,000)	200,000	225,000	(25,000)
Job # 4	55,000	65,000	(10,000)	40,000	45,000	(5,000)	15,000	20,000	(5,000)
Job # 5	95,000	60,000	35,000	60,000	50,000	10,000	35,000	10,000	25,000
Job # 6	250,000	150,000	100,000	225,000	200,000	25,000	25,000	(50,000)	75,000
Job # 7	400,000	275,000	125,000	350,000	295,000	55,000	50,000	(20,000)	70,000
Job # 8	285,000	310,000	(25,000)	200,000	225,000	(25,000)	85,000	85,000	-
Job # 9	325,000	350,000	(25,000)	210,000	205,000	5,000	115,000	145,000	(30,000)
Job # 10	385,000	365,000	20,000	300,000	270,000	30,000	85,000	95,000	(10,000)
Total	2,825,000	2,725,000	100,000	2,160,000	2,165,000	(5,000)	665,000	560,000	105,000

Gross Profit Analysis

Job # 1, Job # 2, Job # 3, Job # 4, Job # 5, Job # 6, Job # 7, Job # 8, Job # 9, Job # 10

■ Budgeted Gross Profit   ■ Actual Gross Profit

Purpose: To summarize gross profit data for several jobs

Distribution: Senior management

Use: To compare budgeted with actual gross profit

Action to be taken: Identify and correct specific causes of variation.

EXHIBIT 23-12
SUMMARY OF CONTRACTS IN PROGRESS

Contract No.	Billings				Costs			
	Total Estimated	Billed	To Be Billed	% Billed	Total Estimated	Incurred	To Be Incurred	% Incurred
Contract # 1	$1,000,000	$850,000	$150,000	85%	$750,000	$300,000	450,000	40%
Contract # 2	850,000	425,000	425,000	50%	500,000	450,000	50,000	90%
Contract # 3	1,200,000	1,150,000	50,000	96%	800,000	400,000	400,000	50%
Contract # 4	1,650,000	400,000	1,250,000	24%	1,200,000	300,000	900,000	25%
Contract # 5	900,000	600,000	300,000	67%	900,000	500,000	175,000	74%
Contract # 6	1,200,000	900,000	300,000	75%	1,500,000	975,000	525,000	65%
Contract # 7	300,000	65,000	235,000	22%	275,000	250,000	25,000	91%
Contract # 8	2,500,000	250,000	2,250,000	10%	2,400,000	400,000	2,000,000	17%
Total	9,600,000	4,640,000	4,960,000	48%	8,100,000	3,575,000	4,525,000	44%

Purpose: To summarize financial status of contracts in progress

Distribution: Senior management

Use: To determine if billing percentage matches cost incurred percentage

Action to be taken: Improve procedures to bill as costs are incurred.

Contracts in Progress

EXHIBIT 23-13
GRAPHIC ANALYSIS OF CONTRACTS IN PROGRESS

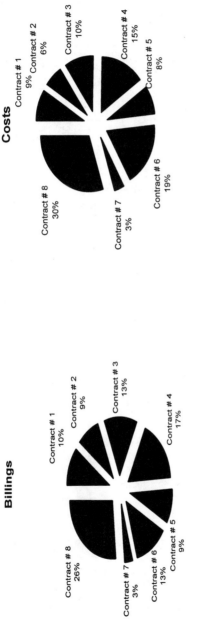

Billings

Costs

Contract Billings and Costs

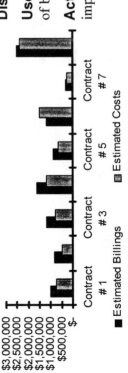

Purpose: To clarify financial status of contracts

Distribution: Senior management

Use: To determine the percentage and dollar amounts of billings and costs

Action to be taken: If costs exceed billings, improve billing procedures.

EXHIBIT 23-14
CONTRACTS IN PROGRESS: PERCENTAGE OF COMPLETION METHOD

Contract No.	Estimated Billings	Billed To Date	Estimated Expenses	Costs Incurred To Date	% Contract Completed	Revenue Recognized	Costs Recognized	Gross Profit Recognized	Over/(Under) Billings
Contract # 1	$1,800,000	$850,000	$640,000	$300,000	47%	$843,750	$300,000	$543,750	$6,250
Contract # 2	850,000	425,000	500,000	450,000	90%	765,000	450,000	315,000	(340,000)
Contract # 3	1,200,000	1,150,000	800,000	400,000	50%	600,000	400,000	200,000	550,000
Contract # 4	750,000	400,000	1,200,000	300,000	25%	187,500	300,000	(112,500)	212,500
Contract # 5	900,000	600,000	675,000	500,000	74%	666,667	500,000	166,667	(66,667)
Contract # 6	1,200,000	900,000	1,500,000	975,000	65%	780,000	975,000	(195,000)	120,000
Contract # 7	300,000	65,000	650,000	250,000	38%	115,385	250,000	(134,615)	(50,385)
Contract # 8	2,500,000	250,000	2,000,000	400,000	20%	500,000	400,000	100,000	(250,000)
Total	9,500,000	4,640,000	7,965,000	3,575,000	45%	4,458,301	3,575,000	883,301	181,699

Purpose: To summarize contracts in progress using the percentage of completion method

Distribution: Senior management

Use: To identify over- or under-billing

Action to be taken: Improve procedures for and identify causes of underbilling.

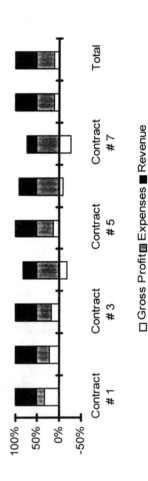

Gross Profit - Contracts In Progress

□ Gross Profit ▨ Expenses ■ Revenue

EXHIBIT 23-15
OVER/(UNDER) BILLINGS: CONTRACTS IN PROGRESS

Contract No.	Estimated Billings	Billed To Date	% Contract Completed	Revenue Recognized	Over/(Under) Billings
Contract # 1	$1,800,000	$850,000	47%	$843,750	$6,250
Contract # 2	850,000	425,000	90%	765,000	(340,000)
Contract # 3	1,200,000	1,150,000	50%	600,000	550,000
Contract # 4	750,000	400,000	25%	187,500	212,500
Contract # 5	900,000	600,000	74%	666,667	(66,667)
Contract # 6	1,200,000	900,000	65%	780,000	120,000
Contract # 7	300,000	65,000	38%	115,385	(50,385)
Contract # 8	2,500,000	250,000	20%	500,000	(250,000)
Total	9,500,000	4,640,000	45%	4,458,301	181,699

Over/Under Billings

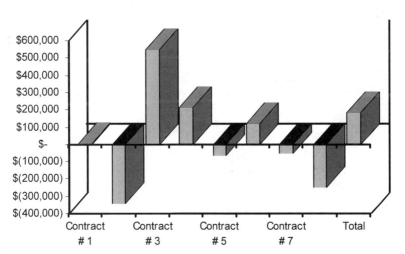

Purpose: To monitor billing status of contracts in progress

Distribution: Senior management

Use: To identify contracts where additional amounts should be billed

Action to be taken: Bill contracts that are under-billed.

EXHIBIT 23-16
CONTRACT IN PROGRESS: COMPLETED CONTRACT METHOD

Contract No.	Estimated Billings	Billed To Date	Estimated Expenses	Costs Incurred To Date	% Contract Completed	Estimated Gross Profit	Over/(Under) Billings
Contract # 1	$1,800,000	$850,000	$640,000	$300,000	47%	$1,160,000	$550,000
Contract # 2	850,000	425,000	500,000	450,000	90%	350,000	$(25,000)
Contract # 3	1,200,000	1,150,000	800,000	400,000	50%	400,000	$750,000
Contract # 4	750,000	400,000	1,200,000	300,000	25%	(450,000)	$100,000
Contract # 5	900,000	600,000	675,000	500,000	74%	225,000	$100,000
Contract # 6	1,200,000	900,000	1,500,000	975,000	65%	(300,000)	$(75,000)
Contract # 7	300,000	65,000	650,000	250,000	38%	(350,000)	$(185,000)
Contract # 8	2,500,000	250,000	2,000,000	400,000	20%	500,000	$(150,000)
Total	9,500,000	4,640,000	7,965,000	3,575,000	45%	1,535,000	1,065,000

Purpose: To summarize contracts in progress where revenue is recognized using the completed contract method

Distribution: Senior management

Use: To identify over/(under) billings

Action to be taken: Bill contracts that have not yet covered expenses.

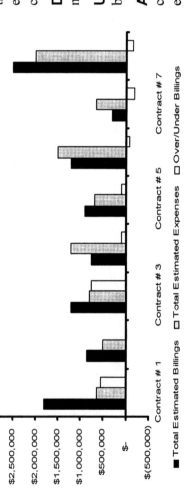

Legend: Total Estimated Billings ■ | Total Estimated Expenses □ | Over/Under Billings □
Contract # 1, Contract # 3, Contract # 5, Contract # 7

CHAPTER 24

Cost Analysis and Allocation Reporting

Cost analysis and allocation provides useful data for (a) product costing, (b) pricing and bidding, (c) evaluation of managerial performance and control, and (d) making special decisions.

- Exhibit 24-1 provides a comprehensive list of cost drivers for allocating various costs. *Just-in-time (JIT)* and *activity-based costing (ABC)* have been two major developments in cost analysis. The JIT philosophy simplifies accounting procedures and helps managers control their costs. An ABC system assigns costs to products based on the product's use of activities, not on its volume. ABC product costing has proven to be more accurate.

- Exhibit 24-2 compares traditional and JIT systems in terms of performance measures.

- Exhibit 24-3 shows the pros and cons of ABC, while Exhibit 24-4 compares overhead costs charged under the traditional volume-based system with the one under ABC, a multiple, volume/non-volume-based cost driver system.

- Break-even and cost-volume-profit (CVP) analysis deal with how profit and costs change with a change in volume, looking specifically at the effects on profits of changes in such factors as variable costs, fixed costs, selling prices, volume, and mix of products sold. By studying the relationships of costs, sales, and net income, management can make better planning decisions. Exhibit 24-5 and 24-6 analyze these relationships.

- Finally, in order to be globally competitive today, firms must increase their emphasis on quality. Exhibits 24-7 through 24-9 report on three key quality performance measures. Each category of quality costs is expressed as a percentage of sales.

EXHIBIT 24-1
ALLOCATION BASES

PRODUCTION AND SUPPORT COSTS	ALLOCATION BASIS
Accounting	Number of transactions Labor hours
Bookkeeping	Number of sales invoices Number of lines per invoice for each product
Accounts receivable	Number of customer accounts Number of postings to customer accounts
Billing	Number of invoices
Taxes	Dollars of tax paid
Property taxes	Book value of equipment and inventory
Paying bills	Number of invoices
Security	Number of patrols made
Legal	Research hours for each case
Power and utilities	Number of kilowatt-hours Floor space
Purchasing	Number of orders Cost of orders Number of purchase orders placed Dollar amount of purchases

EXHIBIT 24-1
ALLOCATION BASES, *Cont'd*

PRODUCTION AND SUPPORT COSTS	ALLOCATION BASIS
Quality control	Number of inspections Number of batches produced Number of inspection hours
Account payable	Number of vendor invoices paid
Central cost and budget	Dollars of factory cost and selling expenses
Traffic	Number of freight bills
Internal audit	Audit time reports
Setting up equipment	Number of setups
Inspection and quality control	Number of inspections Number of units inspected
Waste control	Weight of hazardous materials cleaned
Scheduling production	Number of different products
Redesigning products	Number of engineering orders
Shipping	Number of orders
Cafeteria	Number of employees
Data processing	Number of lines entered Number of hours of service
Engineering	Number of change orders Number of hours Periodic evaluation of services rendered Direct labor hours

EXHIBIT 24-1
ALLOCATION BASES, *Cont'd*

PRODUCTION AND SUPPORT COSTS	ALLOCATION BASIS
Production planning and control	Periodic evaluation of services performed Direct labor hours
Rent and office space	Square footage
Factory administration	Labor hours
Insurance	Book value of equipment Average of finished goods
Maintenance	Machine hours Maintenance hours
Materials storeroom	Number of materials moved Pounds of material moved Number of different parts
Payroll	Number of employees or dollar salaries
Personnel	Number of employees

DISTRIBUTION AND ADMINISTRATIVE EXPENSES	ALLOCATION BASIS
Marketing	Sales
Warehousing	Units or tonnage handled
Sales-service costs	Orders and invoices for each product
Direct selling costs (salesperson's salaries, commissions, and bonuses as well as sales or branch office expenses)	Sales value of product

EXHIBIT 24-1
ALLOCATION BASES, *Cont'd*

DISTRIBUTION AND ADMINISTRATIVE EXPENSES	ALLOCATION BASIS
Storage and building costs	Floor space
Credit investigation, postage, stationary, and similar expenses	Number of orders received
Samples	Cost of each product sample
General corporate advertising Newspaper, magazine, and direct mail	Sales value of products
Stenographic expense	Number of letters written
Salespersons' expenses	Number of salespersons' calls
Handling costs	Tonnage handled
Order writing and filling	Number of items on an order
Direct product advertising	Directly to product being advertised
Shipping department sales and supplies	Sales value of each product or relative weight of product sales
Automobile operation, delivery expenses, etc.	Size of product (weighted by quantity sold) Number of miles operated

Purpose: To use appropriate cost drivers to allocate costs

Distribution: Production/operations manager, cost accountant, executive vice president for operations, treasurer, controller, CFO, CEO

Use: To help assign costs for product/service costing, pricing and performance evaluation by matching costs with drivers

Action to be taken: Pick the right cost driver so that the accuracy of cost data is ensured. Distorted cost data will lead to an inappropriate decision regarding product mix, pricing, etc.

EXHIBIT 24-2
PERFORMANCE MEASURES: TRADITIONAL VS.
JUST-IN-TIME (JIT)

TRADITIONAL	JUST-IN-TIME
Direct labor efficiency	Total head count productivity
Direct labor utilization	Return on assets
Machine utilization	Group incentives
Direct labor productivity	Days of inventory

Purpose: To show the difference in how traditional and JIT systems measure performance

Distribution: Production/operations manager, cost accountant, executive vice president for operations, treasurer, controller, CFO, CEO

Use: To determine if JIT is right for you

Action to be taken: Investigate whether installing JIT would benefit your company and whether JIT performance measures philosophy fits your company's needs.

EXHIBIT 24-3
TRADITIONAL VS. ACTIVITY-BASED COSTING (ABC)

	TRADITIONAL	ABC
Cost pools:	One or a limited number	Many, to reflect different activities
Applied rate:	Volume-based, financial	Activity-based, nonfinancial
Suited for:	Labor-intensive, low-overhead companies	Capital-intensive, product-diverse, high-overhead companies
Benefits:	Simple, inexpensive	Accurate product costing, possible elimination of nonvalue-added activities

Purpose: To show the pros and cons of activity-based costing (ABC)

Distribution: Production/operations manager, cost accountant, executive vice president for operations, treasurer, controller, CFO, CEO

Use: To determine if ABC is right for you

Action to be taken: Install ABC if your company fits the criteria.

EXHIBIT 24-4
ACTIVITY-BASED COSTING (ABC) REPORT

Part 1: Determination of Cost Pool Rate

Overhead Cost Pool	Budgeted Overhead Cost	Cost Driver	Predicted Level for Cost Driver	Predetermined Overhead Rate
Machine Setups	$100,000	Number of setups	100	$1,000 per setup
Material Handling	100,000	Weight of raw material	50,000 pounds	$2.00 per pound
Waste Control	50,000	Weight of hazardous chemical used	10,000 pounds	$5.00 per pound
Inspection	75,000	Number of inspections	1,000	$75 per inspection
Other	$200,000	Machine hours	20,000	$10 per machine hour
Total	$525,000			

Part 2: Job or Product Requirements

Machine setups	2
Raw material required	10,000 pounds
Waste material produced	2,000 pounds
Inspections	10
Machine hours	500

Part 3: Overhead Cost Assignment

Overhead Cost Pool	Predetermined Overhead Rate	Level of Cost Driver	Assigned Overhead Cost
Machine setups	$1,000 per setup	2 setups	$2,000
Material handling	$2.00 per pound	10,000 pounds	20,000
Waste control	$5.00 per pound	2,000 pounds	10,000
Inspection	$75 per inspection	10 inspections	750
Other cost	$10 per machine hour	500 machine hour	5,000
Total			$37,750

EXHIBIT 24-4
ACTIVITY-BASED COSTING (ABC) REPORT, *Cont'd*

Part 4: Comparison with Traditional System

ABC	Traditional
$37,750.	Total budgeted overhead cost / Total predicted machine hours
	= $525,000 / 20,000
	= $26.25 per machine hour
	$13,125 ($26.25 per machine hour x 500 machine hours).

Purpose: To compare overhead costs charged under a traditional volume-based system with charges allocated under ABC, a multiple, volume/nonvolume-based cost driver system

Distribution: Production/operations manager, cost accountant, executive vice-president for operations, treasurer, controller, CFO, CEO

Use: To obtain more accurate cost data

Action to be taken: The reason for the wide discrepancy (between $37,750 vs. $13,125) is that special purpose tools require a relatively large number of machine setups and inspections, and produce a large amount of waste. Use of a single predetermined overhead rate obscures that fact. Inaccurately calculating the overhead cost per unit to the extent illustrated can have serious adverse consequences, including poor decisions about pricing, product mix, or contract bidding. A cost accountant needs to weigh such considerations carefully in designing a product costing system. Though a system using multiple cost drivers is more costly to implement and use, it may save millions through improved decisions. Further, ABC forces management to think in terms of simplifying operations. Once activities that are consumed by a product are identified, the process can be evaluated with a view to cut costs.

EXHIBIT 24-5
BREAK-EVEN ANALYSIS REPORT

Volume	Sales	Variable Costs	Fixed Costs	Total Costs	Profit
-	$0	$0	$30,000	$30,000	($30,000)
1,000	25,000	10,000	30,000	40,000	(15,000)
2,000	50,000	20,000	30,000	50,000	-
3,000	75,000	30,000	30,000	60,000	15,000
4,000	100,000	40,000	30,000	70,000	30,000
5,000	125,000	50,000	30,000	80,000	45,000
6,000	150,000	60,000	30,000	90,000	60,000
7,000	175,000	70,000	30,000	100,000	75,000

Given: (1) Unit sales price = $25
         (2) Unit variable cost = $10
         (3) Total fixed costs = $30,000

Break-Even Chart

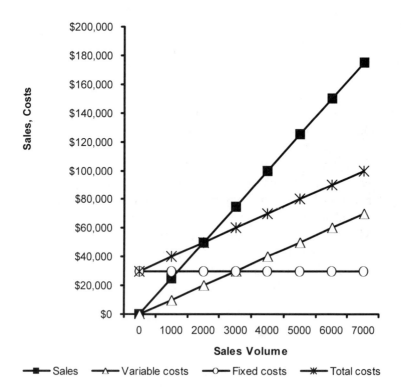

EXHIBIT 24-5
BREAK-EVEN ANALYSIS REPORT, *Cont'd*

Purpose: To determine the level of sales required to break even and see how a change in volume would affect profits

Distribution: Accountants, controller, treasurer, CFO, CEO

Use: To determine a proper sales level for budgeting purposes

Action to be taken: Based on such factors as price, market reaction, advertising to be spent, and target return on investment, determine a feasible level of sales that is within short- and long-term capacity limits.

Profit-Volume Chart

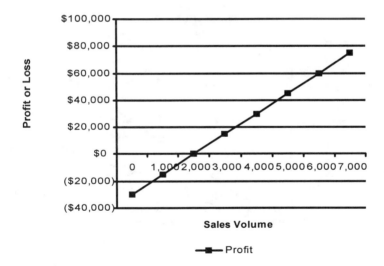

EXHIBIT 24-6
MONTHLY CASH BREAK-EVEN REPORT

Volume	Sales	Variable Costs	Fixed Cash Costs	Total Costs	Profit
-	$0	$0	13,500	$13,500	($13,500)
1,000	25,000	10,000	13,500	23,500	1,500
2,000	50,000	20,000	13,500	33,500	16,500
3,000	75,000	30,000	13,500	43,500	31,500
4,000	100,000	40,000	13,500	53,500	46,500
5,000	125,000	50,000	13,500	63,500	61,500
6,000	150,000	60,000	13,500	73,500	76,500
7,000	175,000	70,000	13,500	83,500	91,500

Given: (1) Unit sales price = $25
        (2) Unit variable cost = $10
        (3) Total cash fixed costs = $13,500

Break-Even Chart

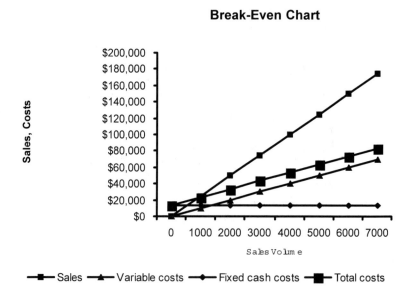

EXHIBIT 24-6
MONTHLY CASH BREAK-EVEN REPORT, *Cont'd*

Purpose: To determine the level of sales required to cover all *cash* expenses during a period (not all fixed costs involve cash payments, e.g., depreciation expense.)

Distribution: Cash managers, accountants, controller, treasurer, CFO

Use: To set a proper sales level for budgeting purposes (The cash break-even point is lower than the usual break-even point, since non-cash charges are deducted from fixed costs.)

Action to be taken: Based on such factors as price, market reaction, advertising to be spent, and a target return on investment, determine a level of sales that is feasible within both short- and long-term capacity limits.

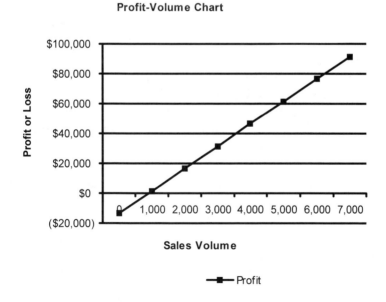

Profit-Volume Chart

EXHIBIT 24-7
QUALITY COST: ONE-YEAR TREND FOR THE YEAR ENDED
MARCH 31, 20--

	Actual Costs 20X2	Actual Costs 20X1	Variance
Prevention costs:			
Quality training	$30,000	$36,000	$6,000
Reliability engineering	79,000	120,000	41,000
Total prevention	109,000	156,000	47,000
Appraisal costs:			
Materials inspection	19,000	33,600	14,600
Product acceptance	10,000	16,800	6,800
Process acceptance	35,000	39,200	4,200
Total appraisal	64,000	89,600	25,600
Internal failure costs:			
Scrap	40,000	48,000	8,000
Rework	34,000	40,000	6,000
Total internal failure	74,000	88,000	14,000
External failure costs:			
Fixed:			
Customer complaints	24,000	33,000	9,000
Variable:			
Warranty	24,000	23,000	(1,000)
Repair	15,000	16,400	1,400
Total external failure	63,000	72,400	9,400
Total quality costs	$310,000	$406,000	$96,000
Percentage of actual sales	10.62%	13.90%	3.29%

Purpose: To compare the current year's quality costs with the previous year's

Distribution: Quality assurance managers, cost accountants, controller, treasurer, CFO

Use: To monitor how quality costs trend over time

Action to be taken: Any unfavorable variance (rising cost) should be investigated and remedied.

EXHIBIT 24-8
PERFORMANCE REPORT FOR THE YEAR ENDED MARCH 31, 20--

	Actual Costs	Budgeted Costs	Variance
Prevention costs:			
Quality training	$30,000	$30,000	0.00
Reliability engineering	79,000	80,000	1,000
Total prevention	109,000	110,000	1,000
Appraisal costs:			
Materials inspection	19,000	28,000	9,000
Product acceptance	10,000	15,000	5,000
Process acceptance	35,000	35,000	-
Total appraisal	64,000	78,000	14,000
Internal failure costs:			
Scrap	40,000	44,000	4,000
Rework	34,000	36,500	2,500
Total internal failure	74,000	80,500	6,500
External failure costs:			
Fixed:			
Customer complaints	24,000	25,000	1,000
Variable:			
Warranty	24,000	20,000	(4,000)
Repair	15,000	17,500	2,500
Total external failure	63,000	62,500	(500)
Total quality costs	$310,000	$331,000	$21,000
Percentage of actual sales	10.62%	11.34%	0.72%

Purpose: To measure actual progress achieved within the period relative to budgeted progress

Distribution: Quality assurance managers, cost accountants, controller, treasurer, CFO

Use: To analyze and direct quality performance over coming periods

Action to be taken: For each cost overrun, ask these questions (1) Is it significant enough for further investigation, e.g., more than 5%? Current practice sets the control limits subjectively, based on judgment and past experience rather than any formal identification of limits. About 45% of the firms surveyed used dollar or percentage control limits. (2) If it is significant, is it controllable? For example, a strike on the part of a sole source supplier leading to material shortage and a price hike is not controllable. (3) If it is controllable, who is responsible for the variance? (4) What is causing the overrun? (5) What can be done about it?

EXHIBIT 24-9
LONG-RANGE PERFORMANCE REPORT FOR
THE YEAR ENDED MARCH 31, 20--

	Actual Costs	Target Costs	Variance
Prevention costs:			
Quality training	$30,000	$14,000	($16,000)
Reliability engineering	79,000	39,000	(40,000)
Total prevention	109,000	53,000	(56,000)
Appraisal costs:			
Materials inspection	19,000	7,900	(11,100)
Product acceptance	10,000	-	(10,000)
Process acceptance	35,000	12,000	(23,000)
Total appraisal	64,000	19,900	(44,100)
Internal failure costs:			
Scrap	40,000	-	(40,000)
Rework	34,000	-	(34,000)
Total internal failure	74,000	-	(74,000)
External failure costs:			
Fixed:			
Customer complaints	24,000	-	(24,000)
Variable:			
Warranty	24,000	-	(24,000)
Repair	15,000	-	(15,000)
Total external failure	63,000	-	(63,000)
Total quality costs	$310,000	$72,900	($237,100)
Percentage of actual sales	10.62%	2.50%	-8.12%

Purpose: To compare the current year's quality cost ratio with the firm's intended long-range quality costs

Distribution: Quality assurance managers, cost accountants, controller, treasurer, CFO

Use: To analyze long-term quality performance

Action to be taken: The optimal quality cost level should be about 2.5% of sales. Remedial action should be taken to stay within the limit. This company has a long way to go to reach the optimal quality level (10.62% versus 2.5%); each category item should be investigated for improvement.

CHAPTER 25

Plant Reporting

Costs can be reduced significantly by monitoring plant activities.

- Exhibit 25-1, the plant capacity utilization report, shows the number of units demanded in different regions, as well as capacity utilization.

- Exhibit 25-2 monitors daily and cumulative plant overhead by its variable and fixed components, with variance analysis.

- Exhibit 25-3 shows how different capacity levels affect profits.

- Exhibit 25-4 shows how capacity levels affect the overhead rate.

- Quarterly machine hours required for various products are analyzed in Exhibit 25-5.

- Exhibit 25-6 shows how effectively equipment is being used, with analysis of idle hours by category.

- Exhibit 25-7 further investigates the causes of idle machine hours.

- Exhibit 25-8 graphs inventory trends.

EXHIBIT 25-1
PLANT CAPACITY UTILIZATION REPORT

	Capacity Available	Units Demanded Domestic	Units Demanded International	Total	% of Capacity
Jan	95,000	75,000	15,000	90,000	95%
Feb	95,000	40,000	20,000	60,000	63%
Mar	95,000	55,000	30,000	85,000	89%
Apr	95,000	60,000	15,000	75,000	79%
May	95,000	70,000	15,000	85,000	89%
Jun	95,000	65,000	10,000	75,000	79%
Jul	95,000	75,000	12,000	87,000	92%
Aug	95,000	30,000	25,000	55,000	58%
Sep	135,000	110,000	20,000	130,000	96%
Oct	145,000	125,000	15,000	140,000	97%
Nov	140,000	128,000	10,000	138,000	99%
Dec	90,000	60,000	8,000	68,000	76%

Purpose: To find out whether plant capacity is being used efficiently

Distribution: Plant manager, sales manager, senior management

Use: To set monthly capacity utilization of plant to meet domestic and international demand

Action to be taken: Take action to stimulate sales in months when capacity is under-used (e.g., December).

EXHIBIT 25-2
DAILY PLANT OVERHEAD CONTROL REPORT

	For July 7, 20X2					Cumulative for July				
	Standard Variable Overhead	Actual Variable Overhead	Variance	Fixed Overhead	Total Overhead	Standard Variable Overhead	Actual Variable Overhead	Variance	Fixed Overhead	Total Overhead
Indirect labor	$950	$865	$85	$410	$1,275	$7,000	$6,300	$700	$2,500	$8,800
Indirect materials	375	385	(10)	150	535	2,800	2,600	200	900	3,500
Depreciation			-	150	150			-	1,050	1,050
Insurance				85	85				595	595
Payroll taxes	165	150	15		150	1,200	900	300		900
Property taxes				10	10				60	60
Rent			-	100	100			-	700	700
Repairs and maintenance	120	140	(20)	30	170	720	980	(260)	250	1,230
Utilities	180	200	(20)	650	850	1,440	1,400	40	5,100	6,500
Other overhead	350	450	(100)	225	675	2,400	3,300	(900)	1,600	4,900
Total	$2,140	$2,190	$(50)	$1,810	$4,000	$15,560	$15,480	$80	$12,755	$28,235

Purpose: To monitor daily and cumulative monthly plant activity

Distribution: Production manager, plant manager

Use: To identify and smooth variations in daily and cumulative monthly overhead

Action to be taken: Use as a planning tool to monitor and control costs.

EXHIBIT 25-3
PROFIT AT VARIOUS LEVELS OF CAPACITY

	60% Capacity	70% Capacity	80% Capacity	90% Capacity	100% Capacity
Sales revenue	$1,200,000	$1,400,000	$1,600,000	$1,800,000	$2,000,000
Variable costs					
Indirect materials	108,000	126,000	144,000	162,000	180,000
Indirect labor	168,000	196,000	224,000	252,000	280,000
Supplies	84,000	98,000	112,000	126,000	140,000
Payroll taxes	25,200	29,400	33,600	37,800	42,000
Fringe benefits	30,240	35,280	40,320	45,360	50,400
Repairs	48,000	56,000	64,000	72,000	80,000
Electric	150,000	175,000	200,000	225,000	250,000
Total variable costs	613,440	715,680	817,920	920,160	1,022,400
Contribution margin	586,560	684,320	782,080	879,840	977,600
Fixed costs					
Depreciation	$65,000	$65,000	$65,000	$65,000	$65,000
Supervisor salaries	235,000	235,000	235,000	235,000	235,000
Insurance	48,000	48,000	48,000	48,000	48,000
Payroll taxes	9,000	9,000	9,000	9,000	9,000
Fringe benefits	7,000	7,000	7,000	7,000	7,000
Rent	33,000	33,000	33,000	33,000	33,000
Electric	8,500	8,500	8,500	8,500	8,500
Total fixed costs	405,500	405,500	405,500	405,500	405,500
Profits	181,060	278,820	376,580	474,340	572,100
% Profits	15%	20%	24%	26%	29%

Purpose: To find out how capacity utilization affects profits

Distribution: Plant manager, senior management

Use: To demonstrate the importance of operating at full capacity

Action to be taken: Motivate salespeople to sell more.

EXHIBIT 25-4
EFFECT OF CAPACITY LEVEL ON PREDETERMINED
OVERHEAD RATE

	Expected Actual Capacity	Normal Capacity	Expected Actual Capacity	Practical Capacity	Theoretical Capacity
% Theoretical Capacity	65%	80%	85%	90%	100%
Variable costs					
Indirect materials	$117,000	$144,000	$153,000	$162,000	$180,000
Indirect labor	182,000	224,000	238,000	252,000	280,000
Supplies	91,000	112,000	119,000	126,000	140,000
Payroll taxes	27,300	33,600	35,700	37,800	42,000
Fringe benefits	32,760	40,320	42,840	45,360	50,400
Repairs	52,000	64,000	68,000	72,000	80,000
Electric	162,500	200,000	212,500	225,000	250,000
Total variable costs	664,560	817,920	869,040	920,160	1,022,400
Fixed costs					
Depreciation	$65,000	$65,000	$65,000	$65,000	$65,000
Supervisor salaries	235,000	235,000	235,000	235,000	235,000
Insurance	48,000	48,000	48,000	48,000	48,000
Payroll taxes	9,000	9,000	9,000	9,000	9,000
Fringe benefits	7,000	7,000	7,000	7,000	7,000
Rent	33,000	33,000	33,000	33,000	33,000
Electric	8,500	8,500	8,500	8,500	8,500
Total fixed costs	405,500	405,500	405,500	405,500	405,500
Total overhead costs	$1,070,060	$1,223,420	$1,274,540	$1,325,660	$1,427,900
Machine hours	16,250	20,000	21,250	22,500	25,000
Overhead rate per machine hour:					
Variable overhead rate	$40.90	$40.90	$40.90	$40.90	$40.90
Fixed overhead rate	24.95	20.28	19.08	18.02	16.22
Total overhead rate	$65.85	$61.17	$59.98	$58.92	$57.12

Purpose: To show how capacity utilization affects overhead costs

Distribution: Production manager, plant manager

Use: To demonstrate the importance of operating at full capacity

Action to be taken: Use in planning to project overhead application rates.

EXHIBIT 25-5
QUARTERLY MACHINE HOUR REQUIREMENTS

Product	First Quarter			Quarter				Total Annual
	Jan	Feb	Mar	1st Quarter	2nd Quarter	3rd Quarter	4th Quarter	
Product 1	1,250	1,450	1,175	3,875	4,500	10,300	8,275	26,950
Product 2	1,400	2,450	1,750	5,600	8,500	9,100	10,000	33,200
Product 3	1,650	2,200	2,400	6,250	8,200	8,500	9,350	32,300
Product 4	1,800	3,100	2,100	7,000	9,350	12,500	14,000	42,850
Product 5	1,100	2,500	2,550	6,150	5,400	7,425	8,500	27,475
Product 6	1,250	2,200	3,500	6,950	5,250	8,925	7,500	28,625
Product 7	1,800	2,300	3,700	7,800	7,800	10,250	10,000	35,850
Product 8	1,650	2,500	2,800	6,950	9,000	10,000	9,500	35,450
Product 9	1,675	1,400	2,350	5,425	8,100	9,250	4,350	27,125
Product 10	2,200	1,950	2,275	6,425	6,500	7,500	9,250	29,675
Product 11	2,400	2,125	3,150	7,675	11,500	15,600	6,000	40,775
Product 12	2,565	2,355	2,985	7,905	12,000	8,550	10,750	39,205

Purpose: To review machine usage for four quarters

Distribution: Production manager, plant manager

Use: To project the number of machine hours likely to be available

Action to be taken: Use in planning to budget unit production and machine hour usage.

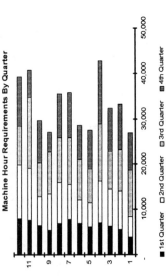

Machine Hour Requirements By Quarter

Product

■ 1st Quarter □ 2nd Quarter ▦ 3rd Quarter ■ 4th Quarter

EXHIBIT 25-6
MONTHLY EQUIPMENT USAGE REPORT

Month	Machine Hours			Machine Hours Not Utilized			
	Available	Utilized	% Utilized	Unassigned	Repairs	Servicing	Total
Jan	1,200	818	68%	230	68	84	382
Feb	1,250	956	76%	112	95	88	295
Mar	1,400	1,010	72%	180	112	98	390
Apr	1,000	699	70%	141	90	70	301
May	2,100	1,578	75%	295	80	147	522
Jun	1,900	1,379	73%	300	88	133	521
Jul	1,450	1,140	79%	140	69	102	311
Aug	1,600	1,198	75%	180	110	112	402
Sep	1,800	1,419	79%	105	150	126	381
Oct	1,400	1,027	73%	170	105	98	373
Nov	1,500	1,168	78%	135	92	105	332
Dec	1,250	868	69%	175	120	88	383

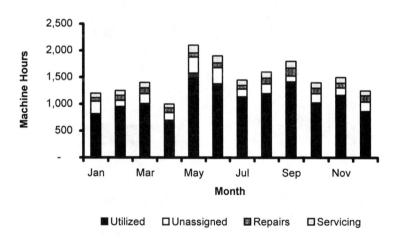

Analysis of Equipment Utilization

Purpose: To analyze monthly equipment utilization

Distribution: Production manager, plant manager

Use: To determine the number of idle machine hours available for production

Action to be taken: Investigate and correct reasons for unassigned machine hours.

EXHIBIT 25-7
ANALYSIS OF IDLE MACHINE HOURS

Machine	Machine Hours				Cause of Idle Machine Hours				
	Available	Utilized	Idle	% Idle	Insufficient Sales	Insufficient Materials	Scheduled Maint.	Unscheduled Repairs	Misc.
Machine A	3,500	2,900	600	17%	250	100	150	75	25
Machine B	4,000	3,000	1,000	25%	-	125	175	550	150
Machine C	2,000	1,900	100	5%	50	-	25	-	25
Machine D	1,000	600	400	40%	-	-	150	250	-
Machine E	6,000	4,000	2,000	33%	1,500	-	200	-	300
Machine F	8,000	7,000	1,000	13%	-	600	400	-	-
Machine G	5,000	4,500	500	10%	300	-	50	100	50
Total	29,500	23,900	5,600	19%	2,100	825	1,150	975	550

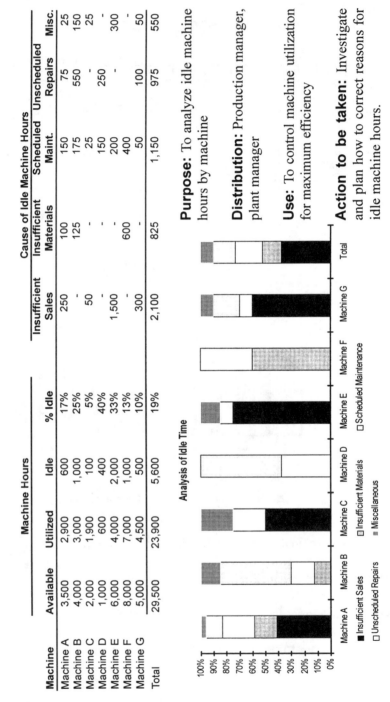

Analysis of Idle Time

Machine A Machine B Machine C Machine D Machine E Machine F Machine G Total

■ Insufficient Sales   □ Insufficient Materials   □ Scheduled Maintenance
□ Unscheduled Repairs   ▦ Miscellaneous

Purpose: To analyze idle machine hours by machine

Distribution: Production manager, plant manager

Use: To control machine utilization for maximum efficiency

Action to be taken: Investigate and plan how to correct reasons for idle machine hours.

EXHIBIT 25-8
INVENTORY TREND

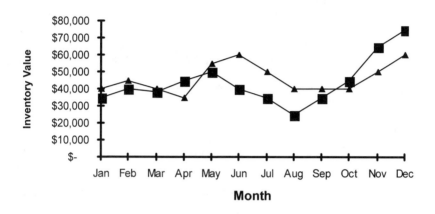

——■—— Actual ——▲—— Budget

	Actual	Budget
Jan	$35,000	$40,000
Feb	40,000	45,000
Mar	38,000	40,000
Apr	45,000	35,000
May	50,000	55,000
Jun	40,000	60,000
Jul	35,000	50,000
Aug	25,000	40,000
Sep	35,000	40,000
Oct	45,000	40,000
Nov	65,000	50,000
Dec	75,000	60,000

Purpose: To monitor inventory buildup

Distribution: Production manager, sales manager, controller

Use: To determine whether actual inventory is being turned over as budgeted (A similar graph may be prepared for work-in-process or raw materials inventory.)

Action to be taken: If the lines diverge, take corrective action.

CHAPTER 26

Research and Development

Crucial as is the research and development function to the future of a company, it is often difficult to monitor.

- Exhibit 26-1 is where it starts, with an appropriation request form designed to justify a project.

- Budgeting is essential to provide overall control: Exhibits 26-2 and 26-3 illustrate types of R&D budgets.

- Exhibits 26-4 through 26-8 illustrate ways to monitor R&D expenditures and progress.

EXHIBIT 26-1
R&D APPROPRIATION REQUEST

Summary of estimated costs and related data:

R&D staff hours   2,300

Total cost	$1,850,000
Project life	3.5 months
Estimated completion date	9/1
Additional capital investment	0
Required additions to staff	0

Estimated return on investment   12.50%

Brief description of major efforts and expected results:
To redesign manufacturing process, which will reduce production time by 5%.

Originated by_____

Approved by _____

Purpose: To justify a proposed R&D project

Distribution: R&D manager, department manager

Use: To document expected costs and savings or benefits of a project

Action to be taken: Required before work begins.

EXHIBIT 26-2
R&D BUDGET DIVISION

| | Exploratory Research | | Product Development | | Cost Reduction | | Total | |
| | Change from | | Change from | | Change from | | Change from | |
Division	Current Year	Last Year	Current Year	Last Year	Current Year	Last Year	Current Year	Last Year
Engineering	$25,000	$5,000	$6,000	$1,000	$8,500	$500	$39,500	$6,500
Machining	0	0	75,000	8,000	6,000	(1,500)	81,000	6,500
Electrical	5,000	1,500	19,000	3,000	3,500	1,000	27,500	5,500
Processing	8,000	2,000	13,500	1,000	8,500	0	30,000	3,000
Total	$38,000	$8,500	$113,500	$13,000	$26,500	$0	$178,000	$21,500

Purpose: To analyze R&D budget by type of expenditure

Distribution: R&D directors, division manager, top management

Use: To monitor R&D costs and contributions to various departments

Action to be taken: Use in conjunction with other reports to help control R&D expenditures.

EXHIBIT 26-3
SUMMARY OF PROPOSED R&D BUDGET

| | Proposed over Life of Project | | | |
Project	Required Staff– Additional	Total Manpower Hours	Project Cost	Estimated Cost for Current Year
5050	0	365	$203,000	$22,000
5062	2	750	528,000	97,000
5068	1	525	392,000	46,000
5071	3	975	729,000	326,000
5074	0	425	455,000	18,500

Purpose: To break out R&D budget by project

Distribution: R&D managers, top management

Use: To monitor project progress

Action to be taken: In conjunction with other reports, use throughout the year to identify and correct deviances.

EXHIBIT 26-4
R&D EXPENDITURE SUMMARY

| | Month | | | Year to Date | | |
	Actual	Budget	Variance	Actual	Budget	Variance
Direct salaries and wages	$16,000	$15,000	$1,000	$122,750	$125,000	$(2,250)
Direct materials and expenses	11,750	12,500	(750)	92,500	97,000	(4,500)
Total direct expense	27,750	27,500	250	215,250	222,000	(6,750)
Indirect salaries and wages	2,000	1,500	500	15,000	12,500	2,500
Depreciation	1,000	1,000	-	8,000	8,000	-
Other overhead	5,500	5,000	500	45,250	42,000	3,250
Total indirect expense	8,500	7,500	1,000	68,250	62,500	5,750
Total expense	$36,250	$35,000	$1,250	$283,500	$284,500	$(1,000)

Purpose: To summarize R&D expenditures for individual projects

Distribution: R&D directors

Use: To compare how well R&D expenditures conform to budget

Action to be taken: Watch for a favorable variance in one area being offset by an unfavorable variance in another. In the above example, the favorable variance of $750 in Direct Materials purchases is offset by the $1,000 unfavorable variance in Direct Wages: Is this because inferior materials are being purchased, causing more work?

EXHIBIT 26-5
REPORT OF R&D PROJECT HOURS

		Budget			Actual	
Division	Hours	Approved Projects	Open Requests	Balance Uncommitted	YTD Hours Expended	Remaining Hours to Expend
A	21,900	10,500	1,990	9,410	9,960	11,940
B	52,600	25,200	2,715	24,685	24,080	28,520
C	38,700	24,600	0	14,100	22,520	16,180
D	11,800	7,100	515	4,185	6,690	5,110
E	16,800	10,900	0	5,900	10,200	6,600
F	26,900	22,100	0	4,800	19,300	7,600
Total	168,700	100,400	5,220	63,080	92,750	75,950

Purpose: To monitor annual budgeted R&D hours for each division against actual hours expended and remaining

Distribution: Divisional managers, R&D directors

Use: To assess whether a division can take on additional work

Action to be taken: Reject all projects if a division has few remaining hours to expend compared with uncommitted hours.

EXHIBIT 26-6
R&D STATUS REPORT

Project	Total Budget	YTD Expenditures	Outstanding Commitments	Total YTD	Remaining Budget	% of Completion
A	$18,500	$8,239	$2,350	$10,589	$7,911	51%
B	22,250	10,533	3,575	14,108	8,142	65%
C	39,500	16,322	12,300	28,622	10,878	70%
D	27,500	13,781	4,075	17,856	9,644	65%
Total	$107,750	$48,875	$22,300	$71,175	$36,575	

Purpose: To assess the status of R&D expenditures by project

Distribution: Project managers, R&D manager

Use: To assess whether a division can take on additional work

Action to be taken: If budget remaining is at variance with % of completion, take corrective action.

EXHIBIT 26-7
R&D PROGRESS REPORT

Program	Actual Expenditures to Date	Approved Expenditures	Future Estimated Expenditures	Total	Original Budget	Over (Under) Committed	Expected Completion Date
Project 1810	$5,500	$600	$3,000	$9,100	$10,000	($900)	3/1
Project 1821	2,100	2,700	6,500	11,300	12,000	(700)	4/15
Project 1824	15,500	3,300	1,500	20,300	20,000	300	5/1
Project 1829	26,700	42,600	77,950	147,250	146,000	1,250	5/1
Project 1832	1,300	12,300	102,500	116,100	127,000	(10,900)	6/30

Purpose: To monitor progress of individual R&D projects

Distribution: R&D director, managers

Use: To compare incurred, committed, and planned expenditures with budget

Action to be taken: In conjunction with other reports for monitoring R&D, find causes of cost overruns and correct them.

EXHIBIT 26-8
R&D PERFORMANCE

Project	Actual Hours	Budgeted Hours	% Actual to Budget	Estimated % of Completion
Project A	92	650	14%	15%
Project B	886	1050	84%	55%
Project C	75	115	65%	60%
Project D	323	950	34%	35%

Purpose: To track efficiency of R&D projects

Distribution: Project managers, R&D manager

Use: To analyze variances in actual versus budgeted hours

Action to be taken: If estimated % of completion is significantly below % actual to budgeted hours, as in project B, find reason for variance and correct if possible.

CHAPTER 27

Marketing

The reports in this chapter are used to monitor how well the marketing department is promoting the firm's products.

- Exhibit 27-1 contains a product budget for the year, which is essential for the development of a marketing plan.
- Exhibits 27-2 and 27-3 are ways to control marketing department expenditures.
- Exhibits 27-3 through 27-6 show how to monitor activities by territories, products, and media.

EXHIBIT 27-1
PRODUCT OPERATING FORECAST

Product	Current Year Forecast					Previous Year Actual
	1st Quarter	2nd Quarter	3rd Quarter	4th Quarter	Total Year	
Product A						
Sales	$215,000	$196,000	$294,300	$256,850	$962,150	$698,296
GP %					24.9	25.9
Contribution margin %					12.6	14.6
Product B						
Sales	$625,400	$526,450	$726,400	$326,900	$2,205,150	$1,652,851
GP %					18.9	19.7
Contribution margin %					10.8	11.0
Product C						
Sales	$126,450	$98,650	$184,520	$221,345	$630,965	$598,354
GP %					29.6	28.4
Contribution margin %					19.4	18.5
Product D						
Sales	$319,400	$415,850	$345,600	$123,850	$1,204,700	$1,542,629
GP %					16.8	15.9
Contribution margin %					10.3	9.8

Purpose: To help draft overall marketing plan

Distribution: Top management, marketing manager, territory manager

Use: To integrate into company-wide marketing plan

Action to be taken: Determine how much marketing effort should be expended on each product to maximize profit.

EXHIBIT 27-2
SUMMARY MARKETING DIVISION BUDGET (in thousands)

	Current Year Plan Quarter					Prior	Increase
	1	2	3	4	Total	Year	(Decrease)
Direct selling	$15,930	$16,240	$16,600	$16,840	$65,610	$61,410	$4,200
Advertising and							
sales promotion	8,820	9,210	9,400	9,610	37,040	35,100	1,940
Warehousing	5,820	5,940	5,940	6,080	23,780	23,000	780
General and							
administration	2,100	2,100	2,100	2,210	8,510	8,300	210
Market research	470	490	490	510	1,960	1,900	60
Customer relations	100	100	100	110	410	430	(20)
Branch offices	1,000	1,010	1,030	1,050	4,090	3,900	190
Total	$34,240	$35,090	$35,660	$36,410	$141,400	$134,040	$7,360
% of net sales					9.6%	9.4%	0.2%

Purpose: To analyze marketing budget by function

Distribution: Top management, marketing manager

Use: To make sure projections stay within same percentage range as previous year

Action to be taken: Determine in which areas expenses may need to be adjusted.

EXHIBIT 27-3
MARKETING BUDGET STATUS REPORT

Category	Total Budget	Actual to 5/31 Expenditures	Commitments	Total	Balance Available
Television	$4,550	$2,022	$522	$2,544	$2,006
Radio	720	319	14	333	387
Consumer magazines	2,250	1,004	79	1,083	1,167
Newspapers	3,075	2,047	376	2,423	652
Business publications	1,525	697	46	743	782
Direct mail	630	412	0	412	218
Total	$12,750	$6,501	$1,037	$7,538	$5,212

Purpose: To monitor advertising budget by medium

Distribution: Top management, marketing manager

Use: To compare against budget and cash flow projections to make sure efficiency is maximized

Action to be taken: Make sure balances are appropriate for planned activities.

EXHIBIT 27-4
COMPARATIVE WEEKLY DOLLAR VOLUMES

Week Ended	This Week	Annual Cumulative	Change This Year/Last Year Weekly Amount	%	Cumulative Amount	%
1/6	$146,560	$146,560	($22,050)	(15.05)	($22,050)	(15.05)
1/13	152,500	299,060	3,455	1.16	(18,595)	(6.22)
1/20	219,455	518,515	14,065	2.71	(4,530)	(0.87)
1/27	192,300	710,815	(3,054)	(0.43)	(7,584)	(1.07)
2/3	308,921	1,019,736	45,022	4.42	37,438	3.67
2/10	185,658	1,205,394	14,058	1.17	51,496	4.27
2/17	258,935	1,464,329	29,354	2.00	80,850	5.52
2/24	219,008	1,683,337	(12,055)	(0.72)	68,795	4.09
3/3	145,355	1,828,692	915	0.05	69,710	3.81

Purpose: To monitor sales volume within territory

Distribution: Top management, marketing manager

Use: With other reports, to make sure activities relate to sales

Action to be taken: See if marketing effort should be adjusted to eliminate any under-performance.

EXHIBIT 27-5
SUMMARY PERFORMANCE BY PRODUCT (in thousands)

Product Line	Actual	Plan	Variance	Percentage
		Year-to-Date		
Product A				
Net sales	$52,522	$50,000	$2,522	5.04
GP	31,214	30,000	1,214	4.05
Contribution margin	14,560	15,000	(440)	(2.93)
Product B				
Net sales	19,245	20,000	(755)	(3.78)
GP	7,055	7,000	55	0.79
Contribution margin	5,102	5,000	102	2.04
Product C				
Net sales	33,020	30,000	3,020	10.07
GP	21,512	20,000	1,512	7.56
Contribution margin	17,041	17,000	41	0.24

Purpose: To monitor the performance of each product

Distribution: Top management, marketing manager

Use: To analyze performance against projections

Action to be taken: Refocus marketing effort to boost under-performing products.

EXHIBIT 27-6
MARKETING REPORT BY MEDIUM

Category	Actual	Budget	Variance	Actual	Budget	Variance
	Current Month			Year-to-Date		
Television	$349	$337	$12	$2,022	$2,075	(53)
Radio	29	55	(26)	319	355	(36)
Consumer magazines	219	181	38	1,004	1,055	(51)
Newspapers	257	276	(19)	2,047	1,625	422
Business publications	159	130	29	697	815	(118)
Direct mail	0	12	(12)	412	355	57
Total	$1,013	$991	$22	$6,501	$6,280	$221

Purpose: To monitor spending by media category

Distribution: Top management, marketing manager

Use: To maintain scheduled expenditures per cash flow projections

Action to be taken: In the light of other reports, adjust media marketing expenditures as needed.

CHAPTER 28

Financial Statements

Managers use financial statements to assess the financial health of a company: how well it is doing, its growth potential, and its vulnerability to risk.

Creditors evaluate a company's financial statements to determine whether the company will be able to pay if they grant it credit.
Investors concentrate on profitability, dividends, and market value measures to see whether an investment is justified.

Accountants and auditors are concerned about whether the company can stay in business and meet its obligations.

Financial statements should be evaluated in the light of the averages for competing companies and the industry as a whole.

- Exhibits 28-1, 28-5, and 28-6 show the income statement along with trend and common-size analysis.

- Balance sheet presentation and analysis are shown in Exhibits 28-2, 28-3, 28-7, and 28-8.

- Exhibit 28-4 is for assessing cash flow from operating, investing, and financing activities.

- Exhibit 28-9 reports inflation-adjusted assets, liabilities, stockholders' equity, sales revenue, cost of sales, and earnings.

EXHIBIT 28-1
INTERIM INCOME STATEMENT

Gross sales			$2,650,000
Less: Sales returns and allowances			100,000
Net sales			2,550,000
Cost of goods sold:			
Interim–Beginning		380,000	
Add: Manufacturing costs			
Direct materials	$510,000		
Direct labor	820,000		
Factoring overhead	950,000	2,280,000	
Cost of goods available		2,660,000	
Less: Inventory–Ending		800,000	
Cost of goods sold			1,860,000
Gross profit			690,000
Operating expenses			
General and administrative expenses		270,000	
Selling expenses		200,000	
Total operating expenses			470,000
Income before interest and taxes			220,000
Interest expense			40,000
Income before taxes			180,000
Income taxes			54,000
Net income			$126,000

Purpose: To determine the profit of the business

Distribution: Management, investors, creditors, directors

Use: To predict earning power by analyzing operating performance

Action to be taken: Reduce excess costs to improve profitability.

EXHIBIT 28-2
INTERIM BALANCE SHEET

Assets
Current assets:

Cash	$70,000	
Trading securities	150,000	
Accounts receivable	450,000	
Inventory	800,000	
Prepaid expenses	20,000	1,490,000

Fixed assets:

Land	1,000,000	
Building	2,000,000	
Equipment	500,000	
Furniture	100,000	
Autos and trucks	250,000	3,850,000

Intangible assets:

Patents	60,000	
Copyrights	20,000	
Trademarks	10,000	90,000

Other Assets:

Deferred startup costs		40,000
Total assets		$5,470,000

Liabilities and stockholders' equity
Liabilities
Current liabilities:

Accounts payable	1,300,000	
Short-term notes payable	1,200,000	
Accrued expenses payable	70,000	2,570,000

Noncurrent liabilities:

Bonds payable	1,500,000	
Mortgage payable	800,000	2,300,000
Total liabilities		4,870,000

Stockholders' equity

Common stock	100,000	
Paid-in-capital	350,000	
Retained earnings	150,000	600,000
Total liabilities and stockholders' equity		$5,470,000

Purpose: To determine what the business owns and owes and its equity position

Distribution: Management, investors, creditors, directors

Use: To appraise the financial status and health of the entity

Action to be taken: Reduce debt exposure.

EXHIBIT 28-3
QUARTERLY REPORTING AND APPRAISAL OF MISCELLANEOUS ASSETS

Types of Asset	Beginning of Quarter	Change	End of Quarter	Major Reasons for Change
Deferred moving costs	$8,000	$20,000	$28,000	Moving to another location.
Deferred startup costs	2,000	12,000	14,000	Starting up a new operation.
Deferred increased fuel costs		1,500	1,500	Expecting to pass on higher rates to another.
Deferred advertising	6,000	(1,000)	5,000	Amortization over period of benefit.
Deferred insurance	3,000	4,000	7,000	Prepayment of policy.
Customer lists		3,000	3,000	Buying a mailing list.
Total	$19,000	$39,500	$58,500	

Purpose: To itemize miscellaneous assets by type

Distribution: Financial analyst, controller

Use: To improve cost-benefit ratio of assets

Action to be taken: Determine the cause for change in deferred asset accounts.

EXHIBIT 28-4
STATEMENT OF CASH FLOWS

Cash flow from operating activities:		
Net income		$100,000
Add (deduct) items not affecting cash:		
Depreciation expense	$10,000	
Decrease in accounts receivable	5,000	
Increase in prepaid expenses	(1,000)	
Increase in accounts payable	20,000	34,000
Net cash flow from operating activities		134,000
Cash flow from investing activities		
Purchase of property	(15,000)	
Sale of available-for-sale securities	20,000	
Purchase of equipment	(3,000)	
Net cash flow from investing activities		2,000
Net cash flow from financing activities		
Issuance of stock	30,000	
Issuance of bonds	40,000	
Payment on long-term debt	(15,000)	
Payment of cash dividends	(10,000)	
Net cash flow from financing activities		45,000
Net Increase in cash		$181,000

Purpose: To determine sources of change for the period

Distribution: Chief financial officer, investors, creditors, financial analyst

Use: To appraise liquidity, sources and uses of cash flow, and state of growth or contraction

Action to be taken: Improve cash management by accelerating cash inflow and delaying cash outflow.

EXHIBIT 28-5
HORIZONTAL (TREND) INCOME STATEMENT

	20X1	20X2	Percent Change
Net sales:	$2,500,000	$2,800,000	12
Cost of goods sold	1,000,000	1,100,000	10
Gross profit	1,500,000	1,700,000	13
Less: Operating expenses			
Selling expenses	200,000	300,000	50
Administrative expenses	100,000	120,000	20
Total operating expenses	300,000	420,000	40
Income from operations	1,200,000	1,280,000	7
Other revenue and gains	50,000	60,000	20
Total	1,250,000	1,340,000	7
Other expenses and losses	40,000	50,000	25
Income before tax	1,210,000	1,290,000	7
Income tax	300,000	330,000	10
Net income	$910,000	$960,000	5

Purpose: To determine trends in income

Distribution: Chief financial officer, investors, creditors, financial analyst

Use: To evaluate the reasons for declining revenue or increasing costs

Action to be taken: Reduce excessive costs.

EXHIBIT 28-6
VERTICAL (COMMON-SIZE) INCOME STATEMENT

	20--	Percentage
Net Sales	$2,800,000	100
Cost of goods sold	1,100,000	39
Gross profit	1,700,000	61
Less: Operating expenses		
Selling expenses	300,000	11
Administrative expenses	120,000	4
Total operating expenses	420,000	15
Income from operations	1,280,000	46
Other revenue and gains	60,000	2
Total	1,340,000	48
Other expenses and losses	50,000	2
Income before tax	1,290,000	46
Income tax	330,000	12
Net Income	$960,000	34

Purpose: To determine the relationship of each income statement item to net sales

Distribution: Chief financial officer, investors, creditors, financial analyst

Use: To see how much expenses or revenues affect profitability

Action to be taken: Implement a cost reduction program.

EXHIBIT 28-7
HORIZONTAL (TREND) BALANCE SHEET

	20--	20--	Percentage of Change
Assets:			
Current assets	$1,200,000	$1,400,000	17
Fixed assets	3,000,000	3,300,000	10
Intangible assets	100,000	120,000	20
Other assets	50,000	60,000	20
Total assets	4,350,000	4,880,000	12
Liabilities:			
Current liabilities	600,000	700,000	17
Noncurrent liabilities	2,000,000	2,400,000	20
Total liabilities	2,600,000	3,100,000	19
Stockholders' equity:	300,000	300,000	0
Capital stock	500,000	550,000	10
Paid-in capital	950,000	930,000	-2
Retained earnings	1,750,000	1,780,000	2
Total stockholders' equity	$4,350,000	$4,880,000	12

Purpose: To determine trends in assets, liabilities, and equity

Distribution: Chief financial officer, investors, creditors, financial analyst

Use: To find why balance sheet items are increasing or decreasing, and the implications thereof

Action to be taken: Improve the mix of debt and equity in financing the business.

EXHIBIT 28-8
VERTICAL (COMMON-SIZE) BALANCE SHEET

	20--	Percentage
Assets:		
Current assets	$1,400,000	29
Fixed assets	3,300,000	68
Intangible assets	120,000	2
Other assets	60,000	1
Total assets	4,880,000	100
Liabilities:		
Current liabilities	700,000	14
Noncurrent Liabilities	2,400,000	49
Total liabilities	3,100,000	64
Stockholders' equity:		
Capital stock	300,000	6
Paid-in capital	550,000	11
Retained earnings	930,000	19
Total stockholders' equity	1,780,000	36
Total liabilities and stockholders' equity	$4,880,000	100

Purpose: To determine the relationship of each asset category to total assets and of each liability or equity category to total liabilities and stockholders' equity

Distribution: Chief financial officer, investors, creditors, financial analyst

Use: To discover the relative importance of each asset, liability, or equity category

Action to be taken: Make cash assets more liquid to pay debt.

EXHIBIT 28-9
INFLATION-ADJUSTED REPORTING

	Historical Dollars	Conversion Index	Current Dollars
Current assets	$300,000	1.2	$360,000
Noncurrent assets	600,000	1.6	960,000
Current liabilities	200,000	1.2	240,000
Noncurrent liabilities	400,000	1.5	600,000
Stockholders' equity	300,000	1.7	510,000
Sales	850,000	1.1	935,000
Cost of sales	450,000	1.1	495,000
Operating expenses	100,000	1.3	130,000
Net Income	$300,000	1.2	$360,000

Purpose: To reveal how inflation affects major balance sheet and income statement categories

Distribution: Chief executive officer, chief financial officer, financial analyst, treasurer

Use: To determine what steps are necessary to minimize the adverse effects of inflation on the business

Action to be taken: Emphasize assets and liabilities that do well in inflationary times.

CHAPTER 29

Financial Statement Analysis

Analyzing a company's financial statements not only helps creditors and investors make informed decisions about the quality of a company, it helps management monitor its own financial status and earnings performance and to reduce risk.

Management wants to present itself in the best possible light because that affects the market price of its stock, its bond rating, and the cost of financing.

Liquidity ratios reveal the firm's ability to pay off short-term debt. Solvency ratios tell whether the company can meet its long-term obligations. Profit is an indicator of the company's earning potential.

- Gross profit and its components are analyzed in Exhibit 29-1.

- Measures of earning power are highlighted in Exhibit 29-2.

- Profit may need to be reconciled in terms of the reasons for its increase or decrease, as shown in Exhibit 29-3.

- Exhibit 29-4 analyzes short-term assets and current liabilities.

- Key liquidity, solvency, operating performance, and market value ratios are presented in Exhibit 29-5.

- Exhibit 29-6 appraises liquidity, while Exhibits 29-7 and 29-8 evaluate solvency and leverage.

- Optimal utilization of assets improves corporate profitability. Asset utilization analysis typically compares sales to specific assets and total asset categories, as shown in Exhibit 29-9.

- If a company is heading towards bankruptcy, management must move promptly to prevent it. Investors and creditors would not want to risk their funds with the company. Thus, it is crucial to monitor the bankruptcy indicators in Exhibit 29-10.

- Exhibit 29-11 is a checklist for management to avoid financing problems leading to business failure.

EXHIBIT 29-1
GROSS PROFIT REPORTING AND APPRAISAL

Product	Revenue			Cost of Sales			Gross Profit			
	Budget	Actual	Variance	Budget	Actual	Variance	Budget	Actual	Dollar Variance	Percentage Variance
Shirts	$600,000	$700,000	$100,000	$320,000	$300,000	$20,000	$280,000	$400,000	$120,000	30
Pants	500,000	460,000	(40,000)	260,000	270,000	(10,000)	240,000	190,000	(50,000)	26
Dresses	800,000	870,000	70,000	410,000	380,000	30,000	390,000	490,000	100,000	20
Sweater	250,000	230,000	(20,000)	110,000	125,000	(15,000)	140,000	105,000	(35,000)	33
Ties	60,000	58,000	(2,000)	27,000	26,000	1,000	33,000	32,000	(1,000)	3
Coats	650,000	680,000	30,000	310,000	335,000	(25,000)	340,000	345,000	(5,000)	1
Total	$2,860,000	$2,998,000	$138,000	$1,437,000	$1,436,000	$1,000	$1,423,000	$1,562,000	$139,000	9

Purpose: To determine the contribution of each product's gross profit

Distribution: Budget analyst, chief financial officer, product manager, plant manager, marketing manager

Use: To ascertain variances to identify problems

Action to be taken: Improve budget estimates and actual performance.

EXHIBIT 29-2
EARNING POWER REPORT

Measure	Company (%)	Industry Norm (%)	Competing Company (%)
Growth rate in earnings			
(change in earnings/beginning earnings)	12	10	11
Return on assets	8	9	11
Return on invested capital	13	12	12
Growth rate in sales	16	15	14
Residual income/net income	15	14	17
Profit margin (net income/sales)	14	13	11

Purpose: To determine the ability of the business to generate future earnings

Distribution: Chief financial officer, investor, financial analyst

Use: To ascertain whether it would be profitable investing in the company over a long period

Action to be taken: Improve profitability by increasing selling price or reducing cost per unit.

EXHIBIT 29-3
INTERIM RECONCILIATION OF PROFITS

Actual earnings	$500,000
Budgeted earnings	450,000
Variance (favorable)	50,000
Reason for increased earnings :	
Increased sales volume	30,000
Manufacturing cost savings	40,000
Difference (favorable)	70,000
Reason for decreased earnings :	
Lower selling price	3,000
Higher selling costs	15,000
Higher administrative costs	2,000
Difference (unfavorable)	20,000
Net difference of actual vs. budget (favorable)	$50,000

Purpose: To explain reasons for deviation of actual from expected earnings

Distribution: Budget analyst, CFO, financial analyst

Use: To ascertain how variances of actual from budget affect corporate profitability

Action to be taken: Improve sales volume, raise selling price, and reduce costs.

EXHIBIT 29-4
SEMIANNUAL ANALYSIS OF CURRENT ASSETS AND CURRENT LIABILITIES

	Budget	Actual	Percentage Change
Current assets:			
Cash	$50,000	$60,000	20
Accounts receivable	30,000	35,000	17
Inventory	70,000	65,000	7
Prepaid expenses	10,000	8,000	20
Total current assets	160,000	168,000	5
Current liabilities:			
Accounts payable	20,000	22,000	10
Notes payable	10,000	10,000	0
Accrued expenses payable	14,000	19,000	36
Total current liabilities	44,000	51,000	16
Working capital (current assets - current liabilities)	$116,000	$117,000	1
Current ratio (current assets/current liabilities)	1.4	1.4	0

Purpose: To evaluate a company's liquidity and working capital status

Distribution: Financial analyst, chief financial officer, treasurer, creditors

Use: To determine whether the business can pay current debt when due

Action to be taken: Accelerate cash inflow and delay cash outflow.

EXHIBIT 29-5
RATIO ANALYSIS

Major Ratios	Company	Industry Average	Major Competitor
Liquidity:			
Current ratio	1.6	1.8	2
Acid-test (quick) ratio	6	5	5.5
Receivables turnover	7	8	7.6
Inventory turnover			
Solvency:			
Total debt to stockholder's equity	40%	36%	32%
Interest coverage	6	5	7
Performance :			
Net income to sales	7%	6%	6.50%
Net income to total assets	12%	11%	13%
Market measures :			
Price-earnings	25	24	30
Earnings per share to market price	5%	4%	4.50%
Dividends per share to market price	2%	3%	1%
Dividends per share to earnings per share	38%	40%	42%

Purpose: To evaluate overall financial position and operating performance of the business

Distribution: Financial analyst, chief financial officer, investor, creditors

Use: To determine whether the business is liquid (solvent), profitable, and provides a good return to stockholders

Action to be taken: Raise cash through better asset management and collections.

EXHIBIT 29-6
ANNUAL LIQUIDITY ANALYSIS REPORT

Liquidity Measure	Current Year	Prior Year	Change	Industry Average
Current ratio	2.6	2.10	0.5	2.2
Quick ratio	1.4	1.10	0.3	1.2
Inventory turnover	6	5	1	4.5
Age of inventory in days	60	72	-12	80
Accounts receivable turnover	8	7	1	9
Collection period in days	45	51	-6	40
Current assets/total assets	0.4	0.36	0.04	0.35
Current liabilities/total liabilities	0.51	0.49	0.02	0.5
Current liabilities/noncurrent liabilities	0.83	0.81	0.02	0.78
Current assets/noncurrent assets	0.63	0.6	0.03	0.54
Cash/total current assets	0.1	0.11	0.01	0.13
Operating cycle in days	105	123	-18	120

Purpose: To determine liquidity as a a basis to convert cash to pay current debt

Distribution: Financial analyst, chief financial officer, treasurer, creditors

Use: To determine if the company's liquid assets are sufficient to meet creditor payments, identify slow-moving merchandise and delinquent customer balances, and identify ways to improve liquidity

Action to be taken: Improve inventory management and collection procedures.

EXHIBIT 29-7
ANNUAL SOLVENCY APPRAISAL REPORT

Solvency Measure	Current Year	Prior Year	Industry Average	Major Competitor
Financial leverage				
(total debt/stockholders' equity)	40%	38%	35%	36%
Noncurrent liabilities/stockholders' equity	24%	20%	21%	19%
Noncurrent assets/total assets	140%	136%	130%	132%
Noncurrent liabilities/total liabilities	70%	72%	68%	71%
Interest coverage				
(income plus interest/interest)	64%	63%	61%	62%
Fixed charge coverage				
(income plus fixed charges/fixed charges)	3.4	3	4.2	4.5

Purpose: To evaluate the company's long-term financial position and level of risk

Distribution: Financial analyst, treasurer, creditors

Use: To ascertain whether earnings are sufficient to pay fixed charges, identify trouble areas, and recommend constructive means to improve the entity's financial status

Action to be taken: Reduce debt position and extend maturity dates of obligations.

EXHIBIT 29-8
LEVERAGE AND DEBT REPORT

Financial Measure	Company	Industry Average	Major Competition
Total liabilities/stockholders' equity	60%	58%	57%
Long-term debt/stockholders' equity	35%	37%	40%
Total liabilities/total assets	73%	68%	64%
Interest/borrowed capital	9%	8%	7%
Current liabilities/total liabilities	25%	30%	26%
Current liabilities/noncurrent liabilities	48%	44%	45%
Total assets/stockholders' equity	150%	152%	149%
Income plus fixed charges/fixed charges	3	3.5	3.8
Income plus interest/interest	6.7	6	5.9
Fixed costs/total costs	73%	70%	68%
Cash flow from operations/total debt	26%	28%	24%

Purpose: To determine debt position as a measure of risk

Distribution: Financial analyst, chief financial officer, creditors

Use: To ascertain the ability to pay debt and maximize return through the use of borrowed funds; can the company withstand adverse business conditions?

Action to be taken: Lengthen the maturity of debt, and improve cash flow.

EXHIBIT 29-9
ASSET UTILIZATION REPORT

Asset Utilization Ratios	Company	Industry Average	Major Competition
Sales to cash	30	26	28
Sales to accounts receivable	12	10	9
Sales to inventory	9	17	8
Sales to working capital	20	23	24
Sales to fixed assets	3.5	2.6	3.8
Sales to total assets	1.5	2	2.4
Sales to intangible assets	6	5	4

Purpose: To determine how well assets generate revenue

Distribution: Financial analyst, chief financial officer, investor

Use: To ascertain (1) which assets are achieving good or poor returns and the reasons why and (2) to identify ways to make assets more profitable

Action to be taken: Improve efficiency of assets.

EXHIBIT 29-10
BANKRUPTCY INDICATORS

1.   E. Altman's Z-Score Model:

$$Z = 1.2X1 + 1.4X2 + 3.3X3 + .6X4 + .999X5$$

where:
   X1 = working capital/total assets
   X2 = retained earnings/total assets
   X3 = earnings before interest and taxes/total assets
   X4 = market value of equity/book value of debt
   X5 = sales/total assets

Guidelines in predicting bankruptcy:

Z-Score	Probability of Failure
1.8 or less	very high
1.81 - 2.99	not sure
3.0 or higher	unlikely

2.   Wilcox's Gambler's-Ruin Prediction Formula:

   Liquidation value equals
   (Cash + marketable securities at market value)
   + (Inventory + accounts receivable + prepaid expenses)
       at 70% of book value
   + (Other assets at 50% of book value)
   - Current liabilities
   - Noncurrent liabilities
   = Liquidation value

3.   Beaver's Cash Ratio:

   Net income + depreciation/total liabilities

   If the ratio is below 1, the company is likely to go bankrupt within 2 years.

Purpose: To predict whether a company is likely to go bankrupt

Distribution: Management, chief executive officer, chief financial officer, financial analyst

Use: To avoid business failure and to ascertain what the firm is worth in liquidation

Action to be taken: Take steps to correct financial problems to avoid bankruptcy.

EXHIBIT 29-11
CHECKLIST FOR AVOIDING FINANCIAL PROBLEMS

- Diversify geographically, over time, economically, and by industry.
- Vertically integrate operations.
- Do not overextend, financially or operationally.
- Have adequate insurance.
- Enter into futures contracts to guard against drastic price changes.
- Restrict expansion during downturns.
- Finance assets with liabilities of similar maturity.
- Sell unprofitable assets.
- Manage assets prudently to balance return and risk.
- Keep lines of credit open.
- Avoid heavy debt.
- Make expenditures required for future growth.
- Automate where possible.
- Use latest technology.
- Reengineer, downsize, and outsource when appropriate.
- Conduct regular financial and operational audits.

Purpose: To assure the continued financial success of the business

Distribution: CEO, financial analyst, financial manager

Use: To prevent financial problems before they hurt the entity

Action to be taken: Correct financial deficiencies immediately.

CHAPTER 30

Reporting on Operating Expenses

Expenses must be tracked to prevent excessive spending and to improve profit through careful cost reduction. Any variances between budgeted and actual costs should be closely monitored.

Operating expenses are typically analyzed monthly or quarterly, so that any needed corrective steps may be implemented promptly.

• Exhibit 30-1 presents a quarterly report listing major operating expenses and showing for each the deviation between expected and actual amounts.

• Exhibit 30-2 shows a bi-weekly expense report.

• Exhibit 30-3 is a monthly analysis of general and administrative costs.

• The various types of selling costs are appraised monthly using Exhibit 30-4.

• Exhibit 30-5 presents a quarterly advertising expense report.

• Exhibit 30-6 analyzes monthly delivery charges by examining such items as delivery costs to merchandise shipped, losses experienced on deliveries, insurance premiums, and how long deliveries take.

EXHIBIT 30-1
QUARTERLY EXPENSE REPORT

Expense	Current Quarter				Prior Quarter	
	Actual	Estimated	Deviation	Actual	Estimated	Deviation
Salaries	$5,000	$4,000	$(1,000)	$4,700	$4,400	$(300)
Rent	3,000	3,500	500	3,100	3,000	(100)
Telephone	200	300	100	260	320	60
Advertising	500	425	(75)	410	400	(10)
Insurance	1,000	1,000	0	1,050	1,000	(50)
Electricity	240	210	(30)	200	180	(20)
Heating	140	150	10	220	120	10
Supplies	400	420	20	390	360	(30)
Inspection	315	300	(15)	245	250	5
Repairs and maintenance	600	400	(200)	410	350	(60)
Total	$11,395	$10,705	$(690)	$10,985	$10,380	$(495)

Purpose: To see how expenses trend over time

Distribution: Budget analyst, chief financial officer, controller, department manager

Use: To identify why a particular expense item is significantly higher or lower relative to a comparable prior period

Action to be taken: Reduce excessive costs.

EXHIBIT 30-2
BIWEEKLY EXPENSE REPORT FOR JANUARY 20--

	First Two Weeks of Month	Last Two Weeks of Month	Total for Month	Budgeted for Month
Telephone	$500	$600	$1,100	$1,000
Advertising	200	150	350	400
Insurance	125	140	265	250
Salaries-regular	2,375	4,425	6,800	7,000
Salaries-overtime	260	375	635	600
Fringe benefits	580	465	1,045	1,000
Rent	450	500	950	800
Utilities	140	120	260	200
Entertainment	180	285	465	450
Commissions	435	625	1,060	1,000
Office supplies used	110	130	240	200
Postage	90	115	205	250
Stationary	75	80	155	150
Travel	140	160	300	280
Bad debts	80	0	80	50
Depreciation	225	300	525	540
Total	$5,965	$8,470	$14,435	$14,170

Purpose: To determine the expenses incurred biweekly by major type

Distribution: Controller

Use: To ascertain the trend in costs over time, possible areas of cost containment, and whether particular costs are excessive

Action to be taken: Reduce excessive expenses.

EXHIBIT 30-3
MONTHLY ANALYSIS AND REPORTING OF GENERAL AND
ADMINISTRATIVE EXPENSES

	Current Month	Prior Month	Month of Prior Year
Officers' salaries	$40,000	$40,000	$37,000
Office salaries	100,000	96,000	90,000
Legal and professional fees	20,000	18,000	16,000
Utilities	1,000	900	800
Insurance	1,800	1,800	1,500
Depreciation on office equipment	2,000	2,000	1,700
Stationary and postage	600	500	400
Total	$165,400	$159,200	$147,400

Purpose: To determine the costs of administering the business

Distribution: Management, investors, creditors

Use: To evaluate trends in administrative costs by type and to ascertain reasons for charges so proper steps, if needed, may be implemented

Action to be taken: Reduce excessive administrative costs.

EXHIBIT 30-4
MONTHLY APPRAISAL AND REPORTING OF SELLING EXPENSES

	Current Month			Prior Month of Current Year			Same Month Last Year		
	Budget	Actual	Change	Budget	Actual	Change	Budget	Actual	Change
Salespeople salaries	$150,000	$160,000	$(10,000)	$140,000	$142,000	$(2,000)	$120,000	$110,000	$10,000
Salespeople commissions	20,000	22,000	(2,000)	18,000	19,000	(1,000)	15,000	12,000	3,000
Telephone	2,000	1,800	200	2,000	2,100	(100)	1,500	1,000	500
Salespeople auto expenses	5,000	4,600	400	5,000	4,800	200	4,000	5,000	(1,000)
Advertising and promotion	7,000	7,000	0	7,000	7,300	(300)	6,000	7,500	(1,500)
Entertainment	4,000	4,100	(100)	4,000	3,600	400	3,500	4,000	(500)
Freight on shipped goods	900	850	50	800	900	(100)	800	700	100
Free samples	600	600	0	500	450	50	350	400	(50)
Total	$189,500	$200,950	$(11,450)	$177,300	$180,150	$(2,850)	$151,150	$140,600	10,550

Purpose: To analyze selling expenses by type for control purposes

Distribution: Sales manager, financial manager, chief financial officer, budget analyst

Use: To identify causes of variances between actual and budgeted selling expenses and to ascertain ways to get more out of each dollar of selling expense

Action to be taken: Reduce costs.

EXHIBIT 30-5
QUARTERLY ADVERTISING EXPENSE REPORT

	Product A	Product B	Service X	Service Y	Total Actual	Total Budgeted
Television	$20,000	$15,000	$10,000	$8,000	$53,000	$50,000
Radio	9,000	6,000	7,000	2,000	24,000	25,000
Newspapers	4,000	3,000	11,000	1,000	19,000	16,000
Public magazines	5,000	9,000	3,000	4,000	21,000	20,000
Trade journals	1,000	2,000	4,000	3,000	10,000	11,000
Inflight magazines	500	400	700	800	2,400	2,200
Billboards	500	600	1,300	1,200	3,600	3,500
Other (e.g., Internet)	200	300	500	700	1,700	1,500
Total	$40,200	$36,300	$37,500	$20,700	$134,700	$129,200

Purpose: To determine the cost of promoting each product or service by medium

Distribution: Advertising manager, public relations manager, product manager, service manager, controller

Use: To determine effectiveness of alternate advertising vehicles in generating sales, comparing each medium and product ratio of sales to costs incurred

Action to be taken: Select most effective advertising medium by product.

EXHIBIT 30-6
MONTHLY DELIVERY CHARGE ANALYSIS AND REPORT

	Current Month	Prior Month	Same Month in Prior Year
Delivery costs/cost of merchandise shipped	2.0%	1.70%	2.30%
Delivery costs/selling price of merchandise shipped	1.3%	1.2%	1.6%
Insurance premium on deliveries/delivery charges	3.0%	2.7%	2.5%
Losses incurred on deliveries/cost of merchandise shipped	1.1%	1.6%	1.3%
Percentage of deliveries shipped in-house	60.0	52.0	43.0
Average time in days from time of order to shipment	3	2.5	4
Average time in days from shipment to customer receipt	2	2	3

Purpose: To determine cost, timing, and efficiency of deliveries

Distribution: Shipping manager, product manager, sales manager

Use: To identify delivery problems requiring correction and implement needed improvement

Action to be taken: Redesign logistics as needed.

CHAPTER 31

Financial Analysis

A financial analysis of the entity will reveal whether it is breaking-even in unit and dollar terms and how solid is its margin of safety. This is shown in Exhibit 31-1.

The contribution margin income statement presented in Exhibit 31-2 shows (1) how costs break down between fixed and variable, and (2) the contribution margin earned. In an economic downturn variable costs—but not fixed costs—can be reduced in the short-term.

EXHIBIT 31-1
QUARTERLY BREAK-EVEN ANALYSIS

	Current Quarter	Prior Quarter	Same Quarter, Prior Year
Break-even point in units (fixed costs/unit contribution margin*)	100,000	98,000	95,000
Break-even point in dollars (break-even x selling price)	$1,000,000	$980,000	$855,000
Margin of safety (expected sales - break-even sales/expected sales)	30%	28%	25%
Cash break-even point in units (fixed costs - depreciation/unit contribution margin)	80,000	75,000	71,000

*Unit contribution margin = selling price less variable costs

Purpose: To determine how many units the business must sell for there to be no loss

Distribution: Controller, division manager, product manager, sales manager

Use: To identify products with lower break-even points to make firm profitable

Action to be taken: Lower costs or increase selling price to lower break-even point on less profitable products.

EXHIBIT 31-2
CONTRIBUTION MARGIN INCOME STATEMENT

Sales (500,000 @ $10)		$5,000,000
Less: Variable cost of sales		
Beginning inventory(40,000 @ $5)	$200,000	
Variable cost of goods manufactured (600,000 @ $5)	3,000,000	
Variable cost of goods available	3,200,000	
Less: Ending inventory (140,000 @ $5)	700,000	
Total variable cost of sales		2,500,000
Manufacturing contribution margin		2,500,000
Less: Variable selling costs	400,000	
Variable administrative costs	100,000	
Total variable selling and administrative costs		500,000
Contribution margin		2,000,000
Less : Fixed costs		
Fixed overhead	300,000	
Fixed selling costs	150,000	
Fixed administrative costs	250,000	
Total fixed costs		700,000
Net income		$1,300,000

Purpose: To analyze income statement in terms of fixed and variable components

Distribution: Department manager, chief financial officer, controller, product manager

Use: To appraise performance of the overall company, department managers, and particular programs

Action to be taken: Reduce excessive variable costs to improve contribution margin.

CHAPTER 32

Valuation of a Business

How much is a business worth? It may be necessary to find out to set a suitable purchase or sales price, for estate planning, in litigation, or to resolve a dispute between owners.

- In valuing a business, the first step is to restate earnings as shown in Exhibit 32-1.
- The major methods for valuing a business are set out in Exhibit 32-2.

EXHIBIT 32-1
RESTATEMENT OF EARNINGS REPORT WHEN VALUING A BUSINESS

Reported net income	$800,000
Adjustments:	
Personal expenses	30,000
Extraordinary or nonrecurring gain	(40,000)
Excessive owner's salary	60,000
Dividend revenue	(50,000)
Owner's fringe benefits	20,000
Interest expense	40,000
Excess depreciation	10,000
Low cost rental	(5,000)
Restated net income	$865,000

Purpose: To determine earnings for valuation purposes

Distribution: Chief executive officer, chief financial officer, merger and acquisition analyst

Use: To set a fair value on the business

Action to be taken: Explain items that are out of line.

EXHIBIT 32-2
DIFFERENT METHODS OF VALUING A BUSINESS

Weighted-average 5-year earnings method using a multiplier of 3	$18,500,000
Capitalization of excess earnings method based on a 5-year period with a multiplier of 3	$19,750,000
Gross revenue multiplier method based on the revenue for the most current year and a multiplier of 1	$20,000,000
Present value of future cash earnings method	$17,700,000
Book value of net assets method	$12,000,000
Market value of net assets method	$21,000,000
Integration (mix) of the weighted-average earnings method and the market value of net assets method	$19,500,000

Purpose: To see whether the value of a business changes with different valuation methods

Distribution: Chief financial officer, lender, potential purchaser of the business

Use: To state the worth of a business in connection with litigation, dispute between owners, bank loans, tax valuation, or potential sale of the business

Action to be taken: Choose the most realistic valuation methods based on the circumstances.

CHAPTER 33

Financing the Business

Financial forecasting, an essential element of planning, is the basis for budgeting. Basically, forecasts of future sales and their related expenses help the firm project future needs for financing. The financial officer must then select the best possible source of financing based on the company's situation, taking into account cost of capital, taxes, risk, and capital structure.

Cost of capital is the financing costs of the business. It is defined as the rate of return necessary to maintain the market value of the firm (or the price of its stock). The cost of capital is computed as a weighted average of the various capital components, which are items on the right-hand side of the balance sheet such as debt, preferred stock, common stock, and retained earnings.

- Exhibit 33-1 illustrates the percentage-of-sales method used to predict total future financing needs.

- Exhibits 33-2 and 33-3 analyze alternative financing options.

- Exhibit 33-4 illustrates the computation of the cost of capital.

- Exhibit 33-5 shows how a change in foreign exchange rate can affect the financial position of a company, a useful guide for a multinational corporation.

EXHIBIT 33-1
THE PERCENTAGE-OF-SALES METHOD FOR PREDICTING EXTERNAL FINANCING NEEDS

	Present (20x1)	% of Sales (20x1 Sales=$20)	Projected (20x2 Sales=$24)
ASSETS			
Current assets	2	10%	2.4
Fixed assets	4	20%	4.8
Total assets	6		7.2
LIABILITIES AND STOCKHOLDERS' EQUITY			
Current liabilities	2	10	2.4
Long-term debt	2.5	n.a.	2.5
Total liabilities	4.5		4.9
Common stock	0.1	n.a.	0.1
Paid-in capital	0.2	n.a.	0.2
Retained earnings	1.2		1.92[a]
Total equity	1.5		2.22
Total liabilities and stockholders' equity	6		Total financing available 7.12
			External financing needed 0.08[b]
			Total 7.2

[a]20-- retained earnings = 20x1 retained earnings + projected net income - cash dividends paid
= $1.2 + 5% ($24) - 40% [5% ($24)]
= $1.2 + $1.2 - $0.48 = 2.4 - $0.48 = $1.92

[b]External financing needed = projected assets - (projected total liabilities + projected equity)
= $7.2 - ($4.9 + $2.22) = $7.2 - $7.12 = $0.08

Purpose: To forecast external financing needs

Distribution: Controller, treasurer, CFO, CEO

Use: To arrange early on a least-cost financing plan

Action to be taken: Investigate issuing notes payable, bonds, stock, or any combination of financing sources.

EXHIBIT 33-2
FINANCING OPTION FOR EXPANSION PROJECT

Principal for all Options	$35,000,000	Interest

Option 1: The company will raise funds with a bond issue at a 10.5 percent interest rate.
Long-Term Borrowing

Time (years)	20	
Rate	10.50%	$73,500,000

Option 2: Long-term rates are headed down and short-term borrowing for nine months through commercial paper or the equivalent would let the company float the bond issue nine months later, when interest rates are projected to be at a more reasonable 9 percent.
Short-term borrowing

Time (years)	0.75	
Rate	12.50%	$3,281,250
Long-term borrowing		
Time (years)	19.25	
Rate	9.00%	60,637,500
Total interest costs		$63,918,750

Option 3: The Company will use short-, intermediate-, and long-term borrowing to reduce short-term interest costs.
Short-term Borrowing

Time (years)	0.5	
Rate	13.00%	$2,275,000
Intermediate-term borrowing		
Time (years)	2.5	
Rate	11.80%	10,325,000
Long-term borrowing		
Time (years)	17	
Rate	9.50%	56,525,000
Total interest costs		$69,125,000

Purpose: To determine the least cost financing option for expansion projects

Distribution: Project analyst, controller, treasurer, cash manager, CFO, CEO

Use: To compare various financing scenarios

Action to be taken: Choose the financing option with the least interest charges.

EXHIBIT 33-3
EVALUATION OF ALTERNATIVE FINANCING PLANS

	All Common (a)	All Debt (b)	All Preferred (c)
Earnings before interest and taxes (EBIT)	$1,000,000	$1,000,000	$1,000,000
Interest		200,000	
Earnings before taxes (EBT)	1,000,000	800,000	1,000,000
Taxes (50%)	500,000	400,000	500,000
Earnings after taxes (EAT)	500,000	400,000	500,000
Preferred stock dividend			160,000
Earnings available to common stockholders (EAC)	$500,000	$400,000	$340,000
Number of shares	140,000	100,000	100,000
Earnings per share (EPS)	$3.57	$4.00	$3.40

Options: For the acquisition of special equipment costing $2 million: (a) Sell 40,000 shares of common stock at $50 each; (b) sell bonds at 10 percent interest: or (c) issue preferred stock with an 8 percent dividend. The present EBIT is $1 million, the income tax rate is 50 percent, and 100,000 shares of common stock are now outstanding

Purpose: To achieve optimal capital structure at the lowest overall cost of capital

Distribution: Treasurer, cash manager, controller, CFO, CEO

Use: To evaluate alternative financing plans

Action to be taken: Choose the best financing plan based on an evaluation of the effect on EPS over a range of EBIT levels, starting with the EBIT break-even (indifference) points of the various financing plans.

EXHIBIT 33-4
COST OF CAPITAL REPORT

Source	Market Value	Weights	Cost	Weighted Average
Debt	$22,000,000	33.08%	5.14%	1.70%
Preferred stock	4,500,000	6.77	13.40	0.91
Common stock	32,000,000	48.12	17.11	8.23
Retained earnings	8,000,000	12.03	16.00	1.92
	$66,500,000	100.00		12.77%

Purpose: To determine the firm's overall cost of capital, for all types

Distribution: Project analyst, treasurer, cash manager, controller, CFO, CEO

Use: As a discount rate under the net present value (NPV) method or as a cutoff rate under the internal rate of return (IRR) method to evaluate a proposed capital project

Action to be taken: Accept the project if the cost of capital (12.77%) is below the project's IRR or if the project's net cash flow discounted at 12.77% is above zero.

EXHIBIT 33-5
THE EFFECTS OF CHANGES IN FOREIGN EXCHANGE RATES

	Weak Currency (Depreciation)	Strong Currency (Appreciation)
Imports	More expensive	Cheaper
Exports	Cheaper	More expensive
Payables	More expensive	Cheaper
Receivables	Cheaper	More expensive
Inflation	Fuel inflation by making imports more costly	Low inflation
Foreign investment	Discourage; lower return on investments by international investors.	High interest rates could attract foreign investors
The effect	Raising rates could slow down the economy.	Reduced exports could trigger a trade deficit.

Purpose: To show how a change in foreign exchange rates can affect the financial position of a company, especially a multinational corporation (MNC)

Distribution: Operations manager, trade department manager, divisional manager, executive vice president for operations, treasurer, controller, CFO, CEO

Use: To make tactical and strategic decisions in the best interest of the company to respond to foreign exchange rate changes

Action to be taken: Make operational and financial decisions in light of a strong or weak dollar. For example, a weak dollar will allow a MNC to promote sales overseas more competitively.

CHAPTER 34

Reporting on Liabilities

Liabilities must be tracked to determine how much is owed, to whom, and when it is due. A crucial question is Does the company have sufficient resources to pay its debts?

- An aging of payables is presented in Exhibit 34-1.
- Exhibit 34-2 shows the monthly debt balances in accounts payable.
- Exhibit 34-3 reports on loans taken out by the company, including loan amount, term period, interest rate, and due date.

EXHIBIT 34-1
MONTHLY AGING PAYABLES REPORT

Supplier	Total	1-30 days	31-60 days	Past due 61-90 days	Seriously past due 91-120 days
Kravis	$20,000	$20,000			
Merrill	30,000		26,000		4,000
Blake	15,000	1,000	10,000	4,000	
Winston	40,000		40,000		
Durham	50,000	20,000	25,000	5,000	
Dallas	10,000			10,000	
Lake	5,000				5,000

Purpose: To assist in cash management

Distribution: Financial analyst, accounts payable supervisor, treasurer, CFO

Use: To avoid backlash from unpaid suppliers and other adverse effects on credit rating

Action to be taken: Carefully monitor due dates of payables; give priority to the oldest.

EXHIBIT 34-2
MONTHLY DEBIT BALANCES IN ACCOUNTS PAYABLE
REPORT

Name of Customer	Amount	Reason
Harris Corporation	$60,000	Return of merchandise after payment was made
White Company	50,000	Advance payment before being billed
Mavis, Inc.	30,000	Allowance for defective goods
Westbury Corporation	40,000	Prepayment's before goods were received
Saft, Inc.	20,000	Error in record keeping
Easy Flow, Inc.	15,000	Overpayment

Purpose: To determine how much is owed to the entity by supplier

Distribution: Accounts payable supervisor, treasurer, controller

Use: To monitor and reduce debit balances (If the company prepays before receiving shipment, it loses interest on that money.)

Action to be taken: Install better controls to overpaying suppliers.

EXHIBIT 34-3
REPORTING ON CURRENT LOANS

Amount	Term	Interest Rate (%)	Date of Loan	Due Date of Loan
$100,000	4 years	8	4/1/20x1	4/1/20x5
200,000	3 years	7	7/1/20x1	7/1/20x4
250,000	3 years	10	3/31/20x2	3/31/20x5
400,000	1 year	6	1/1/20x3	1/1/20x4
500,000	2 years	8	6/15/20x3	6/15/20x5
300,000	1 year	9	3/1/20x3	3/1/20x4

Purpose: To show how much a company has borrowed and the dates to maturity

Distribution: Treasurer, chief financial officer, payables manager

Use: To determine the company's ability to payoff loan commitments and reduce financing cost

Action to be taken: Modify loan agreements based on liquidity and cost concerns.

CHAPTER 35

Audit Reporting and Controls

Security issues are a very important part of the audit process.

- Exhibit 35-1, on general security issues, emphasizes the need for a written security policy and mandatory compliance with management controls.

- Exhibit 35-2 is concerned with restricting access to computer data and facilities.

- Exhibit 35-3 analyzes security controls: Is there adequate segregation of incompatible duties? Rotation of personnel? Protection of data? Surprise inspections and periodic internal audits are crucial.

- Exhibit 35-4 deals with people. It highlights the need to check references and verify a prospective employee's background. There should be written policies, and violations should be penalized.

- Exhibit 35-5 highlights contingency planning. It speaks to an organization's preparedness for emergencies. It emphasizes that both long-term and short-term contingency plans should be in writing.

EXHIBIT 35-1
GENERAL SECURITY ISSUES

(No response indicates a potential vulnerability)	Yes	No	Don't Know or Not Applicable
1. Is there a written policy on security management?	☐	☐	☐
2. Is responsibility for computer security assigned to a specific individual or a department?	☐	☐	☐
3. Is each software purchased by the company reviewed for security requirements?	☐	☐	☐
4. Are there written procedures to protect a company's copyrights, patents, and trade secrets?	☐	☐	☐
5. Are contracts with governmental entities reviewed for special security and confidentiality requirements.	☐	☐	☐
6. Are management controls being followed?	☐	☐	☐
7. Is management concerned about antisocial behavior?	☐	☐	☐
8. Does management seem to have ethics?	☐	☐	☐

Purpose: To assess organizational security

Distribution: Security officer, Internal Audit department

Use: To identify potential risks

Action to be taken: Weaknesses in controls should be corrected.

EXHIBIT 35-2
ACCESS SECURITY

(No response indicates a potential vulnerability)	Yes	No	Don't Know or Not Applicable
1. Is access restricted to sensitive data files?	☐	☐	☐
2. Is access to program documentation and source code restricted?	☐	☐	☐
3. Are the password procedures adequate?	☐	☐	☐
4. Are guards used to monitor access to sensitive areas?	☐	☐	☐
5. Are dogs used to restrict access to sensitive areas?	☐	☐	☐
6. Are all employees required to carry an ID card?	☐	☐	☐
7. Is there a security officer?	☐	☐	☐
8. Is there a written security policy?	☐	☐	☐
9. Are password files encrypted?	☐	☐	☐
10. Are controls in place to prevent and detect security violations?	☐	☐	☐
11. Are users given the minimum access needed to perform their duties?	☐	☐	☐
12. Is user access restricted to specific files, applications, or servers?	☐	☐	☐
13. Is modem access secure? Are techniques such as callback used?	☐	☐	☐
14. Is access to live files restricted to programmers?	☐	☐	☐
15. Is file maintenance restricted to specific individuals?	☐	☐	☐
16. Is there a process in place to grant access?	☐	☐	☐
17. Are access levels reviewed by internal auditors on a periodic basis?	☐	☐	☐

Purpose: To assess access security

Distribution: Security officer, Internal Audit department, computer facilities manager, EDP manager

Use: To identify potential risks

Action to be taken: Weaknesses in controls should be corrected.

EXHIBIT 35-3
SECURITY CONTROLS

(No response indicates a potential vulnerability)	Yes	No	Don't Know or Not Applicable
1. Are audit trails maintained throughout application systems?	☐	☐	☐
2. Is there an independent review and testing of application controls?	☐	☐	☐
3. Is authorization required for changes to computer programs?	☐	☐	☐
4. Is there segregation of activities between programming and computer operations?	☐	☐	☐
5. Is there segregation of activities between clerical controls and computer operations?	☐	☐	☐
6. Is program development separate from program testing?	☐	☐	☐
7. Are personnel assignments rotated?	☐	☐	☐
8. Are dual controls used so that it is not possible to commit fraud in the absence of collusion?	☐	☐	☐
9. Are personnel bonded?	☐	☐	☐
10. Is there separation of duties?	☐	☐	☐
11. Is there rotation of duties?	☐	☐	☐
12. Are surprise inspections made?	☐	☐	☐
13. Are there periodic internal audits?	☐	☐	☐
14. Does the company have a written policy that prohibits full-time personnel from obtaining outside employment or moonlighting?	☐	☐	☐
15. Does the company have a written policy prohibiting the acceptance of gifts or entertainment from suppliers, vendors, contractors?	☐	☐	☐
16. Does the company have a written policy prohibiting the bribing of customers?	☐	☐	☐
17. Does the company have a written policy prohibiting the fixing of prices with competitors?	☐	☐	☐
18. Does the company have a written policy prohibiting gambling on the job?	☐	☐	☐
19. Does the company have a written policy prohibiting drug and alcohol abuse?	☐	☐	☐
20. Does the company have a written policy prohibiting the playing of computer games or surfing the net?	☐	☐	☐
21. Does the company have a written policy prohibiting the lending of keys, ID cards, badges, etc. to unauthorized individuals?	☐	☐	☐

EXHIBIT 35-3
SECURITY CONTROLS, *Cont'd*

			Don't Know or
(No response indicates a potential vulnerability)	**Yes**	**No**	**Not Applicable**
22. Does the company have a written policy prohibiting the disclosure of computer passwords to unauthorized individuals?	☐	☐	☐
23. Are there controls for smoke and fire detection?	☐	☐	☐
24. Are there controls for water detection?	☐	☐	☐
25. Are there redundant components in computer system?	☐	☐	☐
26. Are management controls properly designed?	☐	☐	☐
27. Are there audit controls?	☐	☐	☐

Purpose: To assess security controls

Distribution: Security officer, Internal Audit department, computer facilities manager, EDP manager

Use: To identify potential risks

Action to be taken: Weaknesses in controls should be corrected.

EXHIBIT 35-4
CONTINGENCY PLANNING

(No response indicates a potential vulnerability)	Yes	No	Don't Know or Not Applicable
1. Has the responsibility for creating and maintaining contingency plans been established?	☐	☐	☐
2. Is there a long-term contingency plan?	☐	☐	☐
3. Is there a short-term contingency plan?	☐	☐	☐
4. Are there "Hot Sites," "Warm Sites," or "Cold Sites" contingency facilities?	☐	☐	☐
5. Has a cost-benefit analysis been conducted to determine insurance needs?	☐	☐	☐
6. Is an uninterruptible power supply (UPS) used?	☐	☐	☐
7. Is a full-scale standby power facility available for long-term power outages?	☐	☐	☐
8. Are data files backed up periodically?	☐	☐	☐
9. Are backup copies of data files stored in a secure remote site?	☐	☐	☐
10. Are vital records and documentation stored in a secure remote site?	☐	☐	☐
11. Are there redundant pathways in transmission lines?	☐	☐	☐
12. Are there backup dial lines?	☐	☐	☐
13. Have natural disasters, such as earthquakes, floods, tornadoes been considered in contingency planning?	☐	☐	☐
14. Has consideration been given to vital records management, including backup of data files and software?	☐	☐	☐
15. Has consideration been given to intentional and accidental threats such as strikes, sabotage, disgruntled employees, terrorism, and human errors or omissions?	☐	☐	☐
16. Are preventive actions taken to reduce threats and vulnerabilities?	☐	☐	☐
17. Is there a written plan for taking action during an emergency?	☐	☐	☐
18. Have insurance company requirements to maintain coverage been met?	☐	☐	☐
19. Is management aware of its responsibilities under the Foreign Corrupt Practices Act (FCPA)?	☐	☐	☐
20. Is management aware of its responsibilities for retaining records for tax and regulatory purposes?	☐	☐	☐
21. Has software related failures and malfunctions been considered?	☐	☐	☐

EXHIBIT 35-4
CONTINGENCY PLANNING, *Cont'd*

(No response indicates a potential vulnerability)	Yes	No	Don't Know or Not Applicable
22. Has the contingency plan been adequately tested?	☐	☐	☐
23. Has recovery time been determined?	☐	☐	☐
24. Is the contingency plan updated at periodic intervals as necessary?	☐	☐	☐
25. Are personnel aware of their responsibilities under the contingency plan?	☐	☐	☐
26. Are personnel trained on contingency plan, including when subsequent changes are made?	☐	☐	☐
27. Is there equipment insurance coverage when it is in a remote site (such as at a client's office) or in transit?	☐	☐	☐
28. Is there business interruption and extra-expense insurance coverage?	☐	☐	☐
29. Is there insurance coverage for professional liability?	☐	☐	☐
30. When leasing equipment, has the liability for each party been determined?	☐	☐	☐
31. Are insurance needs reviewed on a periodic basis to prevent under or over insurance?	☐	☐	☐
32. Is there crime insurance?	☐	☐	☐
33. Is there errors and omissions insurance?	☐	☐	☐
34. Is there insurance for electrical disturbance?	☐	☐	☐
35. Are there emergency measures in place for recovery after disaster?	☐	☐	☐

Purpose: To assess an organization's ability to deal with a disaster

Distribution: Internal Audit department, computer facilities manager, EDP manager, senior management

Use: To identify potential risks

Action to be taken: Weaknesses should be corrected.

EXHIBIT 35-5
PERSONNEL SECURITY

(No response indicates a potential vulnerability)	Yes	No	Don't Know or Not Applicable
1. Are employees required to sign a confidentiality agreement?	☐	☐	☐
2. Are an applicant's references and background fully checked before employment?	☐	☐	☐
3. Are new personnel trained on company security practices?	☐	☐	☐
4. Are all materials, including ID cards, keys, and passes, returned by employees upon termination?	☐	☐	☐
5. Are educational achievements of applicants verified?	☐	☐	☐
6. Are references checked of applicants?	☐	☐	☐
7. Are previous employers of applicant contacted?	☐	☐	☐
8. Are criminal convictions checked for applicants?	☐	☐	☐
9. Are applicants in sensitive positions required to undergo a polygraph test or voice stress analysis?	☐	☐	☐
10. Are psychological diagnostic tests used?	☐	☐	☐
11. Are new employees required to undergo mandatory security orientation training?	☐	☐	☐
12. Are there written rules of ethical employee behavior?	☐	☐	☐
13. Are there job enrichment programs?	☐	☐	☐
14. Is there tuition reimbursement for employees?	☐	☐	☐
15. Are there written job descriptions?	☐	☐	☐
16. Are there standards for performance?	☐	☐	☐
17. Are performance appraisals conducted on a regular periodic basis?	☐	☐	☐
18. Are personnel penalized for violating security policies?	☐	☐	☐
19. Is there a background security check performed for temporary, part-time, or contract employees?	☐	☐	☐
20. Is a log kept for personnel working after normal business hours?	☐	☐	☐
21. Are personnel guided when performance is below acceptable levels?	☐	☐	☐
22. Are rewards such as pay, benefits, job security, promotion opportunities, etc. perceived to be inadequate?	☐	☐	☐
23. Are job responsibilities clearly defined?	☐	☐	☐
24. Is there accountability in job assignments?	☐	☐	☐
25. Is there recognition for good performance?	☐	☐	☐

EXHIBIT 35-5
PERSONNEL SECURITY, *Cont'd*

			Don't Know or
(No response indicates a potential vulnerability)	**Yes**	**No**	**Not Applicable**
26. Is feedback on job performance adequate?	☐	☐	☐
27. Is mediocre performance considered unacceptable?	☐	☐	☐
28. Are resources needed to meet requirements provided?	☐	☐	☐
29. Do personnel have enough time to complete assignments?	☐	☐	☐
30. Is management fair and impartial in recruiting, compensating, and evaluating employees?	☐	☐	☐

Purpose: To assess personnel related security problems

Distribution: Internal Audit department, personnel manager, security officer, senior management

Use: To identify potential risks

Action to be taken: Weaknesses should be corrected.

CHAPTER 36

Insurance Analysis

How adequate is your company's insurance? Insurance is designed to reduce risk exposure. Inadequate insurance protection can bankrupt a company.

- A quarterly insurance report can be found in Exhibit 36-1, showing for each major asset the insurance premium, replacement cost, insured value, coverage period, risk rating, and number of insurance carriers.

- Exhibit 36-2 provides quarterly statistics for casualties, theft, product liability, malpractice, and employee dishonesty.

- Insurance for major types of asset by geographic region is found in Exhibit 36-3.

- Exhibits 36-4 and 36-5 show a yearly insurance analysis by asset in terms of insurance coverage, fair market value of property, insurance premiums, losses incurred, and insurance recoveries.

- Exhibit 36-6 is a semiannual report on insurance premiums relative to losses.

- Finally, Exhibit 36-7 is an annual report of prepaid insurance listing each insurer, policy number, type of coverage, policy amount and period, and prepayments made.

EXHIBIT 36-1
QUARTERLY INSURANCE REPORT

Insured Asset	Insurance Premium	Expected Replacement Cost	Insured Value	Term of Coverage	Risk Rating	No. of Insurance Carriers
Machinery	$17,000	$580,000	$550,000	1 year	high	2
Office equipment	6,000	290,000	290,000	2 years	low	1
Vehicles	12,000	185,000	175,000	1 year	moderate	3
Building	20,000	690,000	700,000	1 year	moderate	1
Inventory	16,000	405,000	360,000	3 years	high	4
Furniture	10,000	110,000	100,000	2 years	low	2

Purpose: To assure insurance coverage of assets is appropriate

Distribution: Insurance manager, property manager

Use: To bring coverage in line with expected replacement cost to stay within policy terms

Action to be taken: Increase or decrease insured values to maintain adequate insurance protection.

EXHIBIT 36-2
QUARTERLY INSURANCE COVERAGE STATISTICS

Type of Insured Item	Policy Value	Policy Period	Insurance Premiums	Deductible
Casualty	$3,000,000	1 year	$18,000	$100,000
Theft	2,000,000	18 months	15,000	80,000
Product liability	1,000,000	2 years	10,000	75,000
Malpractice	800,000	3 years	7,000	60,000
Employee dishonesty	500,000	6 months	5,000	40,000

Purpose: To monitor insurance coverage

Distribution: Insurance manager, personnel manager, head of law department, property manager

Use: To ascertain if the company is adequately protected against financial losses

Action to be taken: Modify insurance coverage based on experience.

EXHIBIT 36-3
QUARTERLY REPORT OF INSURANCE POLICIES ON ASSETS

Insured Asset	Geographic Area 1	Geographic Area 2	Geographic Area 3	Total
Autos	$100,000	$120,000	$140,000	$360,000
Truck	200,000	210,000	180,000	590,000
Inventory	160,000	150,000	170,000	480,000
Machinery	300,000	260,000	280,000	840,000
Equipment	400,000	300,000	250,000	950,000
Furniture and fixtures	60,000	50,000	60,000	170,000
Building	900,000	1,000,000	800,000	2,700,000
Leasehold improvements	50,000	30,000	10,000	90,000
Total	$2,170,000	$2,120,000	$1,890,000	$6,180,000

Purpose: To determine insurance protection of major assets by region

Distribution: Insurance manager, controller

Use: To appraise adequacy of insurance coverage and risk exposure in different localities

Action to be taken: Modify insurance coverage based on risk exposure.

EXHIBIT 36-4
YEARLY INSURANCE ANALYSIS

Type of Property	Insurance Coverage	Fair Market Value	Total Premiums	Losses Incurred	Insurance Recoveries	Net Losses
Building	$3,000,000	$2,800,000	$35,000	-	-	-
Equipment	1,500,000	1,500,000	26,000	$80,000	$65,000	$15,000
Machinery	1,000,000	900,000	24,000	110,000	100,000	10,000
Autos	130,000	120,000	9,000	25,000	21,000	4,000
Trucks	200,000	185,000	13,000	38,000	35,000	3,000
Furniture	75,000	70,000	2,000	-	-	-

Purpose: To determine the adequacy of insurance protection

Distribution: Insurance manager, property manager

Use: To analyze loss experience and to ascertain whether assets are properly insured

Action to be taken: Increase or reduce coverage or deductibles as needed.

EXHIBIT 36-5
ANNUAL INSURANCE EXPERIENCE

Category of Coverage	Period of Coverage	Number of Losses	Amount of Losses	Reimbursed Amount	Net Loss
Theft	1/1/x2-12/31/x2	2	$80,000	$70,000	$10,000
Casualty	3/1/x2-3/1/x4	3	140,000	110,000	30,000
Product	7/1/x2-7/1/x5	5	250,000	200,000	50,000
Employee dishonesty	1/1/x2-12/31/x3	0	-	-	-
Vehicle	1/1/x2-12/31/x2	4	65,000	63,000	2,000
Malpractice	1/1/x2-12/31/x6	0	-	-	-
Flood damage	1/1/x2-7/1/x3	1	25,000	25,000	-

Purpose: To assess insurance coverage by major type and policy period

Distribution: Insurance manager, financial analyst, controller

Use: To analyze loss incidence and whether the company is being adequately reimbursed by insurers

Action to be taken: Change policy limits and coverage based on loss experience.

EXHIBIT 36-6
SEMI-ANNUAL REPORT ON INSURANCE PREMIUMS RELATIVE TO LOSSES

Insurance Categorization	Period of Coverage	Insurance Premium	Losses	Losses Relative to Premium Paid
Auto and truck	20x1-19x2	$80,000	$30,000	38 %
Property	20x1-19x3	100,000	70,000	70
Product liability	20x1-19x4	60,000	4,000	7
Executive misrepresentation	20x1-19x2	25,000	-	0
Employee liability	20x1-19x2	40,000	50,000	125
Workers compensation	20x1-19x2	6,000	500	8
Life insurance	20x1-19x5	25,000	-	0

Purpose: To compare trends in the sufficiency of insurance relative with losses incurred

Distribution: Insurance manager, financial analyst, CFO

Use: To decide if the business is properly insuring itself

Action to be taken: Adjust coverage based on loss experience.

EXHIBIT 36-7
YEARLY REPORT OF PREPAID INSURANCE

Insurer	Policy Number	Type of Insurance	Coverage	Period	Prepaid Insurance 1/1/2005	Prepayments	Expensed	Prepaid Insurance 12/31/2005
Metropolitan	246802	building	$1,800,000	2 years	$80,000	$15,000	$12,000	$83,000
Prudential	137912	equipment	1,000,000	1 year	60,000	10,000	4,000	66,000
AIG	410614	furniture	700,000	3 years	40,000	5,000	3,000	42,000
Travelers	183712	services	500,000	4 years	25,000	3,000	5,000	23,000
Geico	412913	vehicles	300,000	1 year	20,000	-	4,000	16,000
Colonial	321161	product	2,000,000	2 years	30,000	7,000	6,000	31,000

Purpose: To review the amount of prepaid insurance by type

Distribution: Insurance manager, CFO

Use: To analyze prepaid insurance assets

Action to be taken: Lower insurance costs by revising coverage and terms as needed and by reducing prepayments to previous levels.

CHAPTER 37

Operations Management Reports

Operations management reporting provides a basis for alerting top management on many key areas of concern about the company's financial position as a going concern.

- Exhibits 37-1 through 37-4 cover various key financial and operating ratios including return on assets (ROA), return on equity (ROE), residual/economic value added, book value per share, earnings per share (EPS), market price per share, and growth rates.
- Exhibit 37-7 keys in on profit variances and its main components.
- Going beyond a growth in earnings, Exhibits 37-8 and 37-9 measure the stability and variability of earnings.

Responsibility reporting establishes a basis for segregating costs by responsibility centers. It is a scorecard for assessing how well subunits of the company are doing in controlling the costs and contributing revenues associated with the activities managed.

- Exhibits 37-5 and 37-6 analyze operating results compared with budgets for profit center managers and are useful in monitoring segments of the company such as products, branches, and stores. They summarize divisional results for top management.

Financial ratios provide vital pieces of information about the company's financial condition. Horizontal analysis looks at trends in the accounts over the years. Industry comparisons tell how the company fares in the industry.

- Exhibits 37-9 through 37-11 show these analyses so that the sound financial assessment of the company can be made. A group of selected financial ratios may assist management to predict a company's potential trouble down the road.

- Exhibits 37-14 through 37-16 introduce some powerful bankruptcy prediction models: Altman's Z score, Lambda Index, degree of relative liquidity, and Wilcox's gambler's ruin models.

- Exhibits 37-17 and 37-18 present Du Pont systems. They provide a useful guide for managers' efforts to increase their performance and stockholders' return. By breaking down the return on investment (ROI) into net profit margin and total asset turnover, a weakness can be recognized. By using financial leverage (use of debt), it is possible to increase return to stockholders.

EXHIBIT 37-1
MONTHLY REPORT TO BOARD OF DIRECTORS

	Actual	Budget	Variance
Net sales: Current month	$675,000	$750,000	$(75,000)
Year-to-date (YTD)	4,250,000	3,980,000	270,000
Net income: Current month	75,000	90,000	(15,000)
YTD	310,000	325,000	(15,000)
Net income as % of sales: Current month	11.11%	12.00%	-0.89%
YTD	7.29%	8.17%	-0.87%
Cash	$125,000	$120,000	$5,000
Receivables	562,000	555,550	6,450
Inventory	1,002,500	1,100,000	(97,500)
Current liabilities	785,000	765,000	20,000
Current ratio	1.48	1.65	(0.17)
Property additions: YTD	134,000	135,000	(1,000)
Long-term debt: Additions	97,000	100,000	(3,000)
Pay-offs	45,000	60,000	(15,000)
Return on assets (ROA)	10.00%	11.00%	-1.00%
Return on equity (ROE)	14.00%	15.00%	-1.00%
Book value per share	$4.78	$4.95	$(0.17)
Earnings per share (EPS)	$3.88	$3.95	$(0.07)
Market value per share	$12.50	$13.00	$(0.50)

Purpose: To summarize key financial and operating data for board use

Distribution: Board of directors

Use: To keep board current on the company's financial situation

Action to be taken: Alert the board to reasons for unfavorable or unusual financial measurement and ratios; recommend remedies.

EXHIBIT 37-2
ANNUAL PERFORMANCE REPORT

	Actual	Budget	Actual over Budget
Net sales	$12,678,900	$12,500,000	$178,900
Net income	678,950	700,000	(21,050)
Total debt	1,657,800	1,500,000	157,800
Total equity	4,250,000	4,300,000	(50,000)
Return on assets (ROA)	11.49%	12.07%	-0.58%
Return on equity (ROE)	15.98%	16.28%	-0.30%
Residual income (RI)	$256,000	$250,000	$6,000
Debt/equity ratio	39.01%	34.88%	4.12%
Compound earnings growth-3 yrs	7.88%		
Compound sales growth-3 yrs	13.65%		
Compound asset growth-3 yrs	9.98%		
Debt/equity ratio-3 yrs	1.12		

Purpose: To summarize key financial measures

Distribution: Directors, CEO, chief operation officer, president, top management

Use: To monitor company financial performance

Action to be taken: Alert management to reasons for unfavorable or unusual financial measurements and ratios; make recommendations for remedies.

EXHIBIT 37-3
MONTHLY KEY DATA REPORT

	Actual	Budget	Variance
Total assets	$6,650,000	$6,570,000	$80,000
Asset turnover	3.40	3.50	-0.10
Margin on net sales	4.40%	4.50%	-0.10%
Return on total assets (ROA)	14.96%	15.75%	-0.79%
Economic value added	$450,000	$500,000	$(50,000)
Employees	165	170	-5
Unit sales per employee	$325	$330	$(5.00)
Dollar sales per employee	$12,000,000	$1,180,000	$10,820,000
Order backlog	3,200	3,500	-300
Factory utilization:			
Production line 1	75.00%	80.00%	-5.00%
Production line 2	65.00%	60.00%	5.00%
Production line 3	78.00%	80.00%	-2.00%
Production line 4	70.00%	65.00%	5.00%

Purpose: To summarize key financial and operating data for CEO

Distribution: CEO, chief operation officer, president, top management

Use: To monitor the company's financial situation and facilities utilization

Action to be taken: Alert management to reasons for unfavorable or unusual financial measurements and ratios; make recommendations for remedies.

EXHIBIT 37-4
PERCENTAGE PERFORMANCE REPORT

Budget Item	% of Budget Achieved	Comments and Remarks
Receivables	92%	Strong cash collection efforts reducing receivables
Inventories	98%	Clearance sales
Funded debt	110%	Equipment loans to fund new addition in facility
Property additions	112%	New store
Sales	105%	New store took off faster than anticipated
Cost of sales:		
Direct material	100%	
Direct labor	102%	Higher union demand settled
Factory overhead	104%	Worker's compensation and cleanup costs rose
Gross profit	101%	
Operating expenses:		
Selling expense	98%	Less advertising than planned
General and		
administrative expense	107%	Legal and consulting fees way up
Interest expense	103%	More short-term debt paid off
Net income	102%	

Purpose: To analyze variances of profits and some balance sheet items

Distribution: CEO, chief operation officer, president, top management

Use: To monitor key measures of efficiency

Action to be taken: Alert management to unfavorable or unusual financial measurements and ratios; recommend remedies.

EXHIBIT 37-5
CEO'S MONTHLY OPERATING REPORT

	Actual	Budget	Variance
Net sales	$7,834,500	$7,950,000	$(115,500)
Materials	399,000	400,000	(1,000)
Labor	1,567,890	1,580,000	(12,110)
Overhead	2,546,700	2,450,000	96,700
Selling, general and administrative	734,000	740,000	(6,000)
Operating profits	2,586,910	2,780,000	(193,090)
Non-operating items	234,000	230,000	4,000
Net income before taxes	$2,352,910	$2,550,000	$(197,090)
Backlog:			
Division A	$542,000	$555,000	$(13,000)
Division B	232,000	230,000	2,000
Cash summary:			
Beginning cash	$95,000	$95,000	$-
Collections	654,000	650,000	4,000
Cash disbursements	(589,000)	(600,000)	11,000
Ending cash	$160,000	$145,000	$15,000
Receivables:			
Current	$375,000	$400,000	$(25,000)
Past due	199,000	200,000	(1,000)
Bad debts	(45,000)	(30,000)	(15,000)
Total	$574,000	$600,000	$(26,000)
Inventories	$789,000	$785,000	$4,000
Accounts payable	456,000	450,000	6,000
Head count:			
Division A	123	125	-2
Division B	85	90	-5
Corporate	34	35	-1
	242	250	-8

Purpose: To summarize key financial and operating data

Distribution: CEO, chief operation officer, president, top management

Use: To keep managers current on the company's financial and operating situation

Action to be taken: Alert top managers to unfavorable or unusual financial measurements and ratios; recommend remedies.

EXHIBIT 37-6
PERFORMANCE REPORT BY RESPONSIBILITY CENTER
(in thousands)

	Budget		Variance	
Operating Income and Expense:	**This Month**	**Year to Date**	**This Month**	**Year to Date**
Northern California District				
District manager office expense	$(145)	$(605)	$(8)	$(20)
Berkeley branch	475	1,728	(3)	(11)
Palo Alto branch	500	1,800	19	90
Oakland branch	310	1,220	31	110
Others	600	2,560	47	130
Operating income	$1,740	$6,703	$86	$299
Berkeley Branch				
Branch manager office expense	$(20)	$(306)	$(5)	$4
Store X	48	148	(1)	(5)
Store Y	64	226	9	9
Store Z	38	160	4	10
Other	345	1,500	(10)	(29)
Operating income	$475	$1,728	$(3)	$(11)
Store Y				
Sales	$170	$690	$8	$12
Expenses				
Food expense	40	198	5	14
Supplies	15	62	(3)	(2)
Payroll	24	98	(4)	(5)
Repairs & maintenance	5	21	1	(2)
General	12	45	-	(2)
Depreciation	10	40	-	-
Total expenses	106	464	(1)	3
Operating income	$64	$226	$9	$9

Purpose: To evaluate responsibility center performance

Distribution: CEO, chief operation officer, president, top management

Use: To evaluate performance at various levels

Action to be taken: Alert top management to unfavorable variances for responsibility center.

EXHIBIT 37-7
QUARTERLY PROFIT RECORD

Operating profit:	
Budgeted	$777,450
Actual	710,790
Variance from budget (unfavorable)	$(66,660)
Breakdowns for profit variance:	
Sales volume	21,456
Selling prices	(4,320)
Sales mix	18,765
Material purchase price	2,425
Material usage	4,568
Material mix	4,598
Material yield	3,423
Labor efficiency	8,123
Labor rate	(1,180)
Labor mix	5,400
Overhead spending	3,402
Selling expenses	(2,345)
General and administrative	2,345
	$66,660

Purpose: To analyze profit variance

Distribution: CEO, chief operation officer, president, top management

Use: To evaluate performance against projections

Action to be taken: Alert top management to unfavorable variances for sales, volume, mix, and costs.

EXHIBIT 37-8
INSTABILITY INDEX IN EARNINGS

Year	Quarter	Period	Earnings per Share (EPS)	Earnings Trend*	Difference	Difference Squared
1	1	1	$0.25	$0.17	$0.08	$0.0064
	2	2	0.28	0.22	0.06	0.0036
	3	3	0.29	0.27	0.02	0.0004
	4	4	0.30	0.32	-0.02	0.0004
2	1	5	0.33	0.37	-0.04	0.0016
	2	6	0.34	0.42	-0.08	0.0064
	3	7	0.40	0.47	-0.07	0.0049
	4	8	0.43	0.52	-0.09	0.0081
3	1	9	0.52	0.57	-0.05	0.0025
	2	10	0.61	0.62	-0.01	0.0001
	3	11	0.71	0.67	0.04	0.0016
	4	12	0.85	0.72	0.13	0.0169
					Total	0.0529
				Instability index =		0.0664

*A simple trend equation ($y = a + bt$) solved by regression is used to determine trend earnings.

Purpose: To calculate the stability of earnings

Distribution: Directors, treasurer, controller, chief investment officer, CFO, CEO

Use: To monitor variability in the earnings stream

Action to be taken: Reduce any wide fluctuation in earnings, since it implies corporate instability.

EXHIBIT 37-9
EARNINGS SURPRISES:
EARNINGS ABOVE (BELOW) EXPECTATIONS

Year	Quarter	Period	Earnings per Share (EPS)	Earnings Expectations	Difference	Difference Squared
1	1	1	$0.25	$0.24	$0.01	$0.0001
	2	2	0.28	0.30	-0.02	0.0004
	3	3	0.29	0.30	-0.01	0.0001
	4	4	0.30	0.33	-0.03	0.0009
2	1	5	0.33	0.32	0.01	0.0001
	2	6	0.34	0.30	0.04	0.0016
	3	7	0.40	0.38	0.02	0.0004
	4	8	0.43	0.50	-0.07	0.0049
3	1	9	0.52	0.55	-0.03	0.0009
	2	10	0.61	0.57	0.04	0.0016
	3	11	0.71	0.65	0.06	0.0036
	4	12	0.85	0.75	0.10	0.0100
					Total	0.0246
			Earnings above (below) expectations =			0.0453

Purpose: To calculate variations in earnings against public expectations

Distribution: Directors, treasurer, controller, chief investment officer, CFO, CEO

Use: To monitor variability in the earnings stream against earnings estimates by brokerage house analysts

Action to be taken: Evaluate quality of earnings recognizing that wide fluctuations could be a sign of stock price volatility. Though negative earnings surprises can have a devastating impact on stock prices, upward surprises can be beneficial because they reflect a positive earnings picture.

EXHIBIT 37-10
COMPARATIVE INCOME STATEMENT (in thousands)
FOR THE YEARS ENDED DECEMBER 31, 2002, 2001, 2000

	2002	2001	2000	Incr. or 2002-2001	Decr. 2001-2000	% Incr. 2002-2001	or Decr. 2001-2000
Sales	$98.3	$120.0	$56.6	($21.7)	$63.4	-18.1%	112.0%
Sales Return & Allowances	$18.0	$10.0	$4.0	$8.0	$6.0	80.0%	150.0%
Net Sales	$80.3	$110.0	$52.6	($29.7)	$57.4	-27.0%	109.1%
Cost of Goods Sold	$52.0	$63.0	$28.0	($11.0)	$35.0	-17.5%	125.0%
Gross Profit	$28.3	$47.0	$24.6	($18.7)	$22.4	-39.8%	91.1%
Operating Expenses							
Selling Expenses	$12.0	$13.0	$11.0	($1.0)	$2.0	-7.7%	18.2%
General Expenses	$5.0	$8.0	$3.0	($3.0)	$5.0	-37.5%	166.7%
Total Operating Expenses	$17.0	$21.0	$14.0	($4.0)	$7.0	-19.0%	50.0%
Income from Operations	$11.3	$26.0	$10.6	($14.7)	$15.4	-56.5%	145.3%
Nonoperating Income	$4.0	$1.0	$2.0	$3.0	($1.0)	300.0%	-50.0%
Income before Interest & Taxes	$15.3	$27.0	$12.6	($11.7)	$14.4	-43.3%	114.3%
Interest Expense	$2.0	$2.0	$1.0	$0.0	$1.0	0.0%	100.0%
Income before Taxes	$13.3	$25.0	$11.6	($11.7)	$13.4	-46.8%	115.5%
Income Taxes (40%)	$5.3	$10.0	$4.6	($4.7)	$5.4	-46.8%	115.5%
Net Income	$8.0	$15.0	$7.0	($7.0)	$8.0	-46.8%	115.5%

Purpose: To show common size income statements over time

Distribution: CFO, CEO, chief operating officer, president, top management

Use: To see the trend in various income statement items to determine how a company is doing over time

Action to be taken: Take appropriate corrective actions necessary to fix unfavorable ratios.

EXHIBIT 37-11

COMPARATIVE BALANCE SHEET (in thousands) DECEMBER 31, 2002, 2001, 2000

	2002	2001	2000	Incr. or 2002-2001	Decr. 2001-2000	% Incr. 2002-2001	or Decr. 2001-2000
ASSETS							
Current assets:							
Cash	$28	$36	$36	-8	0	-22.2%	0.0%
Marketable securities	22	15	7	7	8	46.7%	114.3%
Accounts receivable	21	16	10	5	6	31.3%	60.0%
Inventory	53	46	49	7	-3	15.2%	-6.1%
Total current assets	124	113	102	11	11	9.7%	10.8%
Plant and equipment	103	91	83	12	8	13.2%	9.6%
Total Assets	227	204	185	23	19	11.3%	10.3%
LIABILITIES							
Current liabilities	56	50	51	6	-1	12.0%	-2.0%
Long-term debt	83	74	69	9	5	12.2%	7.2%
Total liabilities	139	124	120	15	4	12.1%	3.3%
STOCKHOLDERS' EQUITY							
Common stock, $10 par, 4,600 shares	46	46	46	0	0	0.0%	0.0%
Retained earnings	42	34	19	8	15	23.5%	78.9%
Total stockholders' equity	88	80	65	8	15	10.0%	23.1%
Total liabilities and stockholders' equity	$227	$204	$185	23	19	11.3%	10.3%

Purpose: To monitor income performance over time

Distribution: CFO, CEO, chief operating officer, president, top management

Use: To identify financial performance problems

Action to be taken: Take action to reverse unfavorable ratios.

EXHIBIT 37-12
SUMMARY OF FINANCIAL RATIOS: TREND AND INDUSTRY COMPARISONS

Ratios	Definitions	2002	2003	Industry	Ind.	Trend	Overall
LIQUIDITY							
Net working capital	Current assets - current liabilities	63	68	56	good	good	good
Current Ratio	Current assets/current liabilities	2.26	2.21	2.05	OK	OK	OK
Quick (Acid-test) ratio	(Cash + marketable securities + accounts receivable)/current liabilities	1.34	1.27	1.11	OK	OK	OK
ASSET UTILIZATION							
Accounts receivable turnover	Net credit sales/average accounts receivable	8.46	4.34	5.5	OK	poor	poor
Average collection period	365 days/accounts receivable turnover	43.1 days	84.1 days	66.4 days	OK	poor	poor
Inventory turnover	Cost of goods sold/average inventory	1.33	1.05	1.2	OK	poor	poor
Average age of inventory	365 days/inventory turnover	274.4 days	347.6 days	N/A	N/A	poor	poor
Operating cycle	Average collection period + average age of inventory	317.5 days	431.7 days	N/A	N/A	poor	poor
Total asset turnover	Net sales/average total assets	0.57	0.37	0.44	OK	poor	poor
SOLVENCY							
Debt ratio	Total liabilities/total assets	0.61	0.61	N/A	N/A	OK	OK
Debt-equity ratio	Total liabilities/stockholders' equity	1.55	1.58	1.3	poor	poor	poor
Times interest earned	Income before interest and taxes/interest expense	13.5 times	7.65 times	10 times	OK	poor	poor

EXHIBIT 37-12
SUMMARY OF FINANCIAL RATIOS: TREND AND INDUSTRY COMPARISONS, *Cont'd*

Ratios	Definitions	2002	2003	Industry	Ind.	Trend	Overall
PROFITABILITY							
Gross profit margin	Gross profit/net sales	0.43	0.35	0.48	poor	poor	poor
Profit margin	Net income/net sales	0.14	0.1	0.15	poor	poor	poor
Return on total assets	Net income/average total assets	0.077	0.037	0.1	poor	poor	poor
Return on equity (ROE)	Earnings available to common stockholders/ average stockholders' equity	0.207	0.095	0.27	poor	poor	poor
MARKET VALUE							
Earnings per share (EPS)	(Net income - preferred dividend)/ common shares outstanding	3.26	1.74	4.51	poor	poor	poor
Price/earnings (P/E) ratio	Market price per share/EPS	7.98	6.9	7.12	OK	poor	poor
Book value per share	(Total stockholders' equity - preferred stock)/ common shares outstanding	17.39	19.13	N/A	N/A	good	good
Price/book value ratio	Market price per share/book value per share	1.5	0.63	N/A	N/A	poor	poor
Dividend yield	Dividends per share/market price per share						
Dividend payout	Dividends per share/EPS						

Purpose: To summarize key financial ratio measures

Distribution: Board of directors, CEO, chief operating officer, president, top management

Use: To determine how a company fares in the industry and how it is doing over time

Action to be taken: Take action to reverse unfavorable ratios.

EXHIBIT 37-13
Z-SCORE: PREDICTION OF FINANCIAL DISTRESS[1]

Year	Balance Sheet Current Assets (CA)	Total Assets (TA)	Current Liability/Liability (CL)	Total Liability (TL)	Retained Earnings (RE)	Working Capital (WC)	Income Statement SALES	EBIT[2] or Net worth	Stock Data Market Value (MKT-NW)	Calculations WC/TA (X1)	RE/TA (X2)	EBIT/TA (X3)	MKT-NW/TL (X4)	SALES/TA (X5)	Misc. Graph Values Z Score	TOP GRAY	BOTTOM GRAY	Year
1	3266	5247	1873	3048	1505	1393	8426	719	1122	0.2655	0.2868	0.1370	0.3681	1.6059	3.00	2.99	1.81	1
2	3427	5843	2433	3947	1024	994	6000	-402	1147	0.1701	0.1753	-0.0688	0.2906	1.0269	1.42	2.99	1.81	2
3	2672	5346	1808	3864	600	864	7018	-16	376	0.1616	0.1122	-0.0030	0.0973	1.3128	1.71	2.99	1.81	3
4	1656	3699	1135	3665	-1078	521	4322	-1274	151	0.1408	-0.2914	-0.3444	0.0412	1.1684	-0.18	2.99	1.81	4
5	1388	3362	1367	3119	-1487	21	3600	-231	835	0.0062	-0.4423	-0.0687	0.2677	1.0708	0.39	2.99	1.81	5
6	1412	3249	1257	2947	-1537	155	4861	120	575	0.0477	-0.4731	0.0369	0.1951	1.4962	1.13	2.99	1.81	6
7	1101	2406	988	2364	-1894	113	3508	247	570	0.0470	-0.7872	0.1027	0.2411	1.4580	0.89	2.99	1.81	7
8	698	1925	797	1809	-1889	-99	3357	163	441	-0.0514	-0.9813	0.0847	0.2438	1.7439	0.73	2.99	1.81	8
9	785	1902	836	1259	-1743	-51	3530	219	1011	-0.0268	-0.9164	0.1151	0.8030	1.8559	1.40	2.99	1.81	9
10	1280	4037	1126	1580	150	-154	4082	451	1016	-0.0381	0.0372	0.1117	0.6430	1.0111	1.86	2.99	1.81	10
11	986	3609	761	1257	175	225	4241	303	1269	0.0623	0.0485	0.0840	1.0095	1.1751	2.20	2.99	1.81	11
12	2663	3795	1579	2980	81	1084	3854	111	563	0.2856	0.0994	0.0292	0.1889	1.0155	1.60	2.99	1.81	12
13	2286	3443	1145	2866	332	1141	3259	232	667	0.3314	0.0213	0.0674	0.2326	0.9466	1.84	2.99	1.81	13
14	2472	3627	1152	3289	93	1320	3875	-145	572	0.3639	0.0256	-0.0400	0.1738	1.0684	1.51	2.99	1.81	14
15	2672	5060	1338	4285	-1588	1334	4696	-441	1765	0.2636	-0.3138	-0.0872	0.4119	0.9281	0.76	2.99	1.81	15
16	2870	5056	1810	4239	-1538	1060	5337	158	1469	0.2097	-0.3042	0.0313	0.3466	1.0556	1.19	2.99	1.81	16
17	3310	5566	1111	4696	-1478	2199	6342	262	966	0.3951	-0.2655	0.0471	0.2057	1.1394	1.52	2.99	1.81	17
18	2999	5326	820	4410	-1431	2179	5754	105	738	0.4091	-0.2687	0.0197	0.1673	1.0804	1.36	2.99	1.81	18
19	3203	5516	1267	4496	-1301	1936	6371	242	1374	0.3510	-0.2359	0.0439	0.3055	1.1550	1.57	2.99	1.81	19

[1]To calculate "Z" score for private firms, enter net worth in the MKT-NW column. (For publicly-held companies, enter market value of equity.) [2] EBIT = Earnings before interest and taxes.

Purpose: To monitor potential for bankruptcy

Distribution: Treasurer, cash manager, controller, CFO, CEO

Use: To monitor profitability of a company over time

Action to be taken: If the company is heading for possible trouble, take corrective action, perhaps by curtailing expansion or cutting back on dividends. The Z-score is about 90 percent accurate in forecasting business failure one year in the future; about 80 percent accurate in two years in the future. The following guidelines have been established for classifying firms:

Z-score	Probability of failure
1.8 or less	Very high
1.81 - 2.99	Not sure
3.0 or higher	Unlikely

Z-SCORE GRAPH

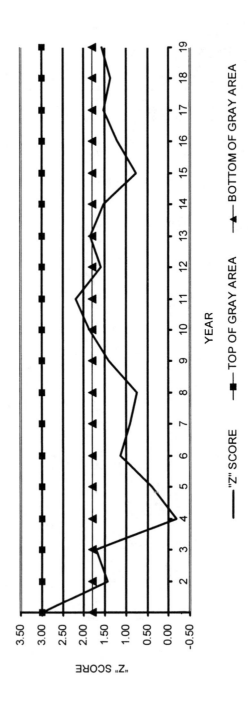

EXHIBIT 37-14
LAMBDA INDEX

Year	1	2	3	4	5	6
Short-term line of credit	$100,000	$100,000	$100,000	$100,000	$100,000	$100,000
Beginning liquid assets	62,933	4,915	15,126	103,197	110,243	253,278
Adjustments						
Initial liquid reserve	162,933	104,915	115,126	203,197	210,243	353,278
Total sources of funds	(58,018)	10,211	88,071	7,046	143,035	(244,843)
Total uses of funds						
Net cash flow	(58,018)	10,211	88,071	7,046	143,035	(244,843)
Ending liquid assets, short-term debt, and adjustments (net)	4,915	15,126	103,197	110,243	253,278	8,435
Ending liquid reserve	104,915	115,126	203,197	210,243	353,278	108,435
Standard deviation	NA	48,245	73,097	59,769	78,245	135,047
Calculated Lambda index	NA	2	3	4	5	1
Additional cash required (remaining) to maintain Lambda of 3.0	NA	29,610	16,095	(30,936)	(118,542)	296,706
Very safe		15	15	15	15	15
Healthy		9	9	9	9	9
Slight - 1 in 20,000		4	4	4	4	4
Low - 1 in 20		2	2	2	2	2

Purpose: To monitor likelihood of bankruptcy   **Distribution:** Treasurer, cash manager, controller, CFO, CEO

Use: To appraise profitability of a company over time

Action to be taken: If a company is heading for possible trouble, take corrective action. The index measures the key aspect of uncertainty in cash-flow measurement by utilizing a sample standard deviation. Guidelines are:

Lambda Score	*Probability of Short-Term Liquidity*
1.64	1 in 20
3.90	1 in 20,000
9.00 or higher	Unlikely

LAMBDA INDEX GRAPH

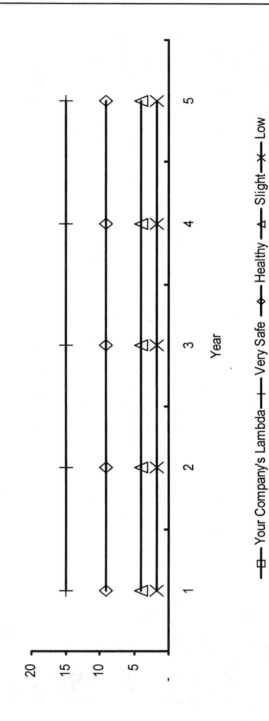

EXHIBIT 37-15
PREDICTING LIQUIDITY PROBLEMS

Year	ACCTS. REC. AR	INVENTORY INV	CURRENT ASSETS CA	CURRENT LIAB. CL	ENDING W.C. E-WC	BEGINNING W.C. B-WC	N.S.V NSV	COST OF SALES COS	NET INCOME NI	NON-CASH EXPENSES NON	OPER. TURNOVER OT=	SALES VALUE OF SVI=	OPERATIONS CASH OCP=	CHANGE WORKING WCC=	TOTAL CASH TCP=	EXPENDI-TURES E=	DEGREE OF RELATIVE DRL=	BASE	Year
1	46746	658880	723684	443752	279932	276638	2252656	1692568	13609	65764	2.4	876910	2138650	3294	2415288	2169989	1.113	1.000	1
2	45050	757051	840686	529690	310996	279932	2234768	1685198	2223	67341	2.1	1003937	2138793	31064	2418725	2134140	1.133	1.000	2
3	29670	649162	816853	400403	416450	310996	2142118	1592984	-25593	66647	2.4	872941	2071704	105454	2382700	1995610	1.194	1.000	3
4	28571	670236	811314	426065	385249	416450	2066589	1499641	30527	38544	2.2	923623	2004580	-31201	2421030	2028719	1.193	1.000	4
5	32614	579651	877937	738837	139100	385249	809457	575467	39297	13216	1.0	815342	778324	-246149	1163573	1003093	1.160	1.000	5
6	32213	509617	583773	412732	171041	139100	2094570	1529598	-53809	56008	2.9	697849	2002150	31941	2141250	2060430	1.039	1.000	6

CALCULATIONS:
OT = NSV / (AR + INV x NSV/COS)
SVI = INV x NSV/COS
WCC = E-WC - B-WC
TCP = B-WC + (OT x SVI)
E = NSV - (NI + NON) - WCC
DRL = TCP / E

Purpose: To calculate relative liquidity

Distribution: Treasurer, cash manager, controller, CFO, CEO

Use: To evaluate the long-term liquidity of the company

Action to be taken: If a company is heading for possible trouble, take corrective action, perhaps by curtailing capital expansion, cutting dividends, or renegotiating debt. The degree of relative liquidity index is used to predict problems. The following guidelines have been established for classifying firms:

DRL Score	*Probability of Short-Term Liquidity*
Less than 1.00	Very high
Higher than 1.00	Unlikely

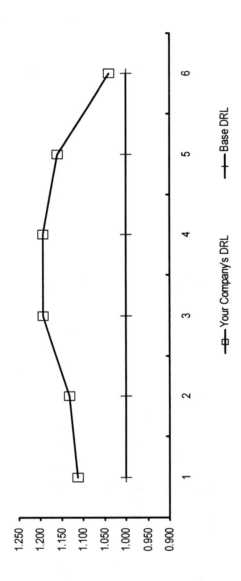

EXHIBIT 37-16
WILCOX'S GAMBLER'S-RUIN FORMULA

Cash	$400,000
Marketable securities	260,000
Accounts receivable ($700,000 x 70%)	490,000
Inventory ($1,000,000 x 70%)	700,000
Prepaid expenses ($300,000 x 70%)	210,000
Other assets ($800,000 x 50%)	400,000
Current liabilities	(900,000)
Long-term liabilities	(1,200,000)
Liquidation value	$360,000

Liquidation value equals:
Cash + marketable securities at market value
Plus: Inventory, accounts receivable, and prepaid expenses at 70% of book value
Plus: Other assets at 50% of book value
Minus: Current liabilities
Minus: Long-term liabilities

Purpose: To project a company's liquidation value

Distribution: Treasurer, cash manager, controller, CFO, CEO

Use: To gauge the solvency of a company by projecting its value in a forced-sale situation (The liquidation value reveals how much will be left to meet creditor claims.)

Action to be taken: If you do not wish to be forced into bankruptcy by creditors, you might want to take remedial actions to increase the company's liquidation value.

EXHIBIT 37-17
RELATIONSHIPS OF FACTORS INFLUENCING RETURN ON INVESTMENT: THE DU PONT FORMULA

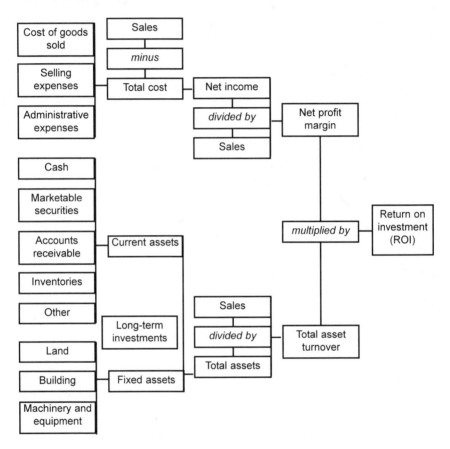

Purpose: To analyze return on investment (ROI) in terms of net profit margin and total asset turnover

Distribution: Treasurer, controller, CFO, CEO

Use: To identify any weakness in margin, turnover, or both

Action to be taken: To improve ROI, you can (a) reduce expenses (for example, improve productivity, automate, or cut down on discretionary expenses); (b) increase assets without decreasing sales (for example, improve inventory control, speed up receivable collections); or (c) increase sales at the same profit margin.

EXHIBIT 37-18
RETURN ON INVESTMENT (ROI) AND RETURN ON EQUITY (ROE)—THE DU PONT AND MODIFIED DU PONT FORMULA

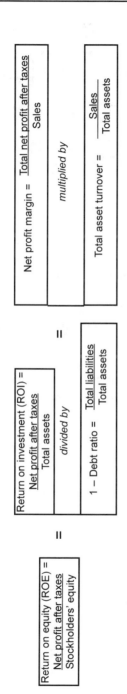

Return on equity (ROE) =

$$\frac{\text{Net profit after taxes}}{\text{Stockholders' equity}}$$

=

Return on investment (ROI) =

$$\frac{\text{Net profit after taxes}}{\text{Total assets}}$$

divided by

$$1 - \text{Debt ratio} = \frac{\text{Total liabilities}}{\text{Total assets}}$$

=

Net profit margin =

$$\frac{\text{Total net profit after taxes}}{\text{Sales}}$$

multiplied by

Total asset turnover =

$$\frac{\text{Sales}}{\text{Total assets}}$$

Purpose: To tie together the ROI and the degree of financial leverage

Distribution: Treasurer, controller, CFO, CEO

Use: To use financial leverage (debt) to increase return to stockholders

Action to be taken: Determine the combination of asset return and leverage that will work best in the company's competitive environment (most companies try to keep at least a level equal to what is considered "normal" within the industry).

CHAPTER 38

Quantitative Analysis, Business Statistics and Mathematics

Managers are decision-makers. They make many choices among alternatives as they deal with the various decision areas. This chapter focuses on basic statistical tools, decision tools, and quantitative models available to accounting and finance managers.

Exhibits 38-1 through 38-7 include expected return, standard deviation, coefficient of variation, decision matrix, decision tree, correlation analysis, regression analysis, Program Evaluation and Review Technique (PERT), Gantt chart, and linear programming. Many of them are *Excel*-based, but linear programming may require a stand-alone software such as *LINDO (Linear Interactive Discrete Optimization)* or *What's Best!*

EXHIBIT 38-1
EXPECTED RETURN, STANDARD DEVIATION, AND COEFFICIENT OF VARIATION

		Project A			
Return (r)	Probability (p)	r p	(r - r)	(r - r)²	(r - r)² p
-5%	0.2	-1%	-24%	5.76%	1.15%
20%	0.6	12%	1%	0.01%	0.01%
40%	0.2	8%	21%	4.41%	0.88%
				Total	2.04%

Expected return = 19.00%
Standard deviation = 14.28%
Coefficient of variation = 1.33

		Project B			
Return (r)	Probability (p)	r p	(r - r)	(r - r)²	(r - r)² p
10%	0.2	2%	-5%	0.25%	0.05%
15%	0.6	9%	0%	0.00%	0.00%
20%	0.2	4%	5%	0.25%	0.05%
				Total	0.10%

Expected return = 15.00%
Standard deviation = 3.16%
Coefficient of variation = 4.74

Purpose: To calculate measures of risk

Distribution: Treasurer, controller, CFO, VP-production, CEO

Use: To monitor variability in sales and earnings (Financial managers can also make important inferences about the future from past data with expected value and standard deviation information. Unstable and erratic sales and earnings mean uncertainty, resulting in greater risk.)

Action to be taken: Choose Project B in this example—the return per unit of risk is higher for Project B.

EXHIBIT 38-2
DECISION MATRIX

Demand (units)	State of Nature				Expected Monetary Value
	0	10	20	30	
Stock (Probability)	0.2	0.3	0.3	0.2	
0	$0	$0	$0	$0	$0.0
10	($100)	$200	$200	$200	$140.0
20	($200)	$100	$400	$400	$190.0 ← Maximum
30	($300)	$0	$300	$600	$150.0
Payoff of decision made with perfect information:	$0	$200	$400	$600	$300.0
Expected Value of Perfect Information (EVPI)					$110.0

Purpose: To make the best possible decision (e.g., how much inventory to stock in face of uncertain demand.)

Distribution: Project analyst, treasurer, controller, CFO, VP-production, CEO

Use: To evaluate different alternatives when demand is uncertain (A decision matrix is a general approach to a wide range of managerial decisions, such as capacity expansion, product planning, process management, and location.)

Action to be taken: Take the optimal stock action, one with the highest expected monetary value (i.e., stock 2 units).The expected value of perfect information can then be computed as: Expected value with perfect information minus the expected value with existing information.

EXHIBIT 38-3
DECISION TREE

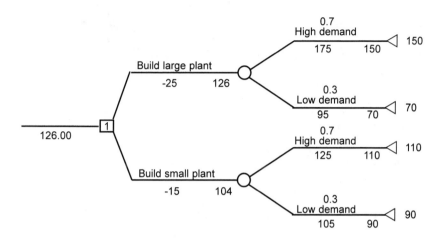

Purpose: To make the best possible decision (e.g., build small plants when future demand is uncertain)

Distribution: Project analysts, treasurer, controller, CFO, VP-production, CEO

Use: To evaluate different capacity expansion alternatives when demand is uncertain and sequential decisions are involved (A decision tree is a general approach to a wide range of managerial decisions.)

Action to be taken: Choose the option that provides the highest expected monetary benefit.

EXHIBIT 38-4
CORRELATION ANALYSIS REPORT

Product	A	B	C	D	E	F
A	1.00	0.26	-0.85	-0.01	-0.07	0.22
B	0.26	1.00	-0.02	-0.07	0.00	0.00
C	-0.85	-0.02	1.00	0.01	0.73	0.23
D	-0.01	-0.07	0.01	1.00	0.01	-0.02
E	-0.07	0.00	0.73	0.01	1.00	0.45
F	0.22	0.00	0.23	-0.02	0.45	1.00

Purpose: To measure the extent to which two variables in a data set covary in a linear fashion

Distribution: Project analysts, product analyst, treasurer, controller, CFO, VP-production, CEO

Use: To identify the strength and direction of an association between two products

Action to be taken: To expand product lines that are negatively correlated in order to ensure product diversification, thus reducing overall risk.

EXHIBIT 38-5
MICROSOFT EXCEL REGRESSION REPORT

Observations	Advertising (in $000s)	Actual Sales (in $000s)
1	$30	$184
2	40	279
3	40	244
4	50	314
5	60	382
6	70	450
7	70	424
8	70	410
9	80	500
10	90	505

SUMMARY OUTPUT
Regression Statistics

Multiple R	0.984444276
R-squared	0.969130533
Adjusted R-square	0.96527185
Standard error	20.42132374
Observations	10

ANOVA

	df	SS	MS	F	Significance F
Regression	1	104739.6003	104739.6003	251.1557537	2.51425E-07
Residual	8	3336.243706	417.0304632		
Total	9	108075.844			

	Coefficients	Standard Error	t Stat	P-value
Intercept	36.34235294	21.98328259	1.653181357	0.136894006
Advertising	5.550294118	0.350222813	15.8478943	2.51425E-07

	Lower 95%	Upper 95%	Lower 95.0%	Upper 95.0%
Intercept	-14.35122039	87.03592627	-14.35122039	87.03592627
Advertising	4.742678341	6.357909894	4.742678341	6.357909894

Purpose: To generate a regression output from MicroSoft Excel

Distribution: Departmental manager, controller, treasurer, CFO, VPs of marketing and production/operations, CEO

Use: To predict sales

Action to be taken: R squared is .9691, or 96.91 percent, which is recognized to mean that almost 97 percent of the total variation of sales is explained by the change in advertising and the remaining 3 percent is accounted for by something other than advertising, such as price and income. R squared tells us how good the estimated regression equation is; the higher the R squared, the more confidence we have in our estimated equation. A low R squared may force you to look elsewhere for the explanation of variations in sales (e.g., price, drop in consumer disposable income, etc.).

EXHIBIT 38-6
PROGRAM EVALUATION AND REVIEW TECHNIQUE (PERT): CRITICAL PATH

Activity	Immediate Predecessors	Description	Time	Earliest Start Times	Earliest Finish Times	Latest Start Times	Latest Finish Time	Slack
A	-	Forecasting Unit Sales	14	0	14	0	14	0**
B	A	Pricing Sales	3	14	17	22	25	8
C	A	Preparing Production Schedules	7	14	21	14	21	0**
D	C	Costing the Production	4	21	25	21	25	0**
E	B, D	Preparing the Budget	10	25	35	25	35	0**

**Critical activities have zero slack.

Purpose: To determine the critical path of a budgeting project

Distribution: Project analyst, cost accountant, project supervisor, treasurer, controller, CFO, CEO

Use: (1) To monitor the progress of a project, using a Gantt chart which is a bar chart that depicts the relationship of activities over time and (2) to answer questions such as (a) When will the project be finished? and (b) What is the probability that the project will be completed by any given time?

Action to be taken: Set goals and priorities for the project, including committed, completion times, and activities; assign areas of responsibility. Budget time and resource requirements. Scheduling establishes time and sequences of the various phases of the project.

NETWORK

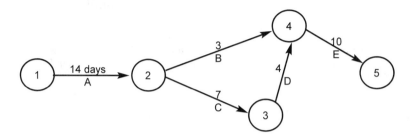

GANTT CHART

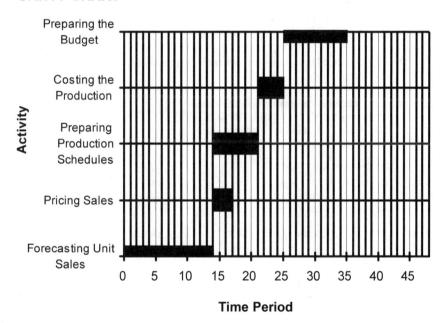

EXHIBIT 38-7
COMPUTER PRINTOUT FOR LINEAR PROGRAMMING

The programming solution is based on the following example:

A furniture maker wishes to find the most profitable mix of two products, desk and table. Both require time in two processing departments, Assembly and Finishing. Data on the two products are as follows:

Processing	Products Desk	Table	Available Hours
Assembly	2	4	100
Finishing	3	2	90
Profit per unit	$25	$40	

The company wants to find the most profitable mix of these two products. Define the decision variables as follows:

x_1 = Number of units of desk to be produced

x_2 = Number of units of table to be produced

The objective function to maximize total profit (Z) is expressed as:

$Z = 25x_1 + 40x_2$

Then, formulate the constraints as inequalities:

$2x_1 + 4x_2 \leq 100$ (Assembly constraint)
$3x_1 + 2x_2 \leq 90$ (Finishing constraint)
$x_1, x_2 \geq 0$

```
                   VARIABLE       ORIGINAL       COEFF.
VARIABLE           VALUE          COEFF.         SENS.
  X 1              20             25             0       Note: X₁ = 20
  X 2              15             40             0             X₂ = 15


CONSTRAINT         ORIGINAL       SLACK OR       SHADOW
NUMBER             RHS            SURPLUS        PRICE
  1                100            0              8.75
  1                90             0              2.50

OBJECTIVE FUNCTION VALUE: 1100      Note: Maximum profit Z = $1,100

                  SENSITIVITY ANALYSIS
             OBJECTIVE FUNCTION COEFFICIENTS
                  LOWER          ORIGINAL       UPPER
VARIABLE          LIMIT          COEFFICIENT    LIMIT
  X 1             20             25             60
  X 2             16.67          40             50

                  RIGHT HAND SIDE
CONSTRAINT        LOWER          ORIGINAL       UPPER
NUMBER            LIMIT          VALUE          LIMIT
  1               60             100            180
  2               50
```

EXHIBIT 38-7
COMPUTER PRINTOUT FOR LINEAR PROGRAMMING, *Cont'd*

Purpose: To allocate scarce resources among competing demands in the most profitable way

Distribution: Operations manager, executive vice president for operations, treasurer, controller, CFO, CEO

Use: To solve planning problems such as (1) finding the least-cost production schedule, taking into account inventory, hiring, layoff, overtime, and outsourcing costs, subject to various capacity and policy constraints, and (2) selecting the least-cost mix of ingredients for manufactured products

Action to be taken: Make sure implementation follows the optimal plan given by a linear programming solution.

CHAPTER 39

Forecasting

The most important function of business is probably forecasting. A forecast is a starting point for planning. The objective of forecasting is to reduce risk in decision-making. In business, forecasts are the basis for capacity planning, production and inventory planning, manpower planning, planning for sales and market share, financial planning and budgeting, planning for research and development, and top management's strategic planning.

- Exhibits 39-1 through 39-7 illustrate some popular forecasting models. These include moving averages, weighted moving averages, exponential smoothing, exponential smoothing and trend effects, and trend analysis.

- Exhibit 39-6 lists the components of the Index of Leading Economic Indicators (LEI), which is used widely to gauge economic activity six to nine months ahead.

- Exhibits 39-7 and 39-8 show how to measure forecasting accuracy of alternative forecasting methods.

EXHIBIT 39-1
MOVING AVERAGE METHOD

Time Period	Number of VCRs Sold	2-Month Moving Average	4-Month Moving Average
1	33	--	--
2	38	--	--
3	31	35.50	--
4	35	34.50	--
5	30	33.00	34.25
6	36	32.50	33.50
7	34	33.00	33.00
8	39	35.00	33.75
9	39	36.50	34.75
10	36	39.00	37.00
11	40	37.50	37.00
12	38	38.00	38.50
13	37	39.00	38.25
14	39	37.50	37.75
15	32	38.00	38.50
16	38	35.50	36.50
17	37	35.00	36.50
18	39	37.50	36.50
19	37	38.00	36.50
20	35	38.00	37.75
21	37	36.00	37.00
22	34	36.00	37.00
23	35	35.50	35.75
24	36	34.50	35.25
	MSE:	6.93	7.66

Number of VCRs Sold   2-Month Moving Avg.
4-Month Moving Avg.

Purpose: To forecast sales

Distribution: Departmental manager, controller, treasurer, CFO, VP-marketing and production/operations, CEO

Use: To make forecasts that are accurate

Action to be taken: Choose the number of periods to use on the basis of the relative importance of older versus current data. For example, one can compare five- and three-month periods.

EXHIBIT 39-2
WEIGHTED MOVING AVERAGE

Time Period	Number of VCRs Sold	2-Month Weighted Moving Average	Weights	
1	33	--	w1	0.500
2	38	--	w2	0.500
3	31	35.50	sum	1.000
4	35	34.50		
5	30	33.00		
6	36	32.50		
7	34	33.00		
8	39	35.00		
9	39	36.50		
10	36	39.00		
11	40	37.50		
12	38	38.00		
13	37	39.00		
14	39	37.50		
15	32	38.00		
16	38	35.50		
17	37	35.00		
18	39	37.50		
19	37	38.00		
20	35	38.00		
21	37	36.00		
22	34	36.00		
23	35	35.50		
24	36	34.50		
	MSE:	6.93		

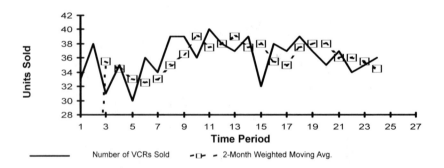

Number of VCRs Sold   2-Month Weighted Moving Avg.

Purpose: To forecast sales

Distribution: Departmental manager, controller, treasurer, CFO, VP-marketing and production/operations, CEO

Use: To make forecasts that are accurate

Action to be taken: Choose proper weights based on accuracy measures as the *mean square error (MSE).*

EXHIBIT 39-3
EXPONENTIAL SMOOTHING METHOD

Time Period	Number of VCRs Sold	Exp. Smoothing Prediction		
			alpha	0.500
1	33	33.00		
2	38	33.00		
3	31	35.50		
4	35	33.25		
5	30	34.13		
6	36	32.06		
7	34	34.03		
8	39	34.02		
9	39	36.51		
10	36	37.75		
11	40	36.88		
12	38	38.44		
13	37	38.22		
14	39	37.61		
15	32	38.30		
16	38	35.15		
17	37	36.58		
18	39	36.79		
19	37	37.89		
20	35	37.45		
21	37	36.22		
22	34	36.61		
23	35	35.31		
24	36	35.15		
	MSE:	8.18		

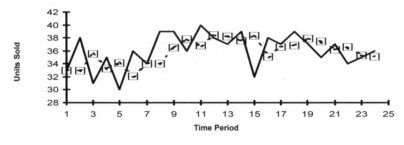

————— Number of VCRs Sold ‑ ‑□‑ ‑ Exp. Smoothing Prediction

Purpose: To forecast sales

Distribution: Departmental manager, controller, treasurer, CFO, VP-marketing and production/operations, CEO

Use: To make forecasts that are accurate

Action to be taken: Use a higher or lower smoothing constant, called alpha, to adjust your prediction as quickly as possible to large fluctuations in the data series.

EXHIBIT 39-4
EXPONENTIAL SMOOTHING WITH TREND EFFECTS

Year	Qtr	Time Period	Actual Sales	Base Level	Trend	Predicted Sales		
2001	1	1	$684.2	684.2	0.0	--	**alpha**	0.119
	2	2	$584.1	672.3	-11.9	$684.2	**beta**	1.000
	3	3	$765.4	672.9	0.6	$660.4		
	4	4	$892.3	699.5	26.6	$673.5		
2002	1	5	$885.4	744.9	45.5	$726.0		
	2	6	$677.0	777.0	32.0	$790.4		
	3	7	$1,006.6	832.5	55.5	$809.0		
	4	8	$1,122.1	915.8	83.3	$888.0		
2003	1	9	$1,163.4	1018.6	102.8	$999.1		
	2	10	$993.2	1106.2	87.6	$1,121.4		
	3	11	$1,312.5	1207.9	101.7	$1,193.8		
	4	12	$1,545.3	1337.5	129.7	$1,309.5		
2004	1	13	$1,596.2	1482.6	145.0	$1,467.2		
	2	14	$1,260.4	1584.0	101.4	$1,627.6		
	3	15	$1,735.2	1691.3	107.3	$1,685.4		
	4	16	$2,029.7	1826.0	134.8	$1,798.6		
2005	1	17	$2,107.8	1978.2	152.2	$1,960.8		
	2	18	$1,650.3	2073.4	95.2	$2,130.5		
	3	19	$2,304.4	2184.8	111.3	$2,168.6		
	4	20	$2,639.4	2336.8	152.1	$2,296.1		
					MSE	47891.7		

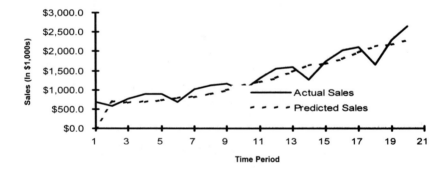

Purpose: To forecast sales

Distribution: Departmental manager, controller, treasurer, CFO, VP-marketing and production/operations, CEO

Use: To make forecasts that are accurate

Action to be taken: Because an upward or downward trend in a time series data causes the exponential smoothing forecast to lag behind (be above or below) the actual occurrence, experiment with two smoothing constants, alpha and beta, to reduce the impact of the error that occurs between the actual and the forecast.

EXHIBIT 39-5
TREND EQUATION

Time Period	Number of VCRs Sold
1	10
2	13
3	16
4	17
5	19
6	23
7	34
8	39
9	45

SUMMARY OUTPUT
Regression Statistics

Multiple R	0.960541436
R-squared	0.92263985
Adjusted R-s	0.909746491
Standard error	3.59342433
Observations	8

ANOVA

	df	SS	MS	F	Significance F
Regression	1	924.0238095	924.0238095	71.55931162	0.000149081
Residual	6	77.47619048	12.91269841		
Total	7	1001.5			

	Coefficients	Standard Error	t Stat	P-value
Intercept	-0.047619048	3.303680464	-0.014413939	0.988967072
Time	4.69047619	0.554477412	8.459273705	0.000149081

	Lower 95%	Upper 95%	Lower 95.0%	Upper 95.0%
Intercept	-8.13143984	8.036201745	-8.13143984	8.036201745
Time	3.333717848	6.047234533	3.333717848	6.047234533
Intercept	-14.35122039	87.03592627	-14.35122039	87.03592627
Advertising	4.742678341	6.357909894	4.742678341	6.357909894

Purpose: To generate a trend equation

Distribution: Departmental manager, controller, treasurer, CFO, VP-marketing and production/operations, CEO

Use: To predict sales

Action to be taken: R squared is .9226, or 92.26 percent, recognized to mean that almost 93 percent of the total variation in sales is explained by the trend equation and the remaining 7 percent is accounted for by something other than trend. A low R squared may force you to find a different factor to explain the variation (e.g., price or change in consumer disposable income). A high R squared indicates sales will rise increasingly.

EXHIBIT 39-5
TREND EQUATION, *Cont'd*

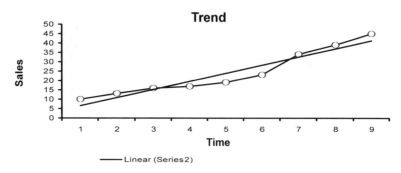

EXHIBIT 39-6
INDEX OF LEADING ECONOMIC INDICATORS

1. Average workweek of production workers in manufacturing
2. Initial claims for unemployment insurance
3. Change in consumer confidence
4. Percent change in prices of sensitive crude materials
5. Contracts and orders for plant and equipment
6. Vendor performance
7. Stock prices
8. Money supply
9. New orders for manufacturers of consumer goods and materials
10. Residential building permits for private housing
11. Factory backlogs of unfilled durable goods orders

Purpose: To forecast economic activity six to nine months ahead

Distribution: Marketing manager, controller, CEO

Use: To aid in predicting economic trends (This series is the government's main barometer for forecasting business trends. Each of the series has shown a tendency to change before the economy makes a major turn—hence, the term *leading indicators.*)

Action to be taken: Adjust business plans if necessary. If the index is consistently rising, even slightly, the economy is chugging along and a setback is unlikely. If the indicator drops for three or more consecutive months, look for an economic slowdown and possibly a recession in the next year or so. A rising (consecutive percentage increases) in an indicator is bullish for the economy and the stock market, and vice versa. The composite figure is designed to tell only the direction business will go, not the magnitude of future ups and downs.

EXHIBIT 39-7
FORECASTING PERFORMANCE REPORT:
ACTUAL VERSUS ESTIMATED

Observations	Advertising (in $000s)	Actual Sales (in $000s)	Est. Sales (in $000s)	Error	Squared Error
1	$30.00	$184.40	$220.00	-35.60	1267.36
2	40.00	279.10	270.00	9.10	82.81
3	40.00	244.00	270.00	-26.00	676.00
4	50.00	314.20	320.00	-5.80	33.64
5	60.00	382.20	370.00	12.20	148.84
6	70.00	450.20	420.00	30.20	912.04
7	70.00	423.60	420.00	3.60	12.96
8	70.00	410.20	420.00	-9.80	96.04
9	80.00	500.40	470.00	30.40	924.16
10	90.00	505.30	520.00	-14.70	216.09

Total squared error = 4369.94
Mean squared error = 436.99

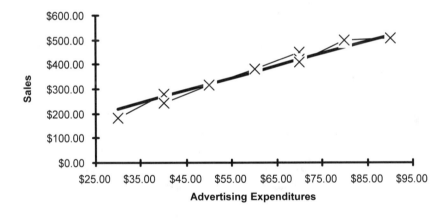

Purpose: To compare actual sales with predicted sales

Distribution: Departmental manager, controller, treasurer, CFO, VP-marketing and production/operations, CEO

Use: To monitor predictive accuracy of a forecasting model

Action to be taken: Choose a forecasting model based on such accuracy measures as the *mean squared error (MSE)*; the lower the MSE, the more accurate the forecasting model is likely to be.

EXHIBIT 39-8
MEASURING ACCURACY OF FORECASTS

Period	Actual(A)	Forecast(F)	e(A-F)	|e|	e^2	Absolute Percent Error	|e|/A
1	217	215	2	2	4	.0092
2	213	216	-3	3	9	.0014
3	216	215	1	1	1	.0046
4	210	214	-4	4	16	.0190
5	213	211	2	2	4	.0094
6	219	214	5	5	25	.0023
7	216	217	-1	1	1	.0046
8	212	216	-4	4	16	.0019
			-2	22	76	.0524

Using the figures,
   Mean absolute deviation (MAD) = Σ |e| /n = 22/8 = 2.75
   Mean squared error (MSE) = Σe^2 / (n - 1)= 76/7 = 10.86
   Root mean squared error (RMSE) = $\sqrt{\Sigma e^2 / n}$ = $\sqrt{76/8}$ = $\sqrt{9.5}$ = 3.08
   Mean absolute percentage error (MAPE) = Σ |e|/A / n = .0524/8 = .0066

Purpose: To evaluate the accuracy of alternative forecasting methods

Distribution: Marketing manager, controller, CEO

Use: To check the performance of a forecast against its own record and against that of other forecasts (The performance of a prediction model is measured in terms of forecasting error, where error is defined as the difference between a predicted value and the actual result. Error (e) = Actual (A) - Forecast (F). Sometimes it is more useful to compute forecasting errors in percentages rather than in amounts.)

Action to be taken: Compare the results of exponential smoothing with alphas and elect the one that gave the lowest MAD or MSE for a given set of data. Use to select the best initial forecast value for exponential smoothing.